Successes of the International Monetary Fund

Also by Ian McDonald

ANGLO-AMERICAN RELATIONS SINCE THE SECOND WORLD WAR

Successes of the International Monetary Fund

Untold Stories of Cooperation at Work

Edited by

Eduard Brau
and
Ian McDonald

palgrave
macmillan

First published 2009 by
PALGRAVE MACMILLAN

Palgrave Macmillan in the UK is an imprint of Macmillan Publishers Limited, registered in England, company number 785998, of Houndmills, Basingstoke, Hampshire RG21 6XS.

Palgrave Macmillan in the US is a division of St Martin's Press LLC, 175 Fifth Avenue, New York, NY 10010.

Palgrave Macmillan is the global academic imprint of the above companies and has companies and representatives throughout the world.

Palgrave® and Macmillan® are registered trademarks in the United States, the United Kingdom, Europe and other countries.

ISBN-13: 978-0-230-20313-6 hardback
ISBN-10: 0-230-20313-2 hardback
ISBN-13: 978-0-230-57809-8 paperback
ISBN-10: 0-230-57809-8 paperback

This book is printed on paper suitable for recycling and made from fully managed and sustained forest sources. Logging, pulping and manufacturing processes are expected to conform to the environmental regulations of the country of origin.

A catalogue record for this book is available from the British Library.

Library of Congress Cataloging-in-Publication Data

Successes of the International Monetary Fund : untold stories of cooperation at work / edited by Eduard Brau and Ian McDonald.
p. cm.
Includes bibliographical references and index.
ISBN-13: 978-0-230-20313-6
ISBN-10: 0-230-20313-2
1. International Monetary Fund—Developing countries. 2. Financial crises—Developing countries—Prevention. 3. Economic assistance—Developing countries. I. Brau, Eduard H., 1942- II. McDonald, Ian, 1938-

HG3881.5.I58S855 2009
332.1"532—dc22 2008034632

10 9 8 7 6 5 4 3 2 1
18 17 16 15 14 13 12 11 10 09

Printed and bound in Great Britain by
CPI Antony Rowe, Chippenham and Eastbourne

Contents

Figures, Tables, and Boxes

Figures

Tables

Boxes

Preface

A reader interested in learning what the International Monetary Fund has done well has a problem. An accessible book about some of the IMF's successes does not exist. Our book is the first, astonishing as that may seem.

There are, however, several recent books, mentioned in the first chapter, that discuss real and perceived failures of the IMF, and we have no problems with these books, although we might have different views on particular points. It is important to discuss failures and weaknesses, so as to learn from them. But it is equally important to learn from what has succeeded, and the IMF has had many successes.

So, we wish to contribute to a better understanding of the IMF and to establish some balance in the literature.

We—the editors—are both retired IMF staff members. We believe we know the IMF well and we seek to be objective about it. We lay out the basis for our arguments so that readers can judge for themselves. We have chosen the topics, invited the authors and discussants, and engaged the publishers independently of the IMF. The editors, authors, and discussants have not accepted any remuneration; proceeds from the book are donated to charity.

Each of the success stories in this book is told by former or present staff members of the IMF who were closely involved with the work they describe. To provide balance and counterpoint, each story is commented upon by a (former) senior government official or an observer also closely involved.

All contributions, including any policy judgments, are the work and responsibility of the individual authors and do not necessarily reflect the views of the IMF or any national authorities.

This book exists only because our 27 authors have readily and graciously accepted our invitation to write nine chapters and commentaries. All of the authors are distinguished professionals who are intimately familiar with their topics. We are profoundly grateful for their contributions.

We have also benefited from the suggestions of many friends and former colleagues who read and commented on drafts. We are grateful for their help and we thank them all.

Notes on Contributors

Leszek Balcerowicz is a former deputy prime minister and minister of finance of Poland and a former governor of the Central Bank of Poland. In June 2008, he was appointed Chairman of Bruegel, a Brussels-based economics think tank.

Tomás J. Baliño is a former deputy director of the IMF's Monetary and Financial Systems Department.

Eduard Brau is a former director of the IMF's Finance Department.

Hugh Bredenkamp is a former senior resident representative of the IMF in Turkey and is currently Assistant Director in the African Department.

Thomas Dawson II is a former director of the IMF's External Relations Department.

Charles Enoch is a former deputy director of the IMF's Monetary and Financial Systems Department and is currently Deputy Director of the Statistics Department.

Arminio Fraga is a former governor of the Central Bank of Brazil and is currently Founding Partner, Gavea Investimentos.

Philip R. Gerson is a former IMF division chief for Brazil and is currently an advisor to the IMF's Deputy Managing Director.

James Gordon is an assistant director in the IMF's Asia and Pacific Department.

Graham Hacche is a former assistant director in the IMF's Research Department and is currently Deputy Director in the External Relations Department.

Mats Josefsson is a former senior economist in the IMF's Monetary and Financial Systems Department.

Kihwan Kim is a former senior official and former Ambassador-at-Large for economic affairs of Korea and is currently Chair of the

Seoul Financial Forum and an international advisor to Goldman Sachs, Asia.

Timothy Lane is a senior advisor in the IMF's Research Department. He will become an advisor to the Bank of Canada in August 2008.

Carl-Johan Lindgren is a former assistant director in the IMF's Monetary and Financial Systems Department.

Ian McDonald is a former chief editor in the IMF's External Relations Department.

Gray S. Mgonja is Permanent Secretary and Paymaster General in the Ministry of Finance of Tanzania. He has been a central figure in the Tanzanian economic reform process.

Hubert Neiss is a former director of the IMF's Asian Department.

Rolando Ossowski is an assistant director in the IMF's Fiscal Affairs Department.

Martin Parkinson is a former deputy secretary in the Australian Treasury and is currently Secretary of the Australian Department of Climate Change.

Lorenzo L. Pérez is a former IMF mission chief and senior resident representative in Brazil and is currently Deputy Director in the Middle East and Central Asia Department.

Massimo Russo is a former director of the IMF's European Department.

Steven Seelig is Advisor in the IMF's Monetary and Capital Markets Department.

Süreyya Serdengeçti is a former governor of the Central Bank of Turkey and is currently a senior lecturer at TOBB Economics and Technology University in Ankara and Director of the Stability Institute at TEPAV, Ankara.

Robert Sharer is Assistant Director in the IMF's Africa Department.

Carlos Steneri is Financial Agent of the Government of Uruguay in the United States and Director of the Management Unit of the Ministry of Finance of Uruguay.

Gilbert Terrier is Assistant Director in the IMF's Western Hemisphere Department.

Wanda Tseng is a former deputy director in the IMF's Asia Department.

José Viñals is Deputy Governor of the Central Bank of Spain.

Martin Wolf is Associate Editor and Chief Economics Commentator, *Financial Times*, London.

Acknowledgments

This book tells stories of successful collaborations between member countries and the International Monetary Fund. Having some of the key participants in these events come together and be willing to give their perspectives is at the heart of this book. The authors and discussants readily accepted our invitations, believing that these stories need telling, and working with them through successive draft chapters was a pleasure. We are profoundly grateful for the contributions of Leszek Balcerowicz, Tomás J. Baliño, Hugh Bredenkamp, Thomas Dawson II, Charles Enoch, Arminio Fraga, Philip R. Gerson, James Gordon, Graham Hacche, Mats Josefsson, Kihwan Kim, Timothy Lane, Carl-Johan Lindgren, Gray Mgonja, Hubert Neiss, Rolando Ossowski, Martin Parkinson, Lorenzo L. Pérez, Massimo Russo, Steven Seelig, Süreyya Serdengeçti, Robert Sharer, Carlos Steneri, Gilbert Terrier, Wanda Tseng, Jose Vinals, and Martin Wolf.

In thinking about how to structure this book and choose among the many possible topics, we benefited from the thoughts of a number of former colleagues. Masood Ahmed, Mark Allen, James Boughton, David Burton, Benedicte Christensen, Sean Culhane, Michel Deppler, Mohsin Khan, Anne Krueger, Michael Kuhn, Anoop Singh, and Teresa Ter-Minassian were generous with their advice and time. We thank them for their help.

Drafts of chapters or paragraphs were read and commented upon by Tomás Baliño, Jack Boorman, Benedicte Christensen, Charles Enoch, Hector Elizalde, James Gordon, Graham Hacche, David Hawley, Russell Kincaid, Carl-Johan Lindgren, Claudio Loser, Jorgé Marquez-Ruarte, John Odling-Smee, Horst Struckmeyer, Donald K. Palmer, and Wanda Tseng. We are grateful for their interest and suggestions. The responsibility for any remaining errors is our own. Members of our families—Saralisa Brau, Anja Brau, Julia Brau, Geoffrey Blanford, Sarah Brau, and Crispina McDonald—also provided helpful ideas on how to keep the material interesting for the general reader.

We are especially grateful to Taiba Batool and Alec Dubber, commissioning editors at Palgrave Macmillan Publishers. They quickly showed interest in publishing this book when they saw the outline of the manuscript and the names of the contributing authors.

We wish to thank Alicia Etchebarne-Bourdin for her skillful preparation of the manuscript and her desktop publishing expertise. We are also grateful to the staff of Macmillan India Limited for shepherding the finished manuscript toward publication.

Eduard Brau and Ian McDonald
Editors

1
Introduction

Eduard Brau and Ian McDonald

Why this book?

The International Monetary Fund (IMF or Fund) is the central institution of the international monetary system—the system of international payments and exchange rates that enables business to take place between countries with different currencies. The organization is much talked about and plays an important role in the economic life of many countries. How well understood is it?

Even dramatic IMF successes are little known. One of us recently gave a talk to a large university audience of economics and political science students. Before the talk, some students came up and asked the speaker to be sure to discuss the role of the IMF in the collapse of the fixed exchange rate regime in Argentina in late 2001 and the subsequent deep economic crisis in that country, an event much discussed in the news and the literature. We chose to open the talk with a question for the audience: could they name a country in which the IMF had a major success in 2002 and 2003?

We were thinking, in particular, of a large economy with substantial external public debt where the incumbent government had successfully pursued important economic reforms, where a presidential election had been pending and the left-of-center opposition candidate had been ahead in the polls, where the cost of the government's borrowing in international capital markets had surged to well over 20 percent per year on fears that economic stability would vanish, and where borrowing by the government in international capital markets to refinance existing debt had become virtually impossible. This situation guaranteed a default on the debt and subsequent economic recession if it persisted for long. Such a default would also have rattled international capital markets and increased the costs for other countries borrowing in these markets.

In these circumstances, the government concluded a support program with the IMF, in consultation and with the support of the political opposition, correctly viewed by many at the time as the likely next administration, to bolster domestic and international confidence. The IMF's support included its largest-ever loan commitment of some $30 billion. The policies carried out under the program by the outgoing and, subsequently, by the new administration succeeded. What could well have been the largest debt default in history was averted, financial stability was restored, and economic growth maintained.

What country were we describing? Not one student in the audience recognized the Brazilian experience of 2002–3, a success story to be told in this book.

The IMF has played a major role in many of the most important economic events of the past decades. It helped steer many of the former Soviet Union countries and others that were formerly centrally planned toward becoming successful market economies. It helped achieve near consensus among economic policy makers on the importance of fiscal responsibility and of keeping inflation low. It provided support to countries at particularly stressful periods, such as when countries fell into financial crises. Surprisingly, given the overall successful performance of the world economy over the past few decades, the IMF has recently been the subject of a number of critiques. To some extent this may be natural, as the IMF has frequently been prepared to take the political heat when domestic politicians wished to assign blame for policies that may have been unpopular in the short term. Also, there have, of course, been IMF policies that with hindsight should have been different.

Recent literature seems to have focused more on the IMF's apparent failings than the successes; indeed, nobody has yet written a book about successes of the IMF. Seeking to achieve a better balance, this book focuses on the positive contributions of the IMF: on its successful support to help economies overcome and recover from financial crises, on its important initiatives to help reduce the occurrence of such crises, and on the IMF's contributions to understanding world economic problems and addressing them more effectively.

When we speak of "successes of the IMF," we mean that the IMF has made a significant positive contribution to the economic policies implemented by one or more of its member countries. The policy-making authorities always have the greatest influence in reaching a positive outcome. The IMF acts from the outside and can make it easier for the authorities to achieve an economic goal.

But how can it be true that there are many IMF success stories and that they are orphans in the literature? Isn't it commonly more productive in life to learn from successes and to disseminate knowledge on what works rather than to dwell mainly on the shortcomings?

Consider some of the recent contributions for general readers by academic authors and financial journalists. For example: Michael Mussa, *Argentina and the Fund: From Triumph to Tragedy* (Peterson Institute for International Economics, 2002); Joseph Stiglitz, *Globalization and Its Discontents* (W.W. Norton and Co., 2002); Paul Bluestein, *The Chastening* (Public Affairs Books, 2003) on the Asian Financial Crises; and Paul Bluestein, *And the Money Kept Rolling In (And Out)* (Public Affairs Books, 2005) on the IMF and Argentina. Without commenting on the substance of these books, we simply note that they deal with one case of a failed IMF-supported program (Argentina), with some IMF-supported programs that are controversial though arguably successful (the Asian financial crises cases in the second half of the 1990s), and with the experience of Russia in moving from a centrally planned to a market economy, aided by one large IMF-supported program that succeeded, and by one that did not succeed.

The point we make is that these publications do not deal with the many successful crisis-resolution programs supported financially by the IMF in this same time span. Nor do they deal with the IMF's many areas of work other than financial support for crisis resolution, much of which is effective; some two-thirds of the staff's time is devoted to this work.

Does the institution itself not tell its success stories? The IMF Web site—www.imf.org—gives access to an extraordinary volume of information among which the success stories are to be found. The trouble is that they are not apparent: they are buried. Finding them requires special prior knowledge on where to look, an ability to read technical material and specialized language, and a lot of time and patience to piece individual stories together from many separate documents. One could also read the official histories of the IMF, which comprise as many as a 1000 pages for each decade up to 1990, and wait for the publication of the volume covering the 1990s. But one will not find an accessible document in which the institution says what it thinks it has done well.

Why are there hardly any contributions for the benefit of a wider audience by current or former members of IMF management, the Executive Board, or staff that discuss the work they have been associated with?

We do not know why, but we speculate that one reason for this absence of contributions may be an understandable reluctance to appear to take individual credit for what is inevitably the success of a team effort jointly between the IMF and the authorities and officials of member countries who are committed to the policies supported by the IMF.

But there is also truth in the adage that a successful IMF crisis-resolution program is usually portrayed to the public as the "country's program," whereas a struggling or failed one is portrayed as the "IMF's program." This is the role in which the IMF is portrayed as a scapegoat. Even though a country has chosen to ask for the IMF's help, some officials may feel embarrassed over being in such a position. There is thus not much advantage for government authorities to publicly praise the IMF; the scapegoating option needs to be held in reserve for possible use at a later time. Nevertheless, to be fair, we are aware of many expressions of appreciation by governments to the IMF, but such appreciations are normally given in private and not publicized.

Finally, there is the highly regarded work of the IMF's Independent Evaluation Office, which was set up in 2001 to conduct objective and independent reviews of IMF policies and programs. This office attempts to learn lessons as it objectively evaluates the IMF's work on topics it has selected. A recent outside evaluation of this office's performance found, however, that its outreach to audiences outside the IMF has thus far been largely ineffective.

The conclusion is that very few authors speak out clearly and accessibly about successes of the IMF.

The IMF's critics therefore have succeeded too often in determining what is known and thought about the institution, with the result that its public image is a poor one. There is little doubt that the IMF's past secrecy about its work contributed significantly to this poor image. Common criticisms are that the IMF applies a one-size-fits-all approach to different countries' problems, that it does the bidding of financial creditors and imposes overly stringent austerity requirements on countries receiving its financial support to help overcome economic crises, that it is too secretive and often arrogant in its dealings with member countries, and that it fails to take account of well-founded criticism.

This poor image is widely held, but is unjustified, in our view. It is often based on misunderstanding of facts and on exaggerated views concerning IMF power and influence. It is also largely based on the criticisms—whether well taken or ill advised—of a few controversial, and sometimes unsuccessful, crisis-resolution programs supported by the IMF. This image does not reflect the many successful programs supported by the IMF that are less well known to the public, nor is it informed by knowledge of the IMF's many areas of successful work in fields other than the resolution of financial crises.

This poor image matters, however. Because it fosters mistaken perceptions, it makes the needed evolution and reform of the IMF more difficult.

Such reforms are especially urgent in the matter of IMF quotas and of the relative voting weights of countries, where the votes of fast-growing middle-income countries and of low-income countries need to increase, largely at the expense of the votes of European countries. The unwritten prerogative of European governments to propose a candidate for the position of the IMF's Managing Director who will be accepted by other member governments needs to be replaced by the principle of selection of the entire management team of the IMF on merit alone.

Reforms of the relative voting weights of countries and of IMF income and budget matters have recently been agreed and will require the approval of the parliaments of a supermajority of member countries. Public opinion matters to parliaments, and it would be unfortunate if mistaken perceptions of the IMF's work and role were to obstruct approval of these reforms.

What does the IMF do?

Developed at the Bretton Woods Conference in July 1944, toward the end of the Second World War, the IMF was born out of the recognition that permanent cooperation was needed between countries to prevent recurrence of the destructive beggar-thy-neighbor policies—such as competitive currency devaluations and exchange controls as well as protectionist trade measures—which had contributed to the worldwide economic disaster of the Great Depression of the 1930s.

Its purposes are, in the words of the IMF's Articles of Agreement, to provide a permanent institution for international monetary cooperation "to facilitate the expansion and balanced growth of international trade, and to contribute thereby to the promotion and maintenance of high levels of employment and real income" by promoting an open system of international payments and a stable system of exchange rates and to provide temporary financial assistance to member countries to resolve balance of payments problems.

The IMF was created together with the World Bank, and their creation was related to what is today the World Trade Organization, and also the United Nations, to provide the framework and institutions through which countries would cooperate on monetary, development, external trade, and security issues of common interest.

Each of the IMF's 185 member countries is represented on the IMF's 24-member Executive Board with a vote weighted according to the size of the country's economy. This Board, exercising powers delegated to it by the IMF's Board of Governors, sets policy and takes all decisions related to the institution's ongoing work. IMF management and staff carry out the work, with room for initiative under the Board's guidelines, and make recommendations for decision by the Board.

In pursuit of its purposes, the IMF's work encompasses three main activities:

- Surveillance: this is a system of oversight and peer review. Under its Articles, the IMF is to "exercise firm surveillance over the exchange rate policies of members" and "oversee the compliance of each member with its obligations" to collaborate with the IMF and other members to promote a stable system of exchange rates. It does this through what is known as bilateral surveillance, which usually involves annual consultations with each member. The IMF is also to "oversee the international monetary system in order to ensure its effective operation" and does this through what is known as multilateral surveillance.
- Technical cooperation and institution building: this comprises the offer of advice and skill transfer to member countries in the areas of macroeconomic and financial sector policy and management, and of economic governance practices to help prevent crises.
- Financial assistance: the provision of temporary loans to members to support policies designed to help overcome balance of payments problems "without resorting to measures destructive of national or international prosperity," in the words of the Articles. The IMF's financial resources derive from countries' quota subscriptions according to the size of each country's economy.

Except for a few mini states, only Cuba and North Korea are now not among the IMF's members. Eastern European countries, the successor states of the Soviet Union, and Switzerland did not become members until the early 1990s. Venezuela's government announced in 2007 it wanted to leave the institution, until it added up the financial impact of self-isolation and put the idea on hold. No country has left the IMF in more than 50 years. On the contrary, middle- and low-income countries strongly demand a larger say in running the IMF.

The IMF is the creation and creature of sovereign countries. It acts in a world of countries with vastly different economic and political power, as reflected in the weighted voting shares of these countries. These power realities are muted to some degree because countries have voluntarily ceded some responsibilities to the IMF; they have agreed to collaborate through the IMF and seek compromise on international monetary and financial issues, because they see it as being in their interest. Also, most of the decisions of the IMF's Executive Board are taken by a broad consensus of the membership, a practice that tends to increase somewhat the influence of smaller countries beyond their formal voting power.

Working with its sovereign country members, the IMF can encourage or criticize; it can offer technical expertise and policy insight from its long and wide-ranging international experience; it can offer incentives or disincentives when it lends; it can provide or withhold loans; but the IMF cannot compel any country to do what that country's government does not wish to do.[1]

A fuller description of the background to, and more detail on, the IMF's operations and areas of work may be found in the Annex.

The stories told in this book

Each story is told from two perspectives by those who were most closely involved: first, by IMF staff members and, second, by a senior government official from the member country or by a representative of the policy community concerned. These authors provide their perspectives side by side. We hope that the composite picture will give readers a faithful account.

The first story relates to the best-known activity of the IMF: the provision of temporary loans to economies in distress.

We have chosen six prominent recent cases of successful IMF assistance to a geographically and economically diverse set of countries that faced different problems over the past decade and a half. These are Korea (1997–98), Poland (1990–91), Turkey (2000–6), Tanzania (1995–2007), Brazil (2002–5), and Uruguay (2002–5). In Korea, the task was to restore confidence and facilitate economic reforms after damage caused by imprudent private-sector external borrowing encouraged by a fixed exchange rate. In Poland, the task was to establish a basis for macroeconomic stability to make possible a transition from its failed centrally planned to a successful market-based economy. In Turkey, the task was to help defeat decades of high inflation that had caused deep-seated problems in the banking and all other major economic sectors and weak economic growth. In Tanzania, the task was to achieve strong sustained economic growth after many years of stagnation caused by overly heavy government interventions that misallocated resources and suffocated private business activity. In Brazil, the task was to reverse quickly a fear-induced closure of the country's access to international capital markets that, if it had persisted, would have destroyed economic stability and growth as a new government was coming into power. Finally, in Uruguay, the task was to overcome massive financial system upheaval caused by large deposit withdrawals from domestic banks triggered by spillovers from a crisis in neighboring Argentina.

Many other excellent examples of successful IMF-supported crisis resolution programs such as Uganda (1987–95); Estonia, Latvia, and Lithuania (1992–98); Mexico (1994–95); Jordan (1995–98); Bulgaria (1996–2000); Mozambique (1996–2005); and Pakistan (2002–5) had to be omitted in the interest of brevity.

The second story covers the transparency revolution, that is, the opening of the economic books of governments and of the IMF.

Until recently, too many governments prevented the timely release of essential economic and financial information to financial markets and the public, and even to the IMF. This materially contributed to the outbreak of financial crises in several countries, since the depth of the economies' problems was shielded from view for too long. Also, the IMF published little about its work. Since the mid-1990s, there has been a dramatic turnabout toward openness. In addition, the IMF and the World Bank have sponsored guidelines and standards on best practices by countries in many important economic policy areas and are monitoring their implementation. The purpose is to build strong economic governance practices that outlive changing officeholders.

The third story deals with initiatives to reduce the incidence of financial crises. Inflexible exchange rates, inadequate discipline in macroeconomic policies, and deep-seated weaknesses in financial systems caused or aggravated the crises in several economies in the 1990s. Most of the affected countries now have adopted more flexible exchange rate policies and are engaged in major self-insurance by accumulating large foreign reserve holdings. The management of macroeconomic policy has also improved in many countries. The crises also made countries receptive to an initiative by the IMF and the World Bank to examine proactively and comprehensively their financial systems. Its purpose is to recommend improvements, in both advanced and developing countries, to strengthen the resilience of these systems when faced with setbacks.

The fourth story deals with the *World Economic Outlook* (*WEO*), the IMF's twice-yearly publication analyzing world economic developments and prospects and making related policy recommendations to governments and central banks. The *WEO* provides the basis for the semiannual discussions of the world economy by finance ministers and central bank governors and for their guidance to the IMF on important related policy issues. It has also been the basis for the analyses prepared by IMF staff for the periodic deliberations on the world economy by the finance ministers of the Group of 7–8 industrial countries and other international forums in which the IMF's Managing Director participates. The *WEO* has been accompanied since 2001 by the *Global Financial Stability Report*, the IMF's main vehicle for analyzing topical issues concerning international capital markets.

In the final chapter, the editors draw conclusions and discuss the conditions and circumstances needed for successful multilateral cooperation through the IMF.

We feature a number of IMF success stories in this book because we are convinced that they have not received the attention they deserve. But this emphasis and space constraints leave out two significant areas of IMF work, which, for completeness, we now discuss briefly.

The first important area is that of the IMF's regular surveillance discussion with each member, following which the IMF publishes its reports if the member country agrees, as most do. The task of the staff and of the Executive Board is to assess candidly the member's macroeconomic and financial policies. Their particular duty is to judge whether the member's exchange rate and other policies with important cross-border effects contribute to international financial stability. If they do not, corrective policies are recommended.

Here independent evaluations have revealed a picture of partial effectiveness. In many cases, the recommendations of the Executive Board to a member turn out to have been broadly appropriate, in hindsight. However, the member may not have followed the advice. In other cases, the advice may not have been the best. In any case, advice is given and ensuring that it is good advice demands the best up-to-date analytical insight and information from the staff to the member and to the Executive Board. In reaching its own recommendations, the Executive Board seeks to weigh the staff's views based on the wide cross-country experience present among Executive Directors and their colleagues in their capitals.

This is an enduring challenge that is not always met by the participants, the member country, the staff, and the Executive Board. What sometimes has been lacking is a willingness to engage in "ruthless truth-telling" in a timely manner for fear not only of precipitating a financial crisis but also of upsetting relationships with a country's authorities and officials. Finding the proper balance between candor and maintaining trusting relationships with members is a constant challenge for the staff. The IMF's most effective tool of persuasion is achieving as successful as possible a track record of insight on important economic developments and policy matters. Being open to debate and discussion, as the IMF strives to be, is an important means to achieving insight that is useful to member countries.

The second area is that of technical cooperation and training, to which the IMF devotes about a quarter of its staff resources. Here independent evaluations show the balance of results to be positive in the large majority of applications.

Technical advice is offered in such fields as economic and financial statistical systems and methodologies; the conduct, instruments and management of monetary policy and of exchange rate policy by central banks and of other central bank functions; the establishment of financial regulation and supervision systems and instruments; the management of national budgets, the setting up and management of efficient taxation systems and instruments, the management of budgetary expenditures, and the review of the efficiency of such expenditures; and in other areas within the mandate of the IMF.

This advice has been free of charge to low-income countries and is valued by them for its generally high quality and political impartiality. Also highly valued by countries is the prompt availability of technical advice because the IMF is the only major economic institution that has most of the needed experts on its staff.

This work of economic and financial institution-building and skill transfer is often relied upon by the international community, for example, in many recent cases of new or newly independent states, or of failed states on the path to economic reconstruction. Sometimes large-scale and multiyear efforts are involved in collaboration with other organizations, as in the 1990s when the IMF led the work to help countries in Eastern Europe and the former Soviet Union establish modern central banks and financial systems.

The balance between IMF successes and failures

The IMF obviously is not right and successful every time; it is far from perfect, misses opportunities and has other weaknesses, like every institution. But we believe it is still broadly effective.

The IMF is a great success if it is judged by the achievement of one of its main statutory purposes, which is "to facilitate the expansion and balanced growth of international trade, and to contribute thereby to the promotion and maintenance of high levels of employment and real income" in the words of the Articles of Agreement.

On the IMF's watch, the international monetary system has experienced strains and stresses, but no difficulties have come close to the calamities suffered by the world economy between the two world wars, which prompted the founding of the IMF. In large parts of the world today, unlike when the IMF was established, currency convertibility is taken for granted and exchange restrictions are an unknown concept to most people. Between 1950 and 2006, world trade volume grew at an average annual rate of about 6½ percent, contributing to growth in real world GDP averaging about 4 percent a year, faster than in any other period in recorded history.

Of course, many factors, influences, and government policies shaped this outcome, including advances in technology, broadly market-oriented policies in most of the world economy, and successive multilateral trade liberalizations achieved under the auspices of the (now) World Trade Organization. Many, therefore, share credit in these successes, but they include the IMF, which has contributed to the expansion of international trade through the liberalization of exchange systems, and to steadier growth and higher employment than in the past through its contributions to crisis prevention, crisis resolution, and improvements in the conduct of economic policies.

The IMF has also succeeded in establishing the permanent "machinery for consultation and collaboration on international monetary problems" in the words of the Articles. Discussions on world monetary issues and needed responses take place regularly among high officials of member countries. The *World Economic Outlook*, discussed in Chapter 10, provides the well-respected basis for this. Collaborative discussions through the IMF have become routine for governments and have survived serious disagreements among them. However, the spirit of internationalism and of accommodation ebbs and flows over time, and effective solutions may not be implemented by governments.

The objective of the regular surveillance of each member's economy, the IMF's main activity, is to seek to prevent financial crises and improve the conduct of economic policies more generally. As indicated earlier, here the record is one of only partial effectiveness. The IMF has anticipated only some crises and has been surprised by others. Even when the IMF proves prescient, however, success in preventing a crisis may still be elusive, as the case of Thailand demonstrates (Box 1.1).

Box 1.1 The case of Thailand

The IMF sometimes fails to persuade a government, through its surveillance discussions, to change its current policies in time to avert a crisis, even though the evidence of a crisis in the making appears very strong to the IMF. When the problem has become so large that the crisis hits, all policy options are unpleasant and the prospects of an easy recovery are diminished.

Thailand showed classic symptoms of vulnerability through unsustainably large deficits on the current account of its balance of payments of nearly 8 percent of GDP in both 1995 and 1996, financed heavily by short-term foreign currency borrowing. Banks and finance companies were encountering problems of nonperforming loans; confidence and capital inflows weakened in 1996 and throughout early 1997, but the central bank continued to defend its fixed exchange rate by spending virtually all of the country's large foreign reserves. These eventually ran out and a float and depreciation of the currency in early July 1997 formed the only remaining option. No other policy actions were taken, and the currency continued to depreciate through end-July; only then did Thailand request an IMF support program, which was put in place in August and included comprehensive policy steps.

Thai policy makers had counted on a return of confidence and of capital inflows and chose not to accept IMF advice to adopt comprehensive corrective policy measures, including adopting a more flexible exchange rate policy. This advice was given in December 1996 in person in Bangkok by then IMF Managing Director Michel Camdessus, in May 1997 by then First Deputy Managing Director Stanley Fischer, and by IMF staff during the annual surveillance discussions in March and in numerous confidential communications. This advice was not made public at the time by the IMF for fear of precipitating the crisis it sought to avoid. In this period, the central bank did not publish data on its true liquid foreign reserve position, and vital information requested by the IMF was withheld, though the staff was aware of heavy reserve losses. When full information on the depleted reserve position was published by the central bank in conjunction with the IMF loan in August 1997, the public was shocked. Exchange market participants began asking whether similar surprises might lurk in other countries.

As part of its surveillance activities to help prevent financial crises, the IMF has introduced the important transparency and financial-sector-assessment initiatives discussed in Chapters 8 and 9. Participation by countries in these demanding programs is voluntary, yet widespread. Most major industrial and middle- and low-income countries would not participate in these programs if they were not of high quality and judged to make important contributions to crisis prevention.

Are the successful crisis resolution programs featured in this book the lone standouts in a sea of failed IMF-supported programs? There is no room here to discuss the large research literature of cross-country studies on the question of the effectiveness of IMF-supported programs in improving the external current account balance, increasing international reserves, lowering inflation, and raising the rate of economic growth.

A broadly representative picture of successes and failures of IMF-supported crisis-resolution programs can be obtained by looking at the ten programs in the decade to 2005 that were supported by the IMF with the largest IMF financing relative to the countries' IMF quota or their GDP (Mexico, 1995–96; Russia, 1996–98; Thailand, 1997–98; Indonesia, 1997–98; Korea, 1997–98; Brazil, 1998–99; Turkey, 2000–6; Argentina, 2000–2; Brazil, 2002–5; and Uruguay, 2002–5).

Five of these programs were successes (even if, in the case of Turkey, success was not evident early on): Mexico, Korea, Brazil 2002–5, Turkey, and Uruguay. The latter four programs are featured as success stories in this book. A good discussion of Mexico is found in *Mexico 1994: Anatomy of an Emerging Market Crash*, edited by Moises Naim and Sebastian Edwards, Carnegie Endowment for International Peace, Washington, DC, 1998.

The Brazil program in 1998–99 did not succeed in its initial defense of a fixed exchange rate; however, a flexible exchange rate policy was quickly adopted and the economy escaped recession and debt default.

Thailand and Indonesia are hotly debated cases. Thailand recovered quickly from its postcrisis recession and Indonesia more slowly. We and many others regard these programs as broadly successful notwithstanding some misjudgments by the IMF (in particular, like others, it initially underestimated the scale of the economic downturn resulting from the Asian crisis) and notwithstanding some policy implementation slippages by the governments. However, other observers believe strongly that significant costs on the way to recovery could have been avoided if the IMF had advised these countries more effectively.

Of the above ten largest IMF-supported crisis-resolution programs since 1995, the program with Argentina in 2000–2 and the program with Russia in 1996–98 can be seen as clear failures, in our view. These programs were based on a variant of a fixed exchange rate policy that reflected the preferences of the authorities. Economic and financial policies to sustain this exchange rate policy were not implemented and failed, the exchange rates depreciated suddenly and sharply, and deep recessions and debt defaults followed. Interestingly, in both Argentina and Russia, the profound trauma of the deep recessions, surge in unemployment, and increase in poverty that followed the program failures induced both governments finally to implement budget policies without IMF support that made subsequent economic growth possible.

As these two cases demonstrate, the cause of failure may be poor policy design, such as IMF agreement to support a fixed exchange rate policy even though a flexible policy was technically preferable in these instances; government and IMF overoptimism in estimating the effects of particular policy measures; intervention of bad luck for which no compensating contingency measures had been agreed upon in advance; governmental nonimplementation of certain agreed policy measures, which led to IMF curtailment of the program; or other reasons.

Finally, as noted earlier, the IMF's extensive work on technical cooperation and institution building shows positive results in the large majority of applications.

In conclusion, in our view, the balance of successes and failures in the IMF's work adds up to a broadly positive record, even though there are areas where improved IMF performance is needed.

There are strong spurs to achieving better performance, as the IMF's work is kept under close review by member countries, by commissions and committees created by parliaments, by academic observers, by journalists and observers from civil society, and by its Independent Evaluation Office. The IMF also has by now achieved, as it should, a strong culture of transparency, learning, and introspection that searches for better answers whenever possible.

Part I IMF Financial Help to Economies in Crisis

How the IMF Helps Its Members

When a country requests the IMF's help in a balance of payments crisis, the IMF's staff and management negotiate with the economic authorities of the country to establish policies the government will implement to overcome the crisis and enable the country to resume economic growth. These policies—budgetary, monetary, exchange rate, and other—are outlined, and for some specific policies quantified, in a so-called letter of intent from the economic authorities to the Managing Director, often referred to as IMF "conditionality." On this basis, the economic authorities request a loan from the IMF, often in the form of a so-called Stand-By Arrangement.

This request, accompanied by a report and recommendation from staff, is presented for approval to the Executive Board. After approval, the IMF loan is normally disbursed in quarterly installments over a period of a year or two, as long as the policies described in the letter of intent are implemented. Reviews by the Executive Board take place at least every six months and revisions in policies are agreed as new information, problems, or opportunities arise. Nowadays, virtually all such letters of intent and staff reports to the Executive Board are published.

The IMF disburses foreign currencies to the country's central bank, increasing its gross foreign reserve holdings. These larger reserves allow aggregate spending by residents on domestic and foreign goods and services that is larger than would otherwise be possible. This additional spending lessens the downturn in economic activity that is normally brought on by a balance of payments crisis, easing the hardship caused by the crisis.

Over the years, the IMF has cumulatively lent several hundred billion US dollars and all such loans have been repaid, except for outstanding arrears of some $2 billion by three countries (Somalia, Sudan, and Zimbabwe). Some $7 billion has been extinguished through debt relief granted to the poorest countries by the IMF, alongside debt relief also granted by other official creditors.

2

The Korean Crisis Ten Years Later: A Success Story

Hubert Neiss, Wanda Tseng, and James Gordon[1]

In late 1997, Korea was engulfed in a financial crisis that became the country's most traumatic event since the Korean War. The crisis in Korea was largely unexpected. The world had long admired Korea's success in transforming what had been an economic basket case into a member of the exclusive club of advanced countries of the Organization of Economic Cooperation and Development (OECD). Although some macroeconomic weaknesses had emerged early in the year, for most of 1997 the economy still appeared to be doing relatively well. Growth had slowed a little amid a cutback in consumption and investment. Export prices had fallen sharply reflecting world semiconductor prices (one of Korea's main exports), but export volumes were still growing strongly. Other macro indicators, such as inflation, the exchange rate, and the fiscal position, were sound.

Strains in corporate and financial sectors emerged, but their impact on the economy was not fully appreciated at the time. Several debt-ridden conglomerates (*chaebols*) went bankrupt, eroding the balance sheets of their creditor banks. But the bankruptcies were also taken as a positive sign that, in a departure from the past, a reform-minded government was not going to bail out financially irresponsible corporations. However, short-term foreign exchange borrowing had ballooned since 1993 when the government liberalized these flows (while maintaining restrictions on longer-term flows); foreign banks readily obliged, enticed by Korea's

[1] Hubert Neiss is a former director and Wanda Tseng a former deputy director in the IMF's Asian Department, and James Gordon is a division chief in the Asian Department. The authors are very grateful to Sharmini Coorey, Ken Kang, Christian Thimann, and Jong-won Yoon for helpful comments, and to Pihuan Cormier for research assistance.

strong macroeconomic fundamentals. The short-term borrowings were on lent for long-term domestic investments, creating maturity mismatches, and the foreign exchange risks were not hedged because a fixed exchange rate was widely assumed. These weaknesses were not taken as an indicator of a major impending crisis, including by an IMF consultation mission team that visited Korea in October 1997.

At the same time, the external environment was deteriorating. A financial crisis wrought havoc in Thailand in July and touched other countries in Southeast Asia. Sentiment was further worsened by volatility in the Hong Kong stock market in late October, after Taiwan abandoned its currency peg. Korea's external short-term borrowing, which had previously been rolled over as a matter of routine, became a source of vulnerability. Markets began to worry that Korea had too much foreign debt and too little foreign reserves as a cushion should foreign banks cut back exposure. These fears were self-feeding. The lower the rollover of maturing loans by foreign banks, the greater the pressure on reserves, and the less inclined other banks were to roll over. By mid-November, markets estimated Korea's reserves to be $20 billion and only half as large as the debt falling due by the end of the year. There were also rumors about an increasing short-forward position. The authorities' secretiveness about debt and reserves statistics only served to fan market fears.

The authorities initially hoped that Korea could get bilateral help from its key allies and avoid seeking IMF assistance. After all, Korea was now an advanced country and going to the IMF was seen as losing economic sovereignty. However, entreaties to Japan for a bilateral loan and for Japanese banks to maintain their credit lines to Korean banks were unsuccessful; requests to the United States met a similar fate. By mid-November, there was widespread speculation that Korea would have to seek an IMF program. The IMF's Managing Director, Michel Camdessus, secretly visited Seoul on November 16 and reached an agreement with Deputy Prime Minister Kyung Shik Kang to announce Korea's request for help from the IMF on November 18. Mr. Camdessus was also informed that reserves were sufficient to last until at least through the end of the year, giving the IMF some, albeit not much, time to act. However, the government's financial reform bills were defeated in Parliament the next day and Mr. Kang was dismissed; the request for IMF assistance was not made. As the turmoil intensified, a public visit by the IMF's First Deputy Managing Director, Stanley Fischer, followed on November 20. On November 21, the Korean authorities announced that they would seek financial assistance from the IMF.

The program supported by the IMF stabilized the foreign exchange market and provided the catalyst for much-needed corporate and financial sector restructuring. The crisis set off a severe economic downturn with widespread bankruptcies and a sharp jump in unemployment. But within a year, the downturn had begun to reverse; the won had stabilized; interest rates had returned to precrisis levels; and foreign exchange reserves had been built up from practically zero to exceed $50 billion. Korea also reentered international bond markets and had started to repay its more expensive IMF loan. Within two years, real GDP exceeded the precrisis level; the won was appreciating; and foreign reserves exceeded $70 billion. Within three years, reserves were almost $100 billion and the IMF-supported program had ended. And within four years, all outstanding IMF loans had been repaid, well ahead of schedule. By any measure, this was a successful program.

Initial emergency program

An advance financial sector team from the IMF arrived in Seoul on November 24, followed by a full team two days later.[2] The team, of which we were a part, was a diverse group, reflecting the IMF's global membership. In all, 11 nationalities from four continents were represented in the team, bringing diverse perspectives, experiences, and expertise. While the group was assembled in haste, we worked closely together as a team under great pressure to confront the greatest challenge of our professional careers.

Our original work schedule was already a tall order. The program was to be considered by the IMF's Executive Board on December 17. The team thus had three weeks to negotiate the program with the authorities, have the program reviewed at headquarters, and prepare and issue the Board documents. The usual timetable for a program was two or even three months. Adding to the difficulties, the crisis had unfolded so rapidly that both sides had had little time to prepare.

It was a crisp and sunny autumn day on November 25, 1997, when we arrived at the Bank of Korea to begin our work. But what we learned at that first meeting turned the following days into darkness. We were stunned to learn that Korea's short-term external liabilities were considerably higher than reported. This is because reported data had not included borrowing by branches of Korean banks incorporated abroad, in keeping with rules about recording external debt statistics. This discovery made the low level of foreign exchange reserves even more worrying. We faxed a handwritten note to headquarters with three options: obtain short-term bridging loan from the central banks of Japan and the United States,[3] obtain emergency permission from Korean banks' creditors to pay Korean banks' foreign obligations in bonds rather than cash, negotiate an emergency rescue program. IMF Headquarters instructed us to negotiate; it was the option we least preferred because a program negotiated in such a rush might not be credible.

The Korean delegation was headed by Deputy Prime Minister Chung Yuel Lim. It included Vice Minister Duck Koo Chung, Assistant Minister Man Soo Kang, Director General Woo Suk Kim, Director Joong Kyung Choi, and Director Kyung Wook Hur of the Ministry of Finance and Economy, and other senior officials. The delegation set up office in the Hilton Hotel where the IMF team was staying, so that discussions could be held anytime, sometimes very late in the evening even past midnight, scheduled at short notice. The Korean officials worked through many nights. As the day in Seoul drew to a close, Washington opened (where Okyu Kwon was Alternate Executive Director for the constituency including Korea on the IMF's Executive Board), and a second round of phone, fax, and e-mail traffic began. There were several nights that week when the team got no sleep at all, but was kept going by the conviction that it was best placed to provide the help that Korea so badly needed.

Tension was injected by the Korean and international press corps camping outside the elevators in the hotel waiting for news on the negotiations. Tired of being ambushed by journalists, we started to use the hotel stairs, going through the kitchen to the conference room in the basement. But the press was persistent, even posing as Ministry of Finance officials on one occasion in an unsuccessful attempt to obtain information. All the while, CNBC Asia was broadcasting news of falling stock prices and the swooning won. And the news was dismal from the Bank of Korea where banks with foreign credit lines that were not being rolled over continued to queue up for emergency support, further depleting reserves. Unless the situation stabilized, Korea would be bankrupt before the end of the year.

The program had to be negotiated with unprecedented speed because remaining foreign exchange reserves were running out, other countries were not willing to provide a quick bridging loan, and the Korean government did not want to declare a default. In the event, the program was approved by the Executive Board on December 4, only a little over a week after the full mission's arrival.

The announcement that a program had been agreed with the IMF was a traumatic event for the Korean people. Official denial about the need for IMF assistance up until just over a week prior did not prepare the public for this news. Many reacted with shock, dismay, and anger.

Headlines in Korean newspapers lamented the ceding of economic control to outsiders, with banners such as "National Humiliation Day" and "Don't Forget the International Trusteeship." "Trusteeship" was associated with strong feelings for Koreans who were proud of their national independence, given the history of Japanese colonialism.

Program content

The program attacked two immediate problems: the foreign exchange problem and the banking problem, but also started longer-term reform efforts in several other areas.

The foreign exchange problem was tackled by a loan of record size from the IMF ($21 billion) combined with loans from the World Bank ($10 billion) and Asian Development Bank (AsDB) ($4 billion). There was also a declaration by G-7 governments to provide additional funds to Korea if needed, a so-called Second Line of Defense (SLOD) of $22 billion. However, it turned out that key countries contributing to the SLOD did not want the program to assume that money would actually be used, meaning that the SLOD was not really available to meet Korea's foreign exchange needs. The initial emergency program was also accompanied by concerted moral suasion by the monetary authorities in creditor countries to urge commercial banks to roll over maturing Korean debt, and eventually by a formal agreement with foreign banks to reschedule Korean debt in January 1998.

So as to defend the exchange rate, the program required that interest rates be raised sharply above their precrisis level of 14–15 percent. This was probably the most hotly debated aspect of the program (as discussed later in the chapter). But economics aside, raising interest rates in Korea turned out to be less than straightforward in practice. To begin with, there was a law that prohibited interest rates from rising above 25 percent in Korea. Since the program envisaged that interest rates might have to rise almost up to 30 percent, this law had to be repealed for the monetary policy understanding to become effective. Moreover, on December 2, with the program almost finalized, the team received a rocket from headquarters asking why Bloomberg data showed interest rates dropping to 6 percent. Were the authorities serious about the program? In fact, interest rates were being raised. However, Bloomberg had changed its interest-rate sample to cover just two small banks making non-market-based transactions. Bad timing to make sample changes, to say the least. We reassured headquarters that monetary policy was being tightened and that emergency foreign exchange support extended to Korea would not go out the door just as fast as it came in.

The program initially also involved fiscal policy measures, including delaying nonpriority investment programs. These measures were mainly intended to cover some of the costs of the financial sector cleanup. However, once the extent of the downturn in the economy became apparent, these measures were quickly recognized as unnecessary and even harmful. Beginning early in 1998, the fiscal target was progressively loosened so as to allow the automatic stabilizers to work and for fiscal policy to become countercyclical.[4]

But while macroeconomic policies were important, the centerpiece of the program was a comprehensive restructuring plan to address the structural weaknesses in the financial and corporate sectors that the crisis had so cruelly exposed. While the structural reforms were later criticized by some as being unnecessary (as discussed later), it is clear that the program would not have been credible nor would it have received the massive level of official support and consensus for rollover by commercial banks without them.

At the heart of the structural reform agenda were measures to stabilize and then rehabilitate the banking system. The IMF flew in Stefan Ingves from the Central Bank of Sweden, who had successfully dealt with a banking crisis there, to give advice. The strategy for banking reforms was based on earlier experiences of banking crises in some European industrial countries and the United States, and broadly followed the pattern adopted by the other Asian crisis countries, and belatedly also by Japan. Legislation was to be introduced to strengthen the central bank act and to bring banking and prudential supervision up to international best practice.

The program also included the following elements:

- A blanket government guarantee to depositors;
- Temporary liquidity credits to banks by the Bank of Korea to finance deposit withdrawals;
- Closure of nonviable merchant banks and commercial banks;
- Temporary nationalization of some commercial banks;
- Government control over some weak banks;
- Establishing a nonperforming asset (NPA) fund, operated by Korean Asset Management Company, to take NPAs from banks;
- Internal reorganization of banks and banking mergers; and
- Strengthening of bank supervision.

Hoping to bolster investor confidence, the program initiated longer-term reform efforts in several other areas. These included trade and capital account liberalization, improving corporate governance and corporate structure, and labor market reforms.

The United States, a key IMF shareholder, argued vigorously that the program should include trade liberalization measures. The team was not fully convinced, given that insufficient openness was not an immediate cause of Korea's difficulties. One element of trade liberalization—the import diversification program—affecting mainly Japanese automobiles and cultural goods (such as movies, TV, and video games) was particularly sensitive. The authorities were adamantly opposed to any trade measures, observing wryly that liberalizing imports in the midst of a foreign exchange crisis seemed a curious strategy. In the end, the program's trade liberalization component largely repeated preexisting World Trade Organization (WTO) commitments, albeit at a faster pace than the authorities would have wished.

The United States also advocated capital account opening, which met with further strong opposition from the authorities. The team did not see the merits of some of the specific suggestions from the United States, such as allowing hostile takeovers and liberalizing foreign investment in retail trade, but saw a need to attract capital to rebuild reserves. Moreover, Korea's troubles could be linked to the practice of channeling international borrowing by companies through the banks, rather than allowing companies directly to access international markets. A case could thus be made for further commitments to capital account liberalization, especially for long-term inflows. The authorities objected strongly, noting that the public already viewed with suspicion the capital account opening that had been agreed as part of OECD accession a year earlier. Recent events suggested that this had occurred without adequate preparation. In the end, we agreed there would be further capital account liberalization, but it would be gradual.

On corporate restructuring, our team relied a great deal on expertise within Korea as this was an area outside the IMF's usual area of involvement. While the World Bank and work by the OECD provided some guidance, the program's conditions for the corporate sector were largely drawn up by the Korean government and reflected its own priorities. The objective was to restore the financial health and competitiveness of the corporate sector and address the practices that made Korea vulnerable to financial crisis. The strategy involved

- Promoting greater competition, both domestic and foreign, by opening markets, liberalizing foreign investment, and strengthening the regulatory role of the Fair Trade Commission;

- Improving the corporate governance system, including stronger investor rights, independent Boards of Directors, transparency in financial accounting and disclosures, and better bankruptcy procedures; and
- Improving capital structure and profitability, including measures to reduce excessive debt levels, eliminate cross-subsidization of weaker affiliates, and facilitate mergers and acquisitions.

The authorities had unsuccessfully tried to introduce labor reforms a year before the crisis, but had backed off in the face of widespread industrial action. The crisis provided them with an opportunity to revisit these reforms. However, since the labor market was again not central to the crisis, and the issue was highly political, the team was careful in keeping its distance. The program included no more than a vague goal to improve labor market flexibility. Thereafter, labor reform evolved within the context of the Tripartite Accord between labor, business, and government, with the IMF as an observer. The charge sometimes heard that the IMF imposed labor reform on Korea is simply not true.

Revised program

After an initial positive reaction to the December 4 program, markets quickly resumed their downward spiral. This was due to a combination of factors. A leak of the program documents revealed actual debt and reserves numbers that showed how close Korea had come to the edge. Markets also questioned whether the SLOD money was really available. As mentioned earlier, the skepticism turned out to be warranted as it transpired that key countries contributing to the SLOD could not vote for the program if the program assumed the money would be used. In addition, there was an election due on December 18, and doubts arose as to whether the next government would feel bound by the program commitments.

Armed with assurances from the new government, the team regrouped in Seoul over Christmas to strengthen the program.[5]At the same time, what turned out to be the critical missing piece of the initial rescue plan, a rescheduling agreement with creditor banks, was being hammered out in New York and other capitals. In conjunction with the stronger program, a consensus by G-7 banks to largely roll over the short-term debt of Korean financial institutions led to a decisive turn in market sentiment. This was followed by a formal rescheduling agreement with creditor banks that helped to stabilize the foreign exchange situation.

Public relations

In a major departure from what had been normal IMF practice at the time, the team engaged in outreach to the media and civil society to explain and help garner support for the program. At the time, IMF mission chiefs were told to keep a low profile and avoid the press. Indeed, while we were flooded with TV cameras and press questions, the standing order was to refer all questions to headquarters. This was totally impractical with so many rumors flying around and given the time difference between Seoul and Washington. We decided to take action to demystify the IMF and explain the program to the public. We allowed coverage of one of our internal mission discussions by YTN (Yonhap Television News), a business news station, and answered questions about the program. We talked with labor unions, university students and faculty, church groups, and representatives of foreign bank branches in Korea. The outreach also included the personal presence of Managing Director Camdessus on several occasions. One incident typified misconceptions about the IMF. During our visit to a labor union, the elevators in the building stopped only on odd-numbered floors. When we asked why, the answer was that the IMF program required electricity conservation! This, of course, was totally untrue. So outreach and public communications became a major task.

The IMF became a household word to signify economic difficulties. IMF lunches and IMF weddings (austere affairs) became popular, and I.M.Fired bespoke of the social distress of the time. Strong anti-IMF feelings prevailed in Korea, and the crisis was and is still called the "IMF crisis." But there was also wide understanding that sacrifices were unavoidable and that the IMF came to Korea's rescue. While the "IMF prescriptions" were bitter, there is an old Korean saying that "bitter medicine is better for the body." On a personal basis, our team members were treated in a most friendly way by the government and the public, and long-term friendships were forged among us. In 2002, President Kim Dae Jung awarded the "Order of Industrial Service Merit" to the mission chief in recognition of the team's work for Korea.

Reflections on the crisis

By now, there is a large body of literature evaluating the Korea program ex post.[6] We do not want to rehash the whole debate nor suggest that all the criticisms which have been voiced were unjustified. We want to highlight some of the key controversies and give our reflections on what we have learned.

It would be naive to think that everything that was done in a rush would be perfect. We were confronted with a crisis situation, and drastic and far-reaching emergency measures had to be adopted urgently, without the luxury of time for much discussion and reflection. Looking back, as we discussed emergency measures with government officials under great time pressure, we still remember the shock on both sides as the crisis unfolded. Nevertheless most of the measures suggested (in particular, financial and corporate sector reforms) were in the longer-term interest of the Korean economy. In a crisis situation, what is most important is constant reassessment and adjustments in the program in light of unfolding events. We recognized this need from the outset, and the Korea program was the most constantly reviewed program ever at the IMF, with real-time monitoring and reassessment by the staff and management and informal biweekly reviews by the IMF's Executive Board.

Controversies surrounded the two major areas of the program: the immediate foreign exchange crisis and the structural reforms. On the first, critics questioned whether the macroeconomic policy response was appropriate, and whether the foreign exchange crisis could have been better addressed with quicker involvement of creditor banks, more official financing, or capital controls. On the second, criticisms were levied against the interferences of major IMF shareholders and the inclusion in the program of too many reforms affecting too many areas in the Korean economy.

High interest rates: This was probably the most controversial policy in the program. Contrary to popular perceptions of a one-size-fits-all approach in the IMF, we vigorously debated interest rates in internal discussions. In mid-December, shortly after the program went into effect, the team in Seoul raised its concern to IMF management that sustained high interest rates and the liquidity squeeze would drive otherwise sound corporations into bankruptcy. The team understood that because of Korea's structural peculiarities, the banking sector was intricately linked to its corporate sector, and the corporate sector was highly leveraged and vulnerable to interest rate increases. The team argued that agreement with foreign banks to restructure Korea's debt was urgently needed to avoid prohibitively high interest rates that would permanently damage Korea's growth potential.

That said, there was probably no other means to stop the precipitate fall in the won than a sharp and short-term rise in interest rates. Other options were either not available (a quick agreement with banks or even larger official financial support) or not desirable (declaring default). And if, amid the market turmoil, we had proposed a lowering of interest rates, it would almost certainly have triggered a further sharp fall of the won and would have further damaged balance sheets of corporations which had large foreign exchange debts. Moreover, key shareholders on the IMF's Executive Board (especially the United States and also some European Directors) strongly advocated high interest rates and would not have approved the program without it. So there was no choice.

Since the crisis, there have been numerous studies on interest rate policy in the program, analyzing the impact of high interest rates on the exchange rate, credit availability, and output, and the conclusions vary. However, what is clear is that because this policy did not get the buy-in from the Korean authorities, interest rates were increased only hesitantly instead of quickly, and then were kept high for too long, because of fear by the IMF that a quick reduction would throw the foreign exchange market again into turmoil. This contributed to the depth of the recession.

A related point is the assumption made by some critics that a soft landing was possible. Critics often suggest that IMF policies caused the recession, whereas a recession was surely inevitable once the crisis broke. It is impossible to know for sure, but the situation for both Korea and the world economy would probably have been even more devastating if there had been a default. Given that the downturn was so short in duration, it is hard to argue that the IMF made the situation worse.

Fiscal tightening: In addition to interest rates, the other leg of the macro response was fiscal policy. The initial rationale for fiscal tightening was to restore confidence in the government's ability to deal with the crisis and leave room for the expected large costs of bank restructuring. However, less than a month after the program was approved, it had become clear that the original target of a balanced budget would be too contractionary. There was opposition within the IMF staff and Executive Board to fiscal relaxation. The case was gradually won with the support of Stan Fischer, whose argument of "letting the automatic stabilizers work" made the policy switch more palatable to the fiscal doctrinaires. In addition, the program provided for higher expenditures for expanding the social safety net, including unemployment insurance. But then, the tables were turned as the Korean authorities were fiscally conservative by tradition and were reluctant to expand expenditure, especially in the social area. Certainly, the lesson is that there should be no knee-jerk reaction that fiscal tightening is the best policy in every situation. We applied that lesson in Korea, but only after the program started.

Inadequate expansion of social protection: As noted earlier, the program provided for higher expenditures for the social safety net, but because of their long-standing philosophy, the authorities themselves were reluctant. Korea had previously enjoyed high economic growth and did not have to deal with problems of serious unemployment. So the actual setting up of an effective social safety net was slow. This was the World Bank's area of expertise. While Joseph Stiglitz, World Bank Chief Economist at the time, has many criticisms for the IMF policy prescriptions, we are not aware that he has ever reflected on whether he could have done a better job in assisting the authorities with establishing an effective social safety net. In contrast, Managing Director Camdessus proposed working with a Tripartite Accord between the unions, employers, and the government, which helped in preserving social and political calm, providing room for the government to implement policies.

What of the other options (such as quicker agreement with creditor banks, more official financial support, and capital controls) that some have argued should have been used to deal with the foreign exchange crisis? Our reflections on these options are as follows.

Creditor banks were bailed-in too late: Critics argue that the initial December 4 program should have "involved the private sector." In the absence of a framework for doing so, this was a sensitive issue. There was fear (justified or not) that convening an emergency meeting of banks at the outset of the crisis and before a program was in place could increase market nervousness and accelerate capital outflows. The problem was the lack of a readily accepted mechanism to deal with such emergencies. Furthermore, the inability to include the SLOD also played a role in the initial program not working. Perhaps if the SLOD had been available, the agreement with the banks might be less urgent.

Lending packages were too small: While the financing package was the largest ever by the IMF, it was insufficient to instill market confidence, especially since the SLOD from bilateral sources was not really usable. The announcement of these supplementary bilateral resources had initially a favorable psychological effect, but markets soon understood that they were unlikely to be forthcoming.

Failure to impose capital controls: Some have suggested that controls on capital outflows should have been applied, like in Malaysia, to arrest the hemorrhaging of reserves. However, the key was to attract capital back to Korea. Moreover, the Korean authorities had themselves decided it was in their national interest to honor their contractual obligations and not default. They did not want to isolate Korea from global financial markets. We proceeded to negotiate the program with the premise of avoiding default.

But it is clear that high interest rates alone could not have stabilized the exchange rate. In this sense, the near-messianic belief in high interest rates by some key IMF shareholders was misplaced, especially in the face of strong opposition from the Korean authorities. A more comprehensive solution to address the source of the foreign exchange market instability—the liquidity squeeze caused by foreign banks cutting off their credit lines to Korean banks—was required. While the international community has tried to find a solution since the crisis, a mechanism for orderly debt restructuring is still not in place. As for quicker disbursement of official financing, the IMF introduced the Contingent Credit Lines, but no country signed up for this facility, and it was allowed to expire in 2003. The IMF is still working on some alternatives, and Asian countries have intensified regional financial cooperation, but we are still far from an effective solution.

Interference of major shareholders in setting program conditions: This contributed to the "excessive and sometimes irrelevant" conditions and created resentment among the Koreans, and among us. The presence of David Lipton, a senior US Treasury official, who chose to stay at the Hilton Hotel with the IMF mission led to the suspicion of the authorities that we were given orders by the United States. This was not the case, but we were informed about what measures the United States would require in the program if it should vote for it. We strove to take into account the suggestions of major shareholders as much as possible, because the vote of major shareholders in the Executive Board was needed for the rescue package to materialize. Many of the suggestions were sound and in line with the team's own thinking, and ex post, the Korean authorities would also agree with them. However, the obvious interference made it more difficult for political leaders to come to terms with what needed to be done, and also tended to erode the legitimacy of the IMF as an international institution.

Structural reforms: The program was notable for a heavy dose of structural reforms. These have been criticized as being too intrusive and distracting attention from crisis management proper. However, the fact was that the Korean government itself recognized the need for reforms and turned the crisis into an opportunity to correct some deep-seated structural flaws that contributed to the crisis. There were some differences on the closure of insolvent merchant banks, trade liberalization, and capital account liberalization, but as noted earlier, in the latter two areas the program included largely preexisting commitments with the WTO or OECD. On the whole, while there were differences of views on exactly how to go about certain reforms, there was not much disagreement on the overall direction of reforms.

Nevertheless the IMF later recognized that reform conditions could be excessive and sometimes irrelevant and introduced changes to streamline the content of programs. However, we should not lose sight of the fact that most reforms would have been needed even without a crisis but would have been more difficult to implement in good times. None of the critics argue now that the reforms implemented during the crisis should have been reversed, and Korea itself has not reversed them. Indeed, they were key to restoring confidence and boosting the credibility of the program, and ultimately were beneficial to the economy.[7]

Recovery and structural transformation

The historical record is clear. The overall strategy of the Korea program, which was aimed at overcoming the crisis quickly and initiating a sustained recovery, was right. At the time, in 1998 and even in 1999, many did not believe this, including serious analysts of the crisis. For example, *Time* magazine of June 21, 1999, had the cover story "Asian Recovery—Don't bet on it," by Paul Krugman.

Decisive political leadership, committed policymakers in both the outgoing and incoming administrations, and public solidarity and sacrifice, were key to the success of the program. During the campaign, Kim Dae Jung mentioned the possibility of a renegotiation with the IMF. However, immediately after being elected, he announced that he would comply fully with the program and moved quickly to form the Emergency Economic Measures Committee, which supervised daily crisis management in consultation with the economic team of the existing administration. Implementation of the program was taken with the utmost seriousness at all levels of government. Most impressive was the national consensus that emerged: the Korean people united and worked to overcome the crisis; grassroots campaigns to collect gold to save the national economy were just one example.

The threats at the height of the crisis—international default, contagion to the global economy, and collapse of the banking system—receded. The recession was short -lived, and strong economic growth resumed. Sweeping reforms have fundamentally transformed the Korean economy, making it more open, competitive, and resilient.

Korea made a quick and spectacular recovery from the crisis. By 1999, output had already recovered to its precrisis level; ten years later, the economy is now nearly 50 percent larger, and per capita income has nearly doubled. Meanwhile, international reserves, which were almost exhausted at the depth of the crisis, now stand close to $250 billion, covering three times short-term debt.

Korea's economic structure has been transformed:

- The banking system is stronger and more diversified. Banking supervision and regulations were brought in line with best international practice. Banking soundness indicators, such as capital adequacy, profitability, and asset quality, now compare favorably with those in other advanced countries. Risk-assessment practices and credit information have been upgraded. The government has reprivatized most of the banks it acquired during the crisis. Banks refocused their activities on profitable lending opportunities, shifting from concentrating their lending to *chaebols*. This has benefited consumers and small and medium enterprises (SMEs) by providing them with access to credit. Households now can buy houses with mortgages, and SMEs can secure loans to start new businesses. Korea now aspires to become a regional financial center—a goal that was unimaginable during the crisis.
- Capital markets have been deepened. *Chaebols* turned to capital markets to raise financing, helping to develop one of the largest bond markets in Asia. The stock market has also grown rapidly, and foreign investors now account for about a third of market capitalization. Financial markets now exercise greater discipline on the *chaebols*; financial risks, rather than being concentrated in the banking system, are now more widely dispersed.
- Corporate finances and governance have been overhauled. Before the crisis, Korea's corporate sector was characterized by high leverage and low profitability. Now, its financial ratios are similar to those in other advanced countries. Corporate governance has also improved with strengthened investor rights, greater transparency in financial accounts and disclosures, and more accountability of managers and major shareholders. Conglomerates such as Samsung and Hyundai have become globally recognized firms, known for innovation, product quality, and competitiveness.

Since the crisis, concerns have risen about job security and social polarization. Nevertheless there is by now widespread agreement in Korea that the reforms have made the economy more transparent, resilient, and globally competitive. This makes Korea better placed to deal with the new challenges in a rapidly changing global economy and provides the potential for a further rise in living standards of the people.

Closing thoughts

Ten years on, we can look back on the crisis and see how Korea faced the danger of financial collapse and turned it into an opportunity for reforms. The IMF was rapidly on the scene and ready to help when massive and quick support was needed. The IMF acted quickly and substantially, and was effective because of the Korean government's decisive crisis management and the willingness of the Korean people to support reforms. While mistakes and oversights unavoidably occurred, constant reviews provided opportunities for correction and adjustment of policies.

While the overall success of the program is evident, the question remains whether Korea's recovery could have been achieved at lower social and economic cost. As is obvious from the section on our reflections, there are still a number of lessons to be learned from this experience by Korea and the larger international community, in particular the IMF. So both the IMF and Korea have to reflect on this experience. As far as we are concerned, being involved in these events provided us with an unforgettable professional challenge, enduring friendships, and a deeper insight in the handling of financial crises.

The Korean Crisis Ten Years Later: A Success Story

Kihwan Kim[1]

It is indeed a great pleasure and honor to comment on "The Korean Crisis Ten Years Later: A Success Story" authored by Hubert Neiss, Wanda Tseng, and James Gordon. The authors are in every sense of the word three outstanding professionals who played key roles in resolving Korea's 1997–98 crisis. Hence they know the subject well. Moreover, they have every right to be highly satisfied with the outcome of their services rendered under the most difficult circumstances ten years ago. As they observe, unlike in 1997–98, Korea today is a dynamic economy making good progress toward becoming a truly advanced economy.

The central theme of their chapter is that the program the IMF implemented to solve Korea's financial difficulties during the 1997–98 crisis was, on balance, an enormous success. In light of both what Korea is today and the historical fact that Korea recovered from the crisis in about two years, it is difficult to disagree with this central theme. Furthermore, this discussant cannot find flaw with most of the counter-arguments the three authors make against several criticisms of the IMF program advanced by a number of writers in recent years.

However, without meaning to diminish their contributions to the resolution of the Korean crisis, their claim and arguments are a bit like a medical doctor relating how he or she successfully treated a young man who suffered from a severe case of the flu some ten years ago. That young man now has become a professional after having attended college

[1] Dr. Kihwan Kim, Ph.D. in economics from the University of California, Berkeley, has held many senior positions in government, and served as Korea's Ambassador-at-large for Economic Affairs during the 1997–98 Asian financial crisis. He currently serves as Chair of the Seoul Financial Forum and as an international adviser to Goldman Sachs, Asia.

and graduate school in the meantime. On the basis of what and how he is now doing, it is difficult to say that the doctor's treatment of the young man was anything but a success. And the treatment of that young man should be considered part of the doctor's highly successful career.

Figuratively speaking, some ten years ago the Korean economy was indeed a young man who had caught a bad case of the economic flu that was sweeping the Asian region. At that time, that young patient was suffering from high fever coupled with a severe case of dehydration, and the doctor's prescriptions, overall, were correct. Otherwise, the young man may not have recovered and be as healthy as he is today.

But it would be a mistake to attribute his present good health entirely to the doctor's treatment ten years ago. It could be that although the young man today is very healthy, he may have suffered far more than necessary, and with a different prescription, the doctor could have contained the flu, particularly the dehydration, at an earlier stage. Moreover, it is possible that due to the bad temperament of the patient, the doctor was unable to prescribe everything he or she would have liked although other doctors who were called in were able to dispense some medicine regardless of the patient's temper.

As this volume is likely to be read in the future as a collection of case studies of financial cures the IMF has administered to different economies of the world, this discussant would like to focus on several complications that not only Korea but also the IMF doctors had to go through while treating the patient.

The first observation has to do with the great difficulty the IMF delegation experienced in negotiating with the Korean government. The authors note that as opposed to the usual two- to three-month period the IMF has had in negotiating rescue packages for individual countries in financial crisis, in the case of Korea, the IMF delegation had less than three weeks to come up with a rescue package acceptable to both the IMF Executive Board and the Korean government. This three-week period included a Thanksgiving holiday. Owing to the shortage of time and the time difference between Seoul and Washington, the three authors recall that there were several nights when the IMF negotiating team had no sleep at all. But the team kept going on the conviction that it was its duty to provide the help that Korea so badly needed.

Actually, in negotiating with the Korean government, the difficulty that the IMF team encountered was not just a shortage of time. The authors are too polite to say that their Korean counterparts were not the easiest people to work with. If the IMF had had its choice, it would have preferred not to work with the Korean delegation headed by

Deputy Prime Minister Chang Yeul Lim. On November 16, 1997, then Deputy Prime Minister Kyong Shik Kang reached an agreement with IMF Managing Director Michel Camdessus that Korea would seek IMF help and make a public announcement to this effect on November 19. But Mr. Kang was dismissed as Deputy Prime Minister on the morning of November 19. However, at the press conference held that afternoon, the new Deputy Prime Minister, Mr. Lim, denied Korea's intention to seek help from the IMF. Needless to say, this created a great deal of confusion and probably some ill will, particularly on the part of the IMF and the US government, which had known about the agreement between Mr. Camdessus and Mr. Kang. It is difficult to say precisely what impact this had on subsequent negotiations, but there is little doubt that its net impact was negative.

Anyhow, Mr. Lim's denial at the press conference was not accidental. There is enough evidence to show that Mr. Lim was aware of the existence of the confidential agreement between Mr. Kang and Mr. Camdessus. His denial had something to do with his own approach to solving the crisis Korea was moving into. He wanted first to seek a substantial bilateral loan from Japan to avoid negotiating with the IMF. He in fact traveled to Japan on November 28 and returned the next day empty handed. Thus, it is difficult to say that DPM Lim was seriously negotiating with the IMF delegation except for the last three to four days preceding the signing of the agreement with the IMF on December 3.

The abrupt appointment of Mr. Lim as Deputy Prime Minister created yet another complication. Before the financial crisis, Mr. Lim had spent some time at the World Bank as Korea's Representative Director. Mr. Lim's tenure at the World Bank overlapped with Lawrence Summers' term as Vice President for Research for the World Bank. Somehow, the encounter between these two gentlemen was not a happy one. To be more specific, Lawrence Summers felt that Mr. Lim would not eagerly embrace the liberal, market-oriented policy reforms that the United States and the IMF would expect from Korea in exchange for an IMF rescue package. Mr. Summers's impression in this regard was probably reinforced by the spirited defense of Korea's highly protectionist policy in the auto industry by Mr. Lim during his visit to Washington in May 1997 in his capacity then as Korea's Minister of Trade and Industry. It may be surmised that due to the poor impression Mr. Summers had of Mr. Lim, the conditions the US government wanted to ask of the IMF and the Korean government in return for an IMF package became far more stringent than would have otherwise been the case.

In any event, it is to the credit of the three authors to note that there were significant differences between the initial IMF program agreed to on December 3 and the second revised program worked out with the Korean government after December 19. Unfortunately, the authors are not very clear about what precisely those differences were. For example, they state that the initial program contained an agreement among monetary authorities in Korea's creditor countries to exercise moral suasion to urge their commercial banks to roll over maturing Korean debt. This discussant has no reason to dispute this point. However, it is legitimate to ask if the parties to the agreement had any intention or ability to implement this agreement in a timely fashion. The authors also fail to note that the first program had certain features that were highly problematic and do not provide the specific background that gave rise to the creation of the second program. The authors seem to imply that the transition from the first to the second program was simply a result of continuous monitoring of the implementation of the first program. This discussant wants to make three points in this regard: (1) whoever was responsible, the first program contained a critical weakness; (2) the primary significance of the second program was to fix it; and (3) this change was in fact the result of US initiative.

To appreciate these points, it is useful to remember that the crisis in Korea was not a traditional balance of payments crisis due to excessive external debt. In other words, the Korean crisis was not due to insolvency; it was rather a liquidity crisis due to serious mismatches in maturity, currency, and the capital structure of the balance sheets of the financial and nonfinancial sectors of the economy. Since the crisis was a liquidity crisis, a rapid infusion of hard currency reserves was more critical than anything else. However, what the IMF and the Korean government agreed upon on December 3, 1997, was a far cry from this.

The total amount of money that the IMF together with other international financial institutions and governments offered to bail out Korea was \$58.4 billion. Out of this, \$23.4 billion was reserved as a so-called Second Line of Defense (SLOD) that would be made available to Korea by G-7 countries only if the initial amount of \$35 billion contributed by the IMF and other multilateral institutions proved inadequate. The disbursement of \$35 billion was to be spread over more than two years lasting until the year 2000, with payment of each installment conditioned upon the progress Korea was to make in structural reforms and the further tightening of its monetary and fiscal policies as required by the agreement. It is also worth noting that the amount Korea was allowed to draw immediately after reaching agreement with the IMF on

December 3 was $5.6 billion. Korea was allowed to draw an additional $3.5 billion on December 18. Thus, the total amount Korea was able to draw during this 15-day period was $9.1 billion. In short, there was not enough front loading of the IMF assistance to meet the immediate liquidity needs of the country. This indeed was the critical weakness of the first program.

In any case, the $9.1 billion available to Korea during the first 15-day period was judged to be altogether inadequate by Korea's foreign creditors, even in terms of meeting the nation's short-term obligations. Given the large amount of short-term obligations and precarious level of official foreign reserves, this judgment became a self-fulfilling prophecy. As rollovers were refused, the limited foreign reserves rapidly depleted. An internal memorandum prepared by the Bank of Korea on December 18, which took into account both the inflows of foreign funds expected during the ensuing 12-day period plus the foreign reserve balance on hand and the outflows expected to take place during the same period, showed that the foreign reserve balance expected on December 31 would be anywhere from negative $600 million to positive $900 million. No wonder foreign creditors further accelerated the withdrawal of their funds from Korea, pushing the country to the verge of a sovereign default in less than two weeks after the initial agreement was signed. Korea was able to avoid this worst possible situation basically with the help from the United States.

On December 19, this discussant in his capacity as Ambassador-at-Large for the Korean government made basically a twofold request of the US government: first, to persuade IMF member countries to further front load IMF rescue funds and, second, to exert its influence on financial institutions from G-7 countries to resume rollovers on their loans to Korea. In exchange, the Korean government would undertake several policy reforms beyond those that had been agreed on December 3. Dubbed "IMF-Plus," these included greater flexibility in the labor market, liberalizing capital account transactions, and allowing hostile takeovers. The US government responded by asking the IMF to enter quickly into a new round of negotiations with the Korean government for further front loading of rescue funds and G-7 monetary authorities to request their financial institutions to roll over their short-term credits to Korea for one month. In return for this favor, G-7 financial institutions were promised opportunities to renegotiate their outstanding short-term loans to Korean institutions with a payment guarantee from the Korean government. In accordance with this arrangement, the Korean government and foreign banks managed to reach an agreement on

January 28, 1998, that led to the restructuring of nearly 95 percent of Korea's short-term debt by March 18, 1998.

To be sure, requesting foreign creditors to resume rollovers of short-term loans and restructure short-term debt was a standing feature of balance-of-payment crisis resolution efforts by the IMF, as it was in other Asian crisis countries as well as in Eastern Europe and earlier in Latin America. But in the case of Korea, the initiative for these actions was taken by the United States. Indeed, high-level US Federal Reserve officials went out of their way to persuade their counterparts in G-7 countries to accelerate actions by their financial institutions in resuming rollovers and restructuring short-term loans to Korea. The announcement of G-7 support on Christmas Day that had a decisive impact on market confidence was basically a result of these efforts by the US.

The key conclusion to be drawn from these observations is that the initial assistance package worked out between the IMF and Korea fell far short of the country's liquidity needs. Moreover, the further front loading of funds agreed to in the second IMF program was also not sufficient to deal with Korea's liquidity needs. Only when foreign creditors were persuaded by the US government to continue rolling over the existing short-term debt in return for an opportunity to renegotiate these debts were Korea's liquidity needs met.

It is worth noting that it was primarily out of security considerations that the United States government took the series of actions it did. The US felt that unless it helped Korea in a big way in a hurry, its security position would be jeopardized, particularly the safety and well-being of some 36,000 US troops then stationed in Korea.

This point has disturbing implications for the IMF and others. Suppose another country with a size similar to that of Korea faces a financial crisis today. Under the existing charter, could the IMF arrange a support package comparable to the one offered to Korea at the end of renegotiations? In addition, who could arrange the kind of international rescue package that was put together under US initiative on such short notice? Furthermore, it is worth asking if the United States would take the initiative for that country if it had no special security relationship comparable to that of the United States and Korea.

Before closing, this discussant would like to make an observation or two on what the three authors call US interference with the IMF's negotiations with the Korean government. It is highly interesting to note that the three authors were rather irritated by the presence of David Lipton in the very same hotel where negotiations were taking place. In their words:

> The presence of David Lipton, a senior US Treasury official, who chose to stay at the Hilton Hotel with the IMF mission led to the suspicion of the (Korean) authorities that we were given orders by the United States. This was not the case, but we were informed about what measures the United States would have to see in the program if it should vote for it. ... However, the obvious interference made it more difficult for (Korean) political leaders to come to terms with what needed to be done and also tended to erode the legitimacy of the IMF as an international institution.

Surely, the authors are justified in expressing their irritation. However, from the perspective of US policy makers, particularly Lawrence Summers, what the authors call obvious interference is quite understandable. It may be recalled that by a strange historical coincidence, Mr. Summers, who was overseeing the US interests at the time of the Korean financial crisis, had little trust in Mr. Lim, the head of the Korean delegation. Besides, when the United States decided to help Korea in a big way following this discussant's meeting with Mr. Summers, the United States had reasons to make sure that Korea kept its promises. Indeed it was immediately after the December 19 meeting that the United States made the decision to send Mr. Lipton back to Seoul. Mr. Lipton's primary mission was to ascertain the intention of both the incumbent and incoming Korean governments with regard to their intentions to honor the "IMF-Plus" offer delivered on December 19. At a December 22 meeting Mr. Lipton had with President-elect Kim Dae Jung, the offer was indeed confirmed. Over the following few days, Mr. Lipton made his own efforts to see whether or not the offer made by the Korean government was reflected in the negotiations between the IMF and the Korean government delegations. Whether one wants to call Mr. Lipton's presence at the hotel interference by a major IMF shareholder depends on one's own perspective. But given the extent of US interests and the discussion between Mr. Summers and this discussant, this discussant is not prepared to characterize Mr. Lipton's presence at the scene of negotiations as an act "that tended to erode the legitimacy of the IMF as an international institution." Of course, one cannot deny that both the style and demeanor of US officials left much to be desired, especially from the point of view of IMF officials.

In conclusion, the IMF program for Korea had good results. Korea quickly recovered from the crisis. It resumed precrisis level growth within two years, and Korea's foreign exchange reserves today are the fifth largest in the world at more than $250 billion. However, it would be inaccurate to say that all of this was the result of the IMF rescue package or the economic restructuring program recommended by the IMF. In the opinion of this discussant, the decisive turn for the better came when the United States intervened in a significant manner, providing leadership in the rescheduling of Korea's large external short-term debt to G-7 nations. It is doubtful that it is within the power of the IMF to provide assistance on a similar scale and in a similar manner should another crisis of a similar scale occur in the future. Needless to say, what this means for the IMF is that before it becomes sensitive about the erosion of its legitimacy as an international institution, it should be more concerned about the need to expand its resource base if it is to remain the lender of last resort in international financial crises.

3

Poland: Stabilization, Transition, and Reform, 1990–91

Timothy Lane, Rolando Ossowski, and Massimo Russo[1]

The IMF played a critical role in supporting countries making the transition from central planning to the market economy in the 1990s. The main task was to help these countries restore and maintain macroeconomic and external stability while undergoing a radical reshaping of their economic institutions. The countries' desire to change stemmed from the clear failure of the Communist system to deliver a satisfactory living standard for their citizens, especially when compared with the market economies of Western Europe. These failures both compounded the difficulties of transition and steeled the determination to face up to them.

Poland's "big bang" in 1990 was an early and dramatic example of a country tackling the challenges of transition—and a particularly successful example of the IMF's involvement in this new and highly uncertain situation. While 1990 was a very difficult year for the Poles, it set them on the path to becoming a dynamic and stable market economy—one of the fastest-growing countries in Europe for most of the decade and among the first group from the region to join the European Union. This outcome testifies to the authorities' courage and steady commitment to change as well as to the international community's keen desire to see Poland succeed.

When the Solidarity-led government—Poland's first post-Communist government—was formed in September 1989, the IMF acted quickly to engage with them. Barely a week after the formation of the new government, a small staff team went to Warsaw to meet the new

[1] The first two authors were economists on the team that worked with the Polish authorities on their 1990–91 stabilization and reform program; the third author was then Director of the European Department.

authorities, explore their intentions, and offer help.[8] The government followed up at the IMF/World Bank Annual Meetings in early October, which offered the opportunity for Poland's new Minister of Finance to meet the finance ministers of all major member countries, to brief them on his policy intentions and secure their support. Then came the work of designing a viable economic program of stabilization and reform, to be launched at the new year. In mid-October, an IMF staff team was dispatched to Warsaw to start this work. Two missions were required to complete the negotiations just before Christmas 1989. The then IMF Managing Director, Michel Camdessus, visited Warsaw personally during the second mission to ascertain the authorities' commitment to the program and their ability to implement it.[9]

The setting

The new government planned its leap to a market economy in the midst of a rapidly deteriorating economic situation. The economy had been stagnating. Inflation was rampant—not only open inflation but also repressed inflation in the shape of long queues outside shops. A large share of Poland's external debt was not being serviced and was at a crushing level that would require debt relief from its external creditors. Moreover, its own citizens' foreign currency deposits at Polish banks, if valued at a realistic exchange rate, would dwarf those banks' capital, requiring a major infusion of government money to maintain the solvency of the banking system. With the budget already in large deficit, this additional burden could not be sustained. Maintaining the status quo was not an option.

This dire situation was a legacy of previous Communist governments, characterized by years of fitful reforms alternating with repression. Cracks had opened in central planning, with labor unrest beginning in the 1970s. Workers in the Solidarity movement continued to agitate for more reforms until 1981, when martial law was declared and tanks rolled into the streets to repress their movement. Beginning in the mid-1980s, the regime of martial law was eased and some economic reforms were introduced to deal with long-standing economic problems, such as chronic shortages and stagnating living standards, and the economic stresses that were emerging—including mounting external debt. Thus, state enterprises were given some autonomy; private enterprises in some areas were encouraged; there was some timid liberalization of prices; and the parallel foreign exchange market was liberalized, with a widening gap between the official exchange rate and that on the street. These reforms lacked a comprehensive framework, were adopted piecemeal, and failed the test of credibility.

In the event, an alarming deterioration in the economic situation ensued. In 1988–89, inflation surged to rates not seen in decades, shortages intensified, and output began to contract. In its final weeks the Communist government in August 1989 eliminated price controls on food. While the move was intended to balance demand and supply in the food economy, curb the subsidy drain on the budget, and spur agricultural production, the resulting surge in food prices caused the overall cost of living to increase by over one-third in a single month. As wages struggled to catch up—and workers' demands met little resistance from management—Poland seemed to be spiraling toward hyperinflation. With rising inflation, other prices that had not been freed became increasingly out of line—particularly those of coal, electricity, and petroleum products which, as was typical in Communist systems, had been kept below market levels; the resulting subsidies were becoming unaffordable. The deteriorating situation meant that the government budget moved further and further into deficit—adding to the government's need for financing and limiting its room for spending to cushion the coming transition.

The dramatic worsening of economic conditions contributed to growing political ferment. This culminated in constitutional reform, the first open elections in more than 40 years, and a historic change in government in September 1989.

While the economic situation inherited by the new government was extraordinarily complex, Poland had some major advantages, relative to other countries in transition. The history of Communism in the country was shorter than in the Soviet Union. Elements of a market economy remained, in small trade and agriculture, as well as in a broader public awareness of markets. Moreover, the fact that Communism had been imposed on the country from the outside gave Poland a stronger sense of national purpose in making the transition. The new government chose a strong economic team, headed by Deputy Prime Minister Leszek Balcerowicz, to stabilize the economy while launching the transition. The new authorities began immediately to implement measures to reduce the fiscal deficit, including by reducing subsidies.

In this setting, what did the IMF team bring to the table? First, the overall analytical framework and experience in applying it to macroeconomic policies in market economies. The team drew, in particular, on the IMF's extensive experience with addressing external imbalances and stopping high inflation. One team member was a distinguished scholar on centrally planned economies, providing extensive knowledge of the system that was to be transformed. More mundane, but no less essential, were the team's skills and persistence in assembling a consistent set of economic data and sorting out anomalies. All these elements were critical to the task of translating the authorities' intentions into concrete and monitorable policy actions, as a basis for channeling financial support from the international community.

The government also had the benefit of an outpouring of support from the Polish Diaspora, and counted some distinguished expatriate academics among its advisers—notably Stanislaw Gomulka and Jacek Rostowski. In addition, then Harvard Professor Jeffrey Sachs was a special adviser to Solidarity, even several months before it took power. Professor Sachs was steeped in the experience of inflation stabilization in Latin America and elsewhere—with the lesson that hyperinflation cannot be, and never has been, tamed gradually, but requires a thoroughgoing change in policy regime. As an academic, he was in a position to argue this position forcefully and he did so effectively, playing a critical part in bringing into being a successful program. Stanley Fischer (then Chief Economist of the World Bank), Jakob Frenkel (then IMF Economic Counselor), and the late Michael Bruno were also called upon for advice, on a personal basis, by the Polish authorities and interacted usefully with the mission during the negotiations.

Designing the program

The initial task facing the Polish economic team and the IMF mission was to devise a program of policies that would bring inflation under control within a reasonable time frame and make decisive steps toward establishing a market economy. Stopping high inflation always requires two main elements: getting the fundamentals right and braking the cycle of inflationary expectations. This is not an easy problem under the best of circumstances—as countless well-intentioned and seemingly well-conceived stabilization plans have failed. In Poland in the fall of 1989, with inflation ranging from 20 to over 50 percent per month and accelerating, the situation was urgent. Resolving it presented some added complexities.

In every big inflation in history, a fiscal deficit has been a key element; a precondition for ending inflation has been to remove the need for the government to finance itself, in effect, through the printing press. Poland in the late 1980s was no exception: the fiscal position was deteriorating as the fiscal basis of a centrally planned economy—the state's revenue from ownership of enterprises—was breaking down. Moreover, many of the steps planned toward a market economy—dismantling subsidies, opening to foreign competition, and freeing the labor market—were likely to worsen the government's finances even further, at least temporarily. In the longer run, of course, the solution would be to establish a new tax system consistent with a market economy; but in the short run, the situation of the state enterprises was critical to avoiding a fiscal meltdown. Here, a key element was wages: given the lack of market discipline on state enterprises, there was a risk that wage increases would endanger their financial position, thereby starving the government budget, and make inflation control impossible. Wage restraint was thus seen as a critical element of the program. There was also a need for tight control of other government spending.

Self-perpetuating inflationary expectations were another key factor. Expectations of high inflation contributed to driving down the market value of the zloty, and also led Poles to shift their money out of zloty deposits into foreign currencies, mostly US dollars. At the end of 1989, foreign currency deposits accounted for 63 percent of broad money. As zloty deposits made up a dwindling share of Polish balance sheets, that made the economy, and especially the banking system, much more fragile. Inflationary expectations also fed into demands for higher wages, contributing to an inflationary spiral.

The solution preferred by the IMF staff was to adopt a heterodox program: such a program tries to break the inflationary cycle by fixing one or more nominal magnitudes—usually the exchange rate, prices, and wages—while tackling the underlying problem through fiscal adjustment, supported by monetary restraint. Heterodox programs had been tried in several countries, including in South America and Israel; some of these programs were successful at the time, although in some cases the results were not sustained. In Poland, fixing prices was not an option, since prices had previously been fixed at distorted levels resulting in the inefficient allocation of resources and shortages—and as a result, major changes in relative prices were needed. Therefore, the stabilization component of the strategy used the exchange rate and wages to break the momentum of inflation. In particular, the authorities agreed with the IMF staff (and a number of outside experts, including Jeffrey Sachs) on the use of the exchange rate as the main nominal anchor of Poland's program. In hindsight, this choice worked out very well, but its success wasn't a foregone conclusion.

Having decided to peg the zloty to the dollar, the next question was, "At what level?" If the zloty were valued too high, it would price

Poland's exports out of the market and would be unlikely to withstand market pressures; too low a value would fuel inflation. Free foreign exchange trading—in thousands of booths called *kantor* located on street corners, barber shops, and the like—provided a market signal, but an unreliable one given the thinness of the market as the bulk of foreign exchange transactions was still carried out at the appreciated official exchange rate.

During the last weeks of 1989, the free foreign exchange market was driven increasingly by speculation about where the official rate would ultimately be pegged, a decision that was also to be guided in part by the market—creating a cycle of self-reinforcing expectations. Such speculation led to wild gyrations in the exchange rate: over the space of a few weeks, the zloty first depreciated markedly only to subsequently recover strongly. The latter development probably also reflected the tightening of fiscal policy that was already under way.

Interest rates were another key element in the strategy. Here, the authorities and the staff agreed that there was a need to ensure that the interest rate exceeded the inflation rate: a positive real interest rate would provide incentives for the public to hold their money in zloty and signal a break from the past when savings were eroded by negligible interest rates. But this raised a definitional question: given that major adjustments of administered prices (coal, petroleum products, and heating) were in store for January 1, 1990, should real interest rates exceed inflation from January 2 on, or from December 31 on? This was a bone of contention between Professor Sachs and the IMF team: Sachs argued forcefully that real interest rates only needed to be positive after the price jump, and that following this approach would transfer resources from the public to cash-strapped state enterprises; the IMF team thought that this distinction, while correct, would likely not be accepted by the public, starting the program off on the wrong foot. In the end, the authorities decided to set monthly interest rates slightly above the average inflation rate projected for January–February. It was also agreed that interest rates could be lowered or increased depending on the increase in foreign exchange reserves. However, it was later discovered that deposit interest rates could only be changed once a month, greatly limiting the ability of the monetary authorities to react promptly to events.

As a complement to exchange rate policy, wage policy became the second most important anchor. It would not have been realistic nor humane to freeze wages, given that inflation in monthly double digits could bring wages to starvation levels within weeks; what was done instead was a rule providing for partial indexation of wages to inflation. This took the form of a restrictive tax-based incomes policy, with state enterprises incurring stiff tax penalties on any increase in their wage bills that exceeded certain ratios to the rates of increase in retail prices. This policy was discussed in advance with the labor movement.

At a more mundane level, a central part of the work of an IMF team with the authorities is to get the numbers right. Before the IMF is allowed to provide financing, the government has to have plans to ensure that its budget can be financed without using up all the country's external reserves, creating more domestic liquidity than the economy can absorb, or unduly squeezing credit to the rest of the economy. These plans are predicated on a view of how the economy is likely to evolve over the next year or so—the "program projections."

Making program projections is a tricky business in every IMF-supported program—but doubly so in Poland, given that the aim was to set up a whole new market economy. There, a major handicap was that many of the official government statistics were designed for the command and control of a planned economy, rather than the macroeconomic management of a market economy. Under these circumstances, it took weeks to assemble a consistent set of figures capturing actual economic developments (prior to using these data to analyze or forecast). For hour after hour, week after week, the staff met with the Polish experts to reconcile the data and worked on spreadsheets long into the night. During October–November 1989, 12 separate meetings were held to discuss balance-of-payments data alone. This was a major investment in a consistent set of data, which was to prove indispensable in guiding economic policy through the turbulent times ahead.

Even once the economic situation became clearer, launching the transition was a great "leap into the unknown," as *Rzeczpospolita*, one of the main Polish newspapers, headlined on January 1, 1990. It was acknowledged that the onset of economic transition, together with the stabilization program, was likely to disrupt economic activity initially, but nobody had any basis for determining by how much. There was simply no prior experience of state enterprises adjusting to a major macroeconomic shock in this kind of institutional limbo—neither central planning nor market. It was assumed, for projection purposes, that GDP would decline by 5 percent in the first year of the program—but this was an arbitrary number that did not change through dozens of permutations of policy plans under consideration.

Given that the transition was likely to result in serious economic dislocation and major shifts in incomes, one question was what could be done to help cushion the Polish population. In Poland, state enterprises had generally acted as the safety net through a promise of lifetime employment. What was to take their place once the enterprises could not do so any more? Here, the Polish authorities and the IMF team (along with colleagues at the World Bank) saw a need to make room in the budget for some social assistance to ameliorate the situation for the most vulnerable segments of society. The measures put in place included the creation of a Labor Fund to provide unemployment benefits and retraining, the revaluation of pensions and family allowances on a quarterly basis, and the creation or strengthening of social assistance programs, including quick-reaction programs to help poor families pay for higher rents and heating costs.

Negotiations continued well into December, to determine key elements of the program. Finally, the authorities and the mission boiled down all the possibilities that had been discussed into two options: a policy of gradualism that would aim to bring inflation down progressively over the course of 1990 or a radical stabilization under which a one-time 55 percent adjustment of the price level would be followed by rapid convergence of inflation into single digits per month by February. About two weeks before Christmas, the authorities met with the IMF team in a large oak-paneled room in the Finance Ministry—the atmosphere heavy with cigar and cigarette smoke—to mull over these options. They considered whether the policies needed to support them could be brought into being, and what would be the consequences for the Polish people. At length, Minister Balcerowicz stated firmly that he intended to pursue the most radical disinflation path. He feared that if inflation persisted at high levels, public support for the program would quickly dissipate.

The IMF supported the government's program in several ways. A Stand-By Arrangement for $720 million was approved in early February 1990. The IMF also helped establish a Stabilization Fund of $1 billion provided by several industrial countries[10] to support the effort—under a considerably more liberal exchange system—to hold the exchange rate unchanged and to use it as an anchor against inflation in a situation where market conditions were expected to be turbulent. Moreover, the IMF provided substantial technical assistance to build capacity and modernize and improve Poland's economic institutions, including in areas such as fiscal policy and fiscal institutions, central banking and monetary policy, and statistics, and helped coordinate technical assistance provided by other countries. Furthermore, an IMF resident representative office was opened in Warsaw in March 1990—the first such office in Eastern Europe. The two IMF Resident Representatives in Warsaw worked closely with the authorities and provided them hands-on advice and support for the implementation of their policies. Finally, agreement with the IMF paved the way for debt reduction and rescheduling with both official and private creditors, eliminating the large debt overhang which stifled growth and discouraged foreign investments. In particular, in April 1991 Poland reached a historic accord with Paris Club creditors which provided for debt reduction in two stages equivalent to 50 percent of creditors' claims in present value terms.

Initial results

The new program was launched as planned on January 1, 1990. The exchange rate was fixed at 9500 zloty per dollar—which the authorities hoped to be able to defend for about six months. Most remaining price controls were removed, and key administered prices—notably energy prices—were increased very substantially. The central bank's refinance rate was increased to 36 percent a month—a level above the projected average inflation rate for January and February. The wage policy went into effect, limiting increases in state enterprises' wage bills to 30 percent of the increase in retail prices in January, and 20 percent in February–April. And the government took action to balance its fiscal position. The main fiscal measures included a drastic reduction of subsidies and transfers, containment of the government's wage bill, and, on the revenue side, the virtual elimination of income tax relief. At the same time, the fiscal program accommodated higher spending on new social safety nets, transfers to the social insurance funds, and partial service of the foreign debt.

The initial results of these measures were dramatic, but they were not quite as envisaged. On the negative side, it soon became clear that the slump in economic activity was going to be much larger than the 5 percent assumed. The initial burst in inflation was also much larger than expected, reaching 78 percent in January alone. Thereafter, as expected, inflation decelerated sharply, dropping into single monthly digits by March; it remained, however, above initial targets throughout the year. On the other hand, shortages disappeared virtually overnight, and within weeks of the implementation of the program many consumer goods (including foreign goods) were on the shelves for the first time in more than a decade.

Poland's external position and the government's fiscal position improved much more than expected. The external current account shifted into small surplus and the foreign exchange reserves of the central bank surged instead of the small decline envisaged in the program. The government fiscal balance swung from a large deficit into surplus, recording an extraordinary improvement of over 10 percentage points of GDP from 1989. These improvements stemmed in part from two factors: first, the exchange rate adjustment had an unexpectedly large effect on the trade balance, partly because state enterprises were able to run down their inventories and increased their exports in the face of weak domestic demand. Second, these enterprises made large "paper profits"—resulting from wage restraint together with capital gains on their existing inventories and on their foreign currency deposits as a result of the inflation and depreciation of the currency—which were the basis for an increase in income tax revenue accruing to the government. The result was that the government's position was much stronger than earlier envisaged.

The initial success of the program was, in part, serendipitous. In hindsight, the exchange rate adjustment turned out to be larger than was needed to reach the targeted improvement in the external balance. Second, due to the fragmentary nature of data on state enterprises, both the authorities and the staff were surprised by the magnitude of the increased government revenues associated with paper profits on inventories. These profits were substantially augmented by the greater-than-expected reduction in real wages—resulting from the partial indexation rule, together with the fact that monthly inflation in January 1990 was about 30 percentage points higher than expected.

The result of these developments was to put Poland in a much stronger position to establish confidence in the new economic regime. The authorities were able to defend the zloty at its initially pegged level for over a year—much longer than expected—without ever tapping the stabilization fund pledged by the international community. Confidence in the zloty rose: the public shifted their money holdings, to a substantial extent, back into zloty—one of the few examples in international experience where dollarization has actually been reversed. The paper profits also helped to recapitalize state enterprises and banks—making them more resilient against subsequent shocks and preparing them for the transition to a market economy.

There was much discussion at the time of the slump in economic activity, which exceeded by a large margin the 5 percent decline initially projected (Figures 3.1 and 3.2). Some (including staff within the IMF) attributed this to a credit crunch associated with the monetary tightening at the onset of the program. There was indeed a substantial decline

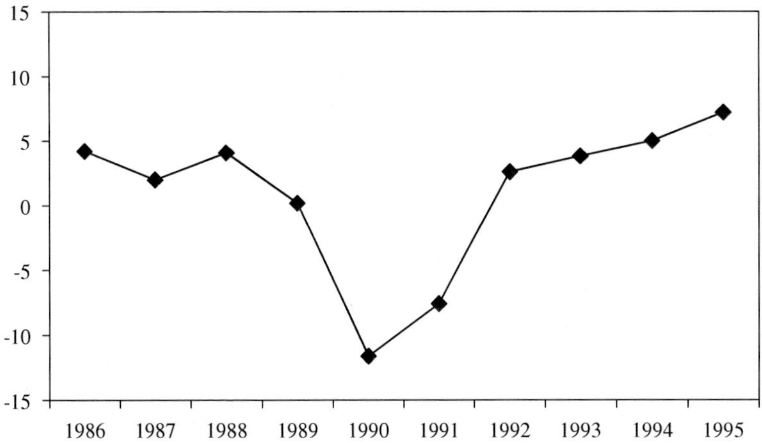

Source: IMF staff reports.

Figure 3.1 Real GDP growth in Poland, 1986–95 (in percent)

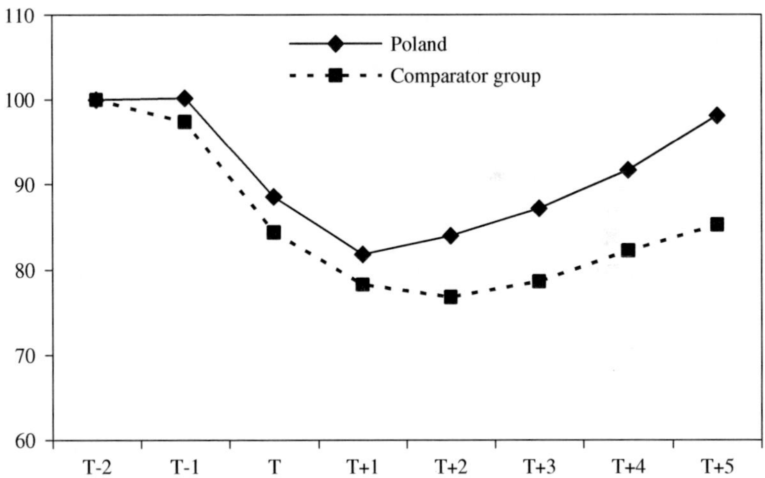

Sources: IMF staff reports.

[1]T refer to the year transition, and GDP at year T-2 is standardized to 100.

[2]The comparator group includes five countries: Bulgaria, Czech Replublic, Hungary, Romania, and Slovakia.

Figure 3.2 Poland's growth in a comparative perspective[1,2] (in percent of the base year GDP)

in credit, in real terms, with the inflationary burst at the onset of the program. However, this decline in credit can also be interpreted as the effect of inflation in erasing the existing debts of state enterprises—a windfall rather than a crunch. In hindsight, while the decline in economic activity was concerning, it was no more severe than in many other transition countries that adopted a variety of other monetary policy strategies.

Given the massive changes taking place in the economy, adaptability was at a premium. Poland's economic program could not be set in stone, but had to be adjusted to changing conditions. A few numerical targets—that is, performance criteria—established in the IMF-supported program were breached, even as the authorities adhered to the same overall policies they had agreed to, because macroeconomic outcomes had changed. Others—notably the government budget balance and international reserves—were overperformed by such wide margins that they became irrelevant (Figure 3.3). During 1990, the IMF staff team traveled to Warsaw frequently, and worked with the authorities to revise the program in light of new circumstances. At times there were differences of opinion on what response was called for. For example, in the summer of 1990 interest rate subsidies to the housing and agriculture sectors were increased, a measure about which the IMF team had misgivings, as it ran counter to moving progressively to market-determined

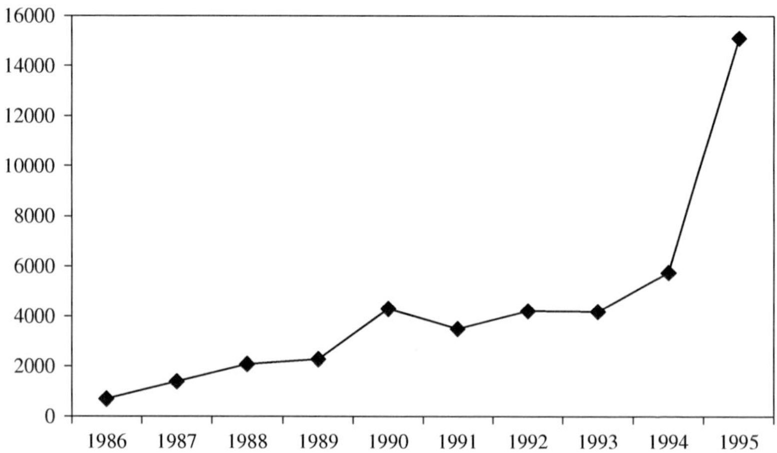

Source: IMF International Financial Statistics database.

Figure 3.3 Net international reserves in Poland, 1986–95 (in US$ million)

prices. As with the negotiations in the fall of 1989, the spirit of these discussions was constructive, guided by the shared objective of helping a stable and strong Polish economy to emerge from this critical period. By the end of 1990 and throughout 1991, monthly inflation continued to exceed targets, and it was feared that it would accelerate again, especially when financial policies were eased. However, macropolicies remained prudent, thus putting the economy on a sound footing for the resumption of growth in subsequent years.

Alongside these macroeconomic developments, there were important changes in the structure of the economy, some of which were associated with the collapse of barriers to movements of people and goods in central Europe more generally. Within a few months, there was tangible evidence of the new, more open, economy that was emerging: for the first time in years, Poles could travel by car to West Berlin, bringing back merchandise to satisfy their compatriots' cravings. The grounds of the Palace of Science and Culture—a massive edifice built as Stalin's gift to the Polish people—ironically turned into a huge street market, where foreign and Polish goods were being sold from improvised stalls. While open unemployment rose from negligible levels to 6 percent of the labor force by end-1990, employment in the private sector surged by 30 percent, mirroring the very strong growth in private activity. While privatization proceeded more slowly than anticipated, important progress was made in preparing the groundwork, building institutions, and enacting enabling legislation for systemic reform. The IMF was particularly active in the areas of the budget, taxation and banking legislation, and monetary policy instruments.[11]

Longer-term developments

The 1990 stabilization program put Poland on the road to becoming a stable market economy, which by May 2004 was ready for membership in the European Union as one of the first group of new entrants. However, that road turned out to be a bumpy one, owing to a combination of external shocks and policy slippages.

In 1991, Poland—like other Central and Eastern European countries—faced a major shock associated with the collapse of trade among the former members of the Council on Mutual Economic Assistance (CMEA) and the economic turmoil associated with the breakup of the Soviet Union. Poland's economic activity slumped further, with GDP declining by 7½ percent. The slump bottomed out the following year, and growth resumed. Economic growth averaged 5 percent during the second half of the 1990s, making Poland one of the fastest-growing economies in Europe.

Poland's stabilization program was successful in preventing a recurrence of high inflation, although the results were not as quick and decisive as had been hoped. After the near-hyperinflationary levels of 1989, annual inflation had declined to about 35 percent in 1993, but it did not reach single digits until 1999. The slow progress in bringing down inflation appears to have reflected a combination of structural factors—notably weak financial discipline on the remaining state enterprises—and shifts in monetary and exchange rate policy (Figure 3.4 and Table 3.1).

The fixed exchange rate—the main anchor of the stabilization program—was adjusted in mid-1991 to bring it into line with the inflation that had occurred and help adjust to the shock of the CMEA collapse. The peg was maintained much longer than originally planned, contributing to building confidence in the zloty and reversing the dollarization that had occurred. The authorities' subsequent pragmatism in adjusting the exchange rate and moving to a "crawling peg" arrangement may have contributed to the delayed success in bringing down inflation further. At the same time, though, it enabled Poland to avoid the "exchange-rate based stabilization syndrome" suffered by some Latin American countries—the trap of chronic overvaluation

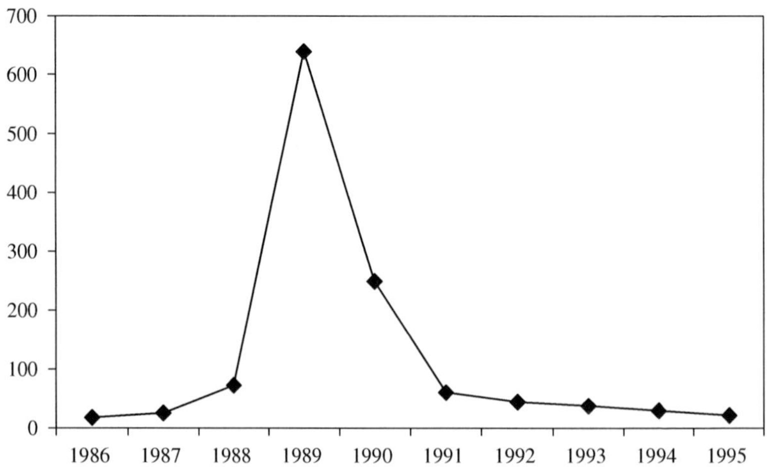

Source: IMF staff reports.
[1]Data refer to percentage changes in the end of period Consumer Price Index.

Figure 3.4 Inflation in Poland, 1986–95[1] (in percent)

Table 3.1 Poland: Selected economic indicators, 1986–95

	Percentage changes, unless indicated otherwise									
	1986	1987	1988	1989	1990	1991	1992	1993	1994	1995
Real GDP	4.2	2.0	4.1	0.2	−11.6	−7.6	2.6	3.8	5.2	7.0
Consumer prices (end of period)	17.7	25.2	72.9	639.7	249.3	60.4	44.4	37.6	29.5	21.6
External current account (in percent of GDP)	−0.9	−0.6	−0.8	−2.7	1.1	−2.9	−0.3	−2.7	−1.2	−1.9
International reserves (US$ million)	689	1,384	2,075	2,278	4,306	3,497	4,222	4,183	5,753	15,102
Foreign direct investment, net (US$ million)	−6	4	−18	−12	10	136	284	580	542	3,617
Export growth	0.2	2.4	12.3	−47.3	45.7	27.6	3.0	1.5	21.7	39.2
Monetary indicators										
Money and quasi-money	34.1	58.3	133.0	239.4	117.9	47.4	57.5	36.0	33.8	39.4
Credit to nongovernment	16.9	17.8	46.4	220.6	179.2	63.8	32.7	33.2	25.3	35.1
General government balance (in percent of GDP)	−0.3	−0.8	0.0	−7.4	3.1	−6.5	−6.6	−2.9	−2.5	−2.3
External debt in convertible currencies (in US$ billion)	34	40	39	40	49	48	49	49	42	44

Sources: IMF staff reports, International Financial Statistics database, and World Economic Outlook database.

which undermined growth and ultimately led to crises, in the absence of an exit strategy from a fixed exchange rate.

After a rapid start with liberalization in 1990, Poland made gradual progress toward market reforms across a broad spectrum during the rest of the decade. It adopted an eclectic and gradual approach to privatization, in which enterprise insiders (managers and workers' councils) were closely involved. This approach resulted in a slower process than in other countries, but at the same time, it reduced the risks of widespread fraud and financial instability associated with some of the more rapid privatization schemes implemented elsewhere. A thriving stock market was established—ironically, located in the previous Communist Party headquarters. Poland's banking system was reformed and modernized, mainly through consolidation of existing institutions, with limited injections of foreign capital.

The IMF's involvement in Poland changed over the 1990s. Following the initial financial arrangement to support the stabilization program, a new three-year arrangement was negotiated in February 1991 to provide support for a program of basic structural reforms. Within a few months, however, the IMF-supported program was off track, and only a small fraction of the agreed financing was actually provided. Economic activity turned out lower than projected, partly as a result of a larger impact from the collapse of the CMEA trade than expected, which put pressure on the fiscal position as corporate taxes weakened. The interruption of the program was mainly due to differences of view between the authorities and the IMF on fiscal and structural policies—which in turn partly reflected political changes, as successive administrations varied in their commitment to continuing reforms under the difficult conditions Poland faced. Fresh one-year arrangements were approved in 1993 and 1994, and implemented with greater success, though albeit with more limited ambitions. Following these arrangements, the IMF continued to maintain a dialogue with the authorities on various economic policy options. In addition, throughout the 1990s the IMF continued to provide technical assistance on a wide range of topics, including central banking and the financial system, fiscal policy, and statistics.

Conclusion

With the benefit of hindsight and despite initial concerns on its feasibility, Poland's 1990 stabilization and reform program can not only be considered a success but also proved to be a pioneering example that influenced the economic strategies subsequently adopted by several transition countries, including Russia. Its immediate objectives, namely, halting hyperinflation, resolving the external payments crisis, eliminating shortages, liberalizing foreign trade, and establishing current account convertibility, were all achieved.

The broad approach proved right. Given the uncertainties, it was difficult to set parameters right, notably the exchange rate. Based on the initial goals, it was probably depreciated too much, but erring on that side turned out for the best—one of only a few cases of dedollarization in history. Erring on the other side would have been worse: pushing the newly transitional economy into a Latin American-style cycle of high inflation and failed stabilization.

The program set the stage for a remarkable recovery and reforms during the 1990s. This rebound can be considered in part a "phoenix miracle" from the ashes of the disastrous situation that characterized the 1980s. After the failures of these years, it was essential to strengthen perceptions of a regime shift. A fundamental change in expectations was needed to end an unsustainable situation; the alternative may have been continuing chaos and high inflation.

Policy design was only one reason, and perhaps not the most important one, for success. An important factor that greatly added credibility was the large financial support provided by the IMF directly and by catalyzing other sources, including the Stabilization Fund. But most important of all were the widespread domestic political support and trust in the Solidarity-led government, the exceptionally strong ownership of the program by the government, and generally consistent policy implementation.

Poland: Stabilization, Transition, and Reform, 1990–91

Leszek Balcerowicz[2]

The International Monetary Fund (and the World Bank) played an important positive role in Poland's radical transition to a market economy: they were our true partners in this historic undertaking. This is why I have read with great interest the account presented by Timothy Lane, Rolando Ossowski, and Massimo Russo, who were all directly involved on the IMF side in Poland's macroeconomic stabilization, which was an important part of the overall economic program.

The cooperation with the IMF was so productive because both sides shared a similar strategic approach to the stabilization of the Polish economy. With respect to the Polish economic team, this approach was due to the fact that its key members spent years studying the macroeconomic and structural problems of Poland's socialist economy against the background of other economies, and designing the basic strategy of dealing with them, even though nobody assumed that history would give us a chance to put the results of this work into practice. This long study gave my Polish colleagues and me a strong "anti-gradualist" orientation toward stabilizing an economy that was entering hyperinflation and transforming an institutional system that crippled the people through extensive controls. Therefore, the "ownership" of the basic strategy was genuine and provided a good platform for a productive dialogue with the IMF team. We never blamed the IMF for the tough measures necessary to stabilize the Polish economy, and

[2] Mr. Balcerowicz served as deputy prime minister and finance minister of Poland from 1989 to 1991 and then again from 1997 to 1999. He is best known as the author of the so-called Balcerowicz Plan, which achieved the rapid transformation of Poland from a centrally planned to a market economy. In 2008 he was appointed chairman of Bruegel, a European think tank based in Brussels.

this probably contributed to the good reputation that the IMF enjoys in Poland. Indeed, the wage controls introduced in 1990 were tougher than those originally proposed by the IMF team. (For more on the earlier work on stabilization and reform on the Polish side, see L. Balcerowicz, *Socialism, Capitalism, Transformation,* Central European University Press, Budapest-London, 1995.)

Regarding the setting, I would say that Poland's economy during 1989 suffered from all the deficiencies of the superficially reformed socialist economy—such as shortages, very low efficiency, and environmental pollution—and from the results of extreme macroeconomic mismanagement, which dated from the excessive foreign borrowing in the 1970s. True, some economic reform measures were adopted in 1988—including lifting the restrictions on private entrepreneurship and introducing the two-tier banking system—but they were not sufficiently comprehensive and they were overshadowed by a catastrophically lax fiscal policy that culminated in hyperinflation. On top of that, Poland was burdened by a huge foreign debt. This combination of the initial economic conditions was much more dramatic than in Hungary or the former Czechoslovakia.

Poland was a pioneer in the political transformation in the Soviet bloc. This included the creation of the "Solidarity" movement in 1980 (to be suppressed by the imposition of martial law in December 1981) and the round-table talks between the representatives of Solidarity and the Communist authorities in early 1989. The members of Poland's future economic team did not participate in these talks, either because they were not regarded as Solidarity experts or because they were critical of the economic demands of the Solidarity side. The economic part of the agreement reached during these negotiations was relatively underdeveloped. In addition, it included overly generous indexation of wages and various concessions to the largest workers' groups (miners, railway men, and others). These concessions had to be largely scrapped in the span of a couple of months, not an easy job for the economic team and the government created in early September 1989.

I doubt, therefore, whether Poland had "some major advantages" relative to other countries in transition, as the authors claim. It is open to speculation whether populations are more ready to accept market-oriented economic reforms when their experience with communist economic systems has been short. Witness, for example, the very radical economic reforms adopted in Armenia, which suffered under Soviet occupation longer than Central and Eastern European countries. Besides, Poland had much stronger trade unions than all other transition economies, which did not facilitate the introduction of the necessary thoroughgoing reforms. During 1990–91, moreover, Poland went through the split in the Solidarity camp and through two election campaigns with the related populist critique of the so-called shock therapy. This experience may be contrasted with that of Hungary, which had elections in both 1990 and 1994. Polish farmers obtained large windfall gains in 1989, thanks to the freeing of the prices of foodstuffs by the last Communist government. The liberalization of the prices of inputs to agriculture, introduced in 1990, took these gains away from them, which, obviously, made the farmers critical of market reforms.

True, Poland benefited from the advice of foreign experts. (Besides those listed by the authors, I would like to mention David Lipton, at that time a colleague of Jeffrey Sachs, who also provided valuable advice.) But the most influential advisers—from my perspective—were the key members of the team that worked on reforms before 1989. They included, among others, Marek Dąbrowski, Stefan Kawalec, and Andrzej Bratkowski.

With respect to the design of the program, I already stressed the fundamental role of the shared strategic approach to stabilization. As far as specifics are concerned, I am largely in agreement with the authors. Tax-based wage controls were, indeed, regarded as an important component of the stabilization effort. One of the most difficult decisions, as the authors rightly point out, was at what level to fix the rate of exchange of the Polish zloty against the dollar. The rate proposed by the domestic experts ranged from 6 to 12 zlotys per dollar, although it was impossible to determine exactly which the correct value was. In my decision on that issue, the risk I most wanted to avoid was the breakdown of the newly introduced convertibility of the zloty, as it would have been tantamount to the bankruptcy of the whole stabilization program.

As the details of the program were worked out with great speed, while we had to deal with the dramatic immediate problems in the last months of 1989, some mistakes were made. One was to introduce overly generous unemployment benefits, which artificially inflated the number of workers seeking these benefits. Another mistake was a too-generous indexation of pensions, which was responsible for the later unsustainable surge in social security expenditures.

Besides macroeconomic stabilization, the program included a massive liberalization of command economy regulations and a deeper institutional restructuring, including the privatization of enterprises. Its pace was slower than planned by the Polish economic team because of the early politicization of the debate and frequent political changes.

Contrary to the views expressed by the authors, the relevant research shows, I believe, that the slower pace has not improved the quality of the privatization process; but it has delayed the restructuring of inefficient enterprises and, thus, hurt Poland's economic performance.

Regarding the initial developments, I would stress that the initial decline in output in 1990 was exaggerated by the statistical apparatus which—given its traditional focus—concentrated on the shrinking part of the economy and was incapable of measuring correctly the rapidly growing private sector. The revised figures showed that the GDP decline in Poland during 1990–91 was in the range of 5–10 percent, less than in Britain after the Second World War during its transition from a wartime to a peacetime economy. However, the inflated official figures of the GDP decline were certainly a shock and required an additional effort on the part of the economic team in persuading critics and other observers that Poland must persist with its stabilization program. Even more effort was required in 1991 when Poland, together with other Central and Eastern European countries, suffered a large shock resulting from the collapse of trade with the formerly centrally planned economies and the related transition to market prices for the oil and gas imported from these economies. Therefore, Poland's stabilization and reform program had to be implemented despite political shocks (two elections and a split in the Solidarity camp) and in the face of large macroeconomic shocks.

In conclusion, let me stress again the good and productive cooperation between the Polish government and the IMF. The IMF team helped us to elaborate the crucial details of the macroeconomic program, and made a very important contribution to the preparations of statistical data. The IMF gave a stamp of credibility to the program; this was crucial for the Polish efforts to obtain the Stabilization Fund for the zloty from G-7 countries, and later to achieve a drastic cut in Poland's external debt.

4

Turkey's Renaissance: From Banking Crisis to Economic Revival

Hugh Bredenkamp, Mats Josefsson, and Carl-Johan Lindgren[1]

On the morning of February 19, 2001, Turkish Prime Minister Bülent Ecevit stormed out of a routine meeting of the National Security Council and declared to the news media "a crisis at the very top of the state." The Prime Minister's spat with President Ahmet Necdet Sezer at that meeting had nothing to do with economic policy. Nevertheless it triggered a meltdown in Turkish financial markets. Investors had been on edge since the previous November, when increasing concerns about policy slippages had combined with fears for the creditworthiness of some local banks to spark a run on the crawling-peg exchange rate regime. That minicrisis was contained, but market confidence remained fragile in the weeks that followed. Consequently, a spike in political tensions—hardly exceptional in the Turkish context—was sufficient to incite a rush for the exits by investors. For three days, the Central Bank (CBT) battled to defend the lira, as overnight interest rates soared to 4500 percent. But, on February 22, the authorities conceded defeat, and the lira was allowed to float, depreciating immediately by some 40 percent. The collapse in confidence, as banks began to default in the market for short-term funds, brought on the worst economic recession

[1] Hugh Bredenkamp is Assistant Director in the IMF's African Department. From 2004 to 2007, he was the IMF's senior resident representative in Turkey. Carl-Johan Lindgren, the IMF's Monetary and Exchange Department's mission chief for Turkey, also had headed a team dealing with the Thai banking crisis in 1997–98. Mats Josefsson had been extensively involved in Thailand after that crisis broke, and remained closely engaged until its final resolution in 2000; he was previously a senior official in the Swedish Financial Supervisory Agency. The authors are grateful to Carlo Cottarelli and Lorenzo Giorgiani for helpful comments, and to Jonathan Manning for research assistance.

in the history of the republic, and required a comprehensive rescue package for the Turkish banking system, at a cost of some $47 billion—one-third of Turkey's national income.

Fast forward to April 2007. President Sezer's term had ended, a new government was in office, and their candidate to replace him was the foreign minister, Abdullah Gül. Secularists, including the military high command, feared that a Gül presidency would herald a rollback in Turkey's strict regulation of religious activity. Late on the night of April 27, the military issued a statement that was interpreted as threatening intervention if needed to protect the secular state. In view of Turkey's history with military coups, a political storm ensued. Although Mr. Gül subsequently took office unimpeded, this was, by common consent, a far more serious political shock than Mr. Ecevit's outburst six years earlier. Yet the markets took it in their stride. The stock market and the lira dipped briefly the following Monday, but quickly stabilized.

Why did market confidence collapse in 2001 but not in 2007? What had happened in the intervening six years to make the economy, and investor sentiment, so much more robust?

The answer is: a radical and wide-ranging transformation in Turkey's economic policies and institutions. This turnaround was launched by one government, sustained and broadened by its successor, and underpinned throughout by extensive IMF support, both financial and technical.

In this chapter, we outline briefly the origins of Turkey's economic weakness in the run-up to the 2001 crisis. We go on to describe the key elements of the postcrisis transformation, with a particular focus on the rescue and rehabilitation of the banking system. The latter was a critical component of the recovery program, and an area where IMF staff provided direct, hands-on support to their Turkish counterparts. We conclude with some observations on why the post-2001 reform effort, more than any of its predecessors, has succeeded and apparently taken root.

The legacy of the 1980s and 1990s

In the decades following World War II, the Turkish economy, like many of its peers in the developing world, was characterized by heavy regulation, protection from foreign competition, and extensive state involvement in commercial activity. Turkey's relatively poor growth performance and high inflation during this period convinced many that a new paradigm was needed, and a comprehensive reform program was launched under the government of Turgut Özal in the early 1980s.

Growth responded strongly to the liberalization and opening up of the economy. But the impact of the reforms was ultimately undermined by poor financial discipline.[12] The fractious political environment played an important role. During the 1980s and 1990s, Turkey had 15 governments, ten of which were coalitions or minority governments. Agreeing on and sticking with the difficult policy choices that were needed, especially on the budget, proved to be impossible in this setting. The result was chronic budget deficits, financed in part by printing money, leading in turn to inflation in the 30–50 percent range throughout the 1980s, rising to an average of over 75 percent during the 1990s.

At the end of the 1990s, a steep recession and the trauma of the 1998 earthquake appeared to create a political opening for a more serious stabilization effort. Ecevit's coalition government put together a bold program, which the IMF backed under a Stand-By Arrangement approved in December 1999. The government of the day put great emphasis on the corrosive effects of inflation—both on equity and growth. High inflation had deterred long-term investment and stunted the development of Turkey's financial sector. The poor suffered most, especially those on fixed incomes and without access to inflation hedges. Since fiscal profligacy was clearly at the root of the inflation, strong up-front fiscal adjustment was the program's central element. A raft of structural reforms—covering pensions, agricultural subsidies, and privatization—was included to put the budget on a sound footing. To convince financial markets and the public that the value of their liras would no longer be inflated away, the central bank committed to a target path for the exchange rate. This would allow interest rates to come down quickly, which was seen as essential to facilitate the fiscal adjustment and support growth. Banking reforms completed the package: these were slated to reduce borrowing costs and revive the economy, and they included plans to establish an independent bank regulator, tighten prudential regulations, and rehabilitate state-owned banks.

The 2000 program had a positive start: interest rates fell sharply and growth took off, exceeding expectations. But the recovery was unbalanced. Though inflation dropped, interest rates fell even faster. Demand surged, sucking in imports. Together with a 60 percent hike in world oil prices, this pushed the current account from near-balance to a deficit of almost 5 percent of GNP in 2000. Rapid credit expansion aggravated risks in the banking system, as short-term funds (some borrowed in foreign currency) were used to lend at longer maturities in lira.

The IMF urged the government to take budget measures to rein in demand, but the government hesitated, not wanting to stall the recovery. This inaction, together with widespread delays in the implementation of the structural reform agenda, growing concerns about bank soundness, and political uncertainties, created a "perfect storm" that subverted market confidence.[13] With the collapse of the lira peg in February 2001, the economic program had to be recast.

Sowing the seeds of recovery: The design of the 2001 program

The immediate challenge in the aftermath of the February 2001 crisis was how to restore confidence. The government's first step was to create a new economic team, under Kemal Derviş, a senior World Bank staffer. Its task was to design a new economic program that would repair the wreckage in the banking system, stabilize the budget in the face of the huge costs of those repairs, and provide a new anchor for inflation to replace the exchange rate peg. The key elements were

- Radical financial and operational restructuring of the state-owned and failed private banks, with capital infusions from the private sector into weak private banks and a further tightening of bank supervision.
- More ambitious budgetary targets, underpinned by new fiscal measures and improvements in the transparency of the budget accounts.
- A revitalized privatization program, covering the telecommunications, electricity, natural gas, sugar, and tobacco sectors.
- Statutory independence for the CBT, with a mandate to move toward formal inflation targeting.
- Incomes policies, including tight control of public sector pay and a more active role for government in influencing private pay settlements.

The program was to be underpinned by a beefed-up financial support package that would combine a restoration of credit lines from international banks with augmented official financing, notably from the IMF (which increased its $11 billion credit line by $8 billion), so as to begin rebuilding the CBT's depleted reserves.[14]

The reform of the banking system was at the heart of this program and is worth recounting in more depth.

The outbreak of the banking crisis

The week of February 19, 2001, was devastating to Turkey's state banks. During that week, losses in the two largest state banks amounted to a massive $2.5 billion, or about 2 percent of GNP. This was the result of overnight interbank borrowing at stratospheric interest rates as banks sought to avoid default in the daily clearing. Some private banks also incurred losses, while others benefited from the rates the state banks were paying on overnight funds.

How did the state banks end up in this situation? For many years, the politicians had abused these banks, which had been "allocated" to different political parties to provide subsidized credits to their political constituencies. The banks were not compensated for the losses from such lending but were instead forced to book them as claims on the government, as so called duty losses. These claims generated little income and no cash flow, which meant that the banks had to fund themselves increasingly short term in the interbank market. As the liabilities grew, they became more vulnerable to liquidity and interest rate risk. By the end of 2000, the state banks' duty losses had grown to some $19 billion, their short-term liabilities to some $22 billion, and their foreign exchange exposure to $18 billion. Even a small shock could have toppled them—the massive shock that hit them in mid-February was truly catastrophic.[15]

Furthermore, the state banks did not have to provide reserves for bad loans, did not have to comply with prudential regulations applicable to private banks, and were not subject to any serious supervision. This allowed massive distortion in the banking system and it became the subject of bitter complaints by private banks. Many private banks got their revenge in the crisis, however, as the huge losses of the state banks were mirrored in huge windfall profits for banks with excess liquidity. But such positive effects were not evenly distributed—many private banks were also severely hurt by the shocks of mid-February.

The calamity in the banking system was a rude wake-up call for the government, which realized that current bank practices could no longer continue. There was a need for fundamental financial and operational restructuring of the state banks and a strengthening of the regulatory and supervisory framework under which all banks had operated.

Throughout the 1990s, banking supervision had been light, and weak rules on asset valuation allowed banks to overstate their financial positions. Most private banks were owned by families, which used their banks as treasuries to companies owned by them. This was possible as connected lending rules were unusually lax. Most banks borrowed short term in international markets and invested the funds long term in loans to related parties or in government securities.[16] This made them extremely vulnerable to liquidity and market risks. By the late 1990s, eight banks had failed and been taken over by the Savings Deposit Insurance Fund (SDIF), which continued to operate them without corrective actions despite growing losses and distortions. There were no bank runs, however, as depositors and bank creditors were fully protected under a blanket state guarantee in effect since 1994.[17]

In mid-1999, a legal amendment called for the establishment of a new independent supervisory authority, the Banking Regulation and Supervision Agency (BRSA). Until then banking supervision had been split between the CBT (off-site) and the Treasury (on-site). The start-up of the new agency was much delayed, however, owing to political disputes over the appointments of the board and Chairman, and it did not become operational until September 2000, following intense pressure from the IMF and World Bank. During this period, banks were without effective supervision, and there were no efforts to resolve the "intervened" banks (that is, banks that had failed and been taken under SDIF stewardship).

IMF involvement in Turkey's banking reforms

Since 1999, there had been several missions from the IMF's Monetary and Exchange Affairs Department (MAE) to provide technical assistance to the authorities on how to deal with the state-owned and intervened banks, and strengthen the regulatory and supervisory framework. In late 2000, market analysts perceived the reform process to be lagging, as BRSA struggled to identify its role and responsibilities.

Most of the issues to be addressed in the banking sector were not new to IMF staff members, who had dealt with a number of banking crises in the late 1990s in Asia and elsewhere. Since the mid-1990s, MAE had systematically built up its knowledge of such crises and their resolution by drawing on banking-crisis experiences in Latin America and the Nordic countries. A number of experienced senior supervisors were hired, and several policy papers on banking crises and bank restructuring were prepared for the IMF Executive Board during this period.[18]

Prior to the crisis, the Turkish authorities had been reluctant to acknowledge the extent of reforms that were needed. Their policies at this time were also poorly communicated, and with various agencies involved, accountability was unclear. When the new government team took charge after the crisis, the dynamics changed—the restructuring process picked up speed and was implemented with determination and skill.[19]

On February 24, a few days after the crisis had erupted, an MAE mission arrived in Ankara to work closely with the Turkish authorities and IMF European Department colleagues in developing the banking sector reforms that would form part of a new IMF-backed program. The mission stayed in Turkey for almost a month. Their stay coincided with a major religious holiday, and Ankara was more or less closed down for several days, during which the mission members were the sole guests at the Sheraton hotel. The senior Treasury, Central Bank, and BRSA staff stayed at their posts, however, and the work proceeded with a spirit of great cooperation and determination. A central role was played by the new BRSA Chairman, Engin Akçakoca, and his deputy, Teoman Kerman.[20] By late March, agreement was reached on almost all aspects of the banking sector reform program.[21]

The bank restructuring strategy

Restoring confidence in the banking system and credibility to economic management was the top priority. It was clear that financial stability, monetary control, and a lowering of interest rates would not be possible unless the banking problems were credibly addressed. The banking sector reforms, therefore, became the central focus of the program. Turkey learned the hard way that macroeconomic stability and economic growth requires a sound banking system. The immediate focus was on the restructuring of state banks, starting the resolution of the intervened banks and putting pressure on private bank owners to recapitalize their banks. Measures to strengthen the legal and regulatory environment were also included. Policies in support of corporate debt restructuring and asset recovery were to be addressed at a later stage.

Reform of the state banks had become the highest priority.[22] A massive recapitalization was called for. The only credible option was to use transferable government securities issued on market terms, so that the banks would not face renewed losses and liquidity problems. In total, the government injected $19 billion in floating rate notes (in lira and foreign currency), thus making it possible for the state banks to fully eliminate their exposures in foreign currency and to repay their overnight money market debt. This meant that the rollover problem was shifted to the CBT, which was in a position to provide liquidity to the banks through more traditional monetary policy instruments. Based on an aggressive valuation of the banks' assets, the government injected an additional $2.9 billion in government securities to raise the capital adequacy ratios of the two large state banks, Ziraat and Halk, above the required minimum of 8 percent. In addition, the state banks became subject to all BRSA regulations applicable to private banks.

In the operational restructuring, the banks' links to line ministers were cut.[23] Instead, an independent and highly professional joint board was appointed for Ziraat and Halk. It would set uniform deposit rates for the state banks, in consultation with the CBT, and these rates were to be kept below market rates for treasury securities to ensure profitability. Moreover, the staffing and organizational structure of Ziraat and Halk were to be streamlined to reduce operating costs. In less than two years, one-third (829) of all branches were closed and the number of employees was reduced by one-half (30,000).

The resolution of intervened banks was tricky, given conditions in the banking market. It was difficult to liquidate good assets, let alone problematic ones. Up to that point, SDIF had taken over 13 banks and the expectation was that three of them could be sold, while the rest would have to be closed and liquidated. The key question was how to build up managerial skills within SDIF to maximize loan recoveries and minimize the fiscal cost.

While the financial condition of some of the larger private banks had strengthened during the crisis, many other private banks had experienced substantial losses from the high interest rates and the depreciation of the lira. With strict application of loan classification and provisioning rules introduced one year earlier, the level of nonperforming loans was expected to increase sharply for all banks. BRSA agreed to hold individual meetings with all banks to discuss their capital positions with the understanding that banks judged to be undercapitalized would be required to present time-bound plans to raise additional capital. All banks had to suspend dividend payments.

In the legal area, the discussion focused on a strengthening of prudential regulations, especially for connected lending and lending to related parties. Agreement was reached on a regulation that would gradually reduce the limits from 70 percent to the EU-compatible level of 25 percent of own funds by 2006. Accounting standards would be brought in line with international standards from the beginning of 2002, and the legal framework to facilitate corporate restructuring was to be reviewed.

Public support scheme

As part of the initial strategy, all undercapitalized banks were required to submit detailed and time-bound plans on how they would raise additional capital by end-2001. The fact that many bank owners had unlimited personal liability under the law for losses in their banks resulting from connected lending was a strong incentive for them to inject needed capital. In total about $1.1 billion was raised. Six banks failed to raise capital and were taken over by SDIF. The persistently high interest rates continued to cause concerns about the financial conditions of banks, however, and there were market rumors that banks still overvalued their assets and would not be able to raise more capital, if faced with additional losses. To remove damaging uncertainties and protect the core banking system, agreement was reached on a support scheme that would make public funds available to help banks that could not raise new capital on their own. This type of scheme had been used successfully in Thailand in 1998.

No effort was spared to make sure that banks' capital needs were assessed correctly. This required a methodology that would spell out in great detail how asset values should be determined and potential losses identified. The assessment had to be fair, equally applied to all banks, and transparent. Introduction of the scheme required a special law that took weeks to develop, given its complexity. Considerable effort was made to explain the exercise to the banking industry, public, and politicians. On the advice of the MAE mission, a team of experienced outside consultants, headed by Mark Carawan—partner in a major consulting firm and with experience from Asia and Sweden—was hired to develop the asset valuation methodology in close cooperation with BRSA staff.[24] The team produced a detailed reporting system (some 100 pages long). Banks' external auditors were required to confirm in writing that the data reported by the bank was correct. This was followed up by a second team of independent auditors, who were to confirm that the bank had followed the methodology prescribed by BRSA. Finally, BRSA's examiners were to sign off on the assessment. This process was essential to help BRSA face powerful bankers with close political connections. The exercise was initiated in June 2002 and completed two months later.

Under the scheme, banks that could not raise capital on their own would have access to public funds if several stringent conditions were met, including (i) such support should be viewed as a last resort; (ii) existing shareholders or new private investors had to match the public contribution; (iii) there would be no bailout of existing shareholders; (iv) the bank had to have a positive net worth; (v) the government had the right to appoint at least one board member; and (vi) existing shareholders were required to pledge as collateral to the government shares held in the bank equal to the government's contribution. As it turned out, no private bank needed capital assistance from SDIF.[25] The owners of one large bank, Pamuk, could not raise the $2 billion needed to enter the scheme and that bank was intervened. The incentives built into the scheme for shareholders to invest their own resources rather than to give the SDIF a role in managing their bank had the desired effect.[26] The exercise was a great success and very professionally managed by BRSA.

Confidence in the private banking system was restored and there have been no further bank failures—with one major exception. There was a highly embarrassing bank failure in 2003, when a relatively small family-owned bank, Imar, became illiquid owing to massive deposit withdrawals. When BRSA examiners went into the bank, they found that most accounting records had disappeared and that deposit liabilities were ten times higher than officially reported due to an elaborate parallel banking operation. For over 10 years, data had been manipulated through a sophisticated computer program. There had been suspicions surrounding the bank—prompting external audits, regular supervisory inspections by the sworn bank auditors,[27] and investigations by the Treasury, and even by a parliamentary committee—but no wrongdoing had been found. The episode illustrated how a truly sophisticated fraud can escape detection for years. Once it was discovered, it was felt that depositors had to be paid in full, at an initial cost to SDIF of more than $6 billion. The happy ending to the story is that the SDIF was able to recover the full amount by confiscating and liquidating assets of the bank's owning family.

A successful outcome

Following their recapitalization and downsizing under new professional management, the state banks immediately became highly profitable, which allowed them to pay hefty dividends to the Treasury. Ziraat accumulated so much surplus capital that it was able to pay the government a special dividend of $2 billion. The intervened Pamuk was successfully merged into Halk, 25 percent of which was privatized in 2007 for $1.8 billion, indicating a total market value close to $10 billion. Market analysts believe Ziraat's market value to be substantially higher. There is thus a realistic prospect that, once these banks are fully privatized, the government may more than recoup the funds it has had to inject to rehabilitate them. Considering that, in early 2001, the value of these banks was close to zero, this is a measure of the reform's success.

The private banking system's profitability also improved significantly following completion of their restructuring and recapitalization. Further mergers and consolidation followed, including the absorption of some of the banks taken over by SDIF. The passage of a new banking law has brought regulations and supervisory practices fully in line with international best practice. A sign of the confidence shown in the banks is that foreign investors have increased their stake in the Turkish banking system from 6 percent in 2001 to nearly 50 percent today.

The economic recovery

The economy turned around remarkably quickly as the program restored confidence. Industrial production began rising in late 2001, and the first half of 2002 saw the recovery in output gathering strength, combined with a 30-percentage-point drop in inflation. Business confidence surged into positive territory, and—after a sharp drop in the wake of the September 11 events—the stock market took off.

Six years on, no one familiar with the history of the preceding decades could fail to be impressed by the fundamental transformation that has been achieved:

The public finances have been put on a sound footing for the long term: The cumulative impact of fiscal profligacy during the 1990s, together with the massive financial costs of the ensuing crisis and the devaluation of the lira, pushed total government debt to over 100 percent of GNP in 2001. Since then, sustained fiscal adjustment has brought the budget into approximate balance and, with some help from an appreciating real exchange rate, has slashed the debt burden by almost half. Turkey's government is justifiably proud that its fiscal position now meets the European Union's Maastricht criteria, a distinction not yet shared by some EU member states. The funding of its debt has also improved: the government can now borrow on longer maturities and lower spreads, and has reduced its reliance on riskier foreign currency debt. As the cost of debt servicing continues to decline in coming years, this will make room for much-needed tax cuts and infrastructure investments. The recent passage of social security reform legislation, which was essential to address widening deficits in the health and pension systems, will give additional support to the long-run fiscal consolidation effort.

Inflation has been tamed: In the 20 years leading up to the 2001 crisis, the lira had on average lost half of its US dollar value every nine months. Inflation had been in the double or even triple digits for 35 years. This erosion of the currency stunted the growth of Turkey's financial sector and held back economic development more generally. It also hit hardest the poorest members of society, such as pensioners on fixed incomes and those less able to use foreign currency or other inflation-proof assets to protect their savings. Not surprisingly, therefore, Turks generally acknowledge the success in bringing inflation down—it has been in the single digits since 2004—as one of the government's foremost achievements.[28] The newly independent central bank was instrumental in delivering this outcome. They quite quickly built a reputation for competence and strong inflation-fighting credentials, meeting every one of their inflation targets from 2002–05. In so doing, they had to stand fast against considerable public pressure, playing an important advocacy role in favor of monetary discipline, and adherence to the stabilization program more broadly. But their efforts would not have paid off without a strongly supportive fiscal policy, and hence they and the government have shared the credit for defeating inflation.

The banking system is now helping propel development and broaden access to credit: During the 1980s and 1990s, the government's voracious borrowing had absorbed the lion's share of available credit in the economy, leaving little for the private sector. High and unstable inflation, combined with restrictions on making floating rate loans to consumers, also discouraged banks from lending except on very short maturities. This picture has changed dramatically over the past five years. The decline in government borrowing, inflation, and real interest rates, together with wholesale reforms and capital infusions in the banking system, had allowed banks to double their lending to the private sector as a share of (rapidly growing) national income, compared to the 1990s. Lending to households, whose access to credit was almost nonexistent in the early 1990s, has expanded at an even faster pace. The stock of housing loans, which stood at a mere 0.2 percent of GNP as recently as 2003, grew by a factor of 20 in real terms in the three years that followed. Such a rapid transformation entails risks that need to be carefully managed, but the changes were long overdue and a necessary step in Turkey's economic development.

The modernization of the economy has accelerated: At the end of the 1980s, almost half of Turkey's workforce was still employed in agriculture, while the services sector accounted for less than one-third of total employment. By 2006, these ratios had been reversed. The exodus from the rural economy to the more dynamic industrial and services sectors has gathered pace in the present decade, contributing to a surge in economy-wide productivity. Real per capita incomes increased by more than one-third in the five years following the crisis, and continue to grow. The factors driving this structural transformation are many and complex, but the creation of a more market-friendly environment, with stable financial conditions, has undoubtedly played an important part. The declining involvement of the state in commercial activity is another hallmark of a modernizing economy, reflecting the hugely successful privatization program of recent years. These reforms helped draw in more than $50 billion in foreign direct investment during 2004–7, more than double the total inflows of the preceding 20 years.

Notwithstanding the enormous strides that have been made, Turkey still faces significant economic challenges. These will need to be handled adroitly if the economic resurgence is to be sustained. In particular, among emerging market economies, Turkey's exposure to global financial shocks remains relatively high. It relies on foreign investors to finance its large current account deficit, its foreign exchange reserve position is less strong than many of its peers, and its public debt burden is still comparatively large. Fiscal and financial consolidation will therefore need to continue in the years ahead. Persistently high unemployment is another vulnerability, albeit of a different kind. While its causes are unquestionably structural in nature, structural remedies to facilitate faster job creation may prove politically difficult, and governments will need to resist pressures to resort to expansionary fiscal measures as a palliative.

Conclusion

Turkey had launched numerous reform efforts prior to 2001, many of them backed by the IMF, but all eventually foundered. What was different this time that allowed the reforms to be sustained? Two factors, in combination, appear to have been decisive: political determination and a favorable global environment.

The Ecevit government's options were limited in 2001, but the government nevertheless deserves credit for taking courageous decisions, for which it paid a price in the 2002 elections. Those elections then brought to power a new party with a market-friendly philosophy and a pragmatic bent. The AK (or Justice and Development) Party derives part of its core support from the small-business sector in Turkey's heartland and came viscerally predisposed to budget discipline, low inflation, and privatization. The party therefore had little difficulty in embracing and building upon the reforms that were underway. Moreover, it was in a strong position to follow through: it was the first government in more than a decade to rule as a single party, with a strong majority in parliament. Its dominance proved to be less complete than it initially appeared, as the opposition found ways to delay reforms through presidential vetoes and court challenges. But the party's parliamentary majority contributed to greater policy coherence and consistency than Turkey had seen in many years.

Investor confidence received a further boost as the new government declared its intent to push ahead with the long-delayed EU-membership process. Though the government's motives were as much political as economic, investors viewed the EU accession process as helping to anchor economic reforms for the medium term—including beyond the life of the IMF-backed program. This not only underpinned the continued inflows of foreign capital that were needed to sustain the recovery but also helped shift the composition of those flows toward longer-term strategic investments.

Positive economic and political changes in Turkey coincided fortuitously with an increasingly favorable global investment climate. Having slumped following the Asian and Russian financial crises, net private capital flows to emerging market and developing countries took off in 2002; by 2005, they were running at almost 2½ times the level seen during the 1990s. As a result, borrowing costs dropped for emerging markets in general, including Turkey, and equity markets boomed. The sizeable current account deficits that came along with the growth resurgence, and which might have threatened the sustainability of the recovery, thus proved to be readily financed.

The IMF's contribution to the successful outcome is widely acknowledged in Turkey, and by international investors. Are there lessons we can draw from the experience? We would highlight three main ones.

First, the health of the banking system is vitally important. Transparent recognition of losses is essential, followed up if necessary by substantial fiscal support to restore solvency and confidence. Financial and operational weaknesses in banks have to be addressed up front and quickly: gradualism is very risky. Properly designed reforms minimize economic and financial losses and help restore momentum for economic growth.

Second, while fiscal retrenchment in the midst of a crisis may not be optimal in all cases, if there is a need to restore government solvency, bold measures—far from being contractionary—can actually help speed economic recovery by boosting confidence.

Third, like an increasing number of its peers, Turkey has found that central-bank independence, coupled with explicit inflation targets and a coherent fiscal policy, can be very effective in overcoming entrenched expectations of high inflation.

Important as these technical aspects are, however, good policy design counts for nothing without the strong political will to implement it. In this respect, Turkey has been fortunate in recent years in having leaders who recognized what needed to be done and who acted accordingly. Thanks to their efforts, the country now faces a brighter economic future than at any previous time in its modern history.

Turkey's Renaissance: From Banking Crisis to Economic Revival

Süreyya Serdengeçti[1]

This section describes how an economy finally awakened from a coma that resulted from a chronic illness that lasted 30 years. Given the obvious difficulty of telling the whole story in less than 20 pages, the authors chose to concentrate on the banking reform, while mentioning rather briefly other areas such as fiscal policy, monetary policy, or institutional reforms such as central bank independence. In the following comment, I will look at the story from the perspective of a career central banker.

The year 2001 was the turning point when a financial crisis, the last and the deepest of the many crises that had occurred previously, turned into a big opportunity. The Central Bank of Turkey was given its independence from political influence after 30 years of chronic inflation, and of denial of dismal economic reality or hesitation to confront it on the part of successive Turkish parliaments and governments. This marked the end of a long period in which the political system had tried to finance chronic fiscal imbalances through inflation and, when that was not bad enough, through incurring excessive public debt and misusing public sector banks. Throughout this period, the widespread—if mistaken—belief in Turkish political and business circles was that, however bad inflation might be, it was the reason the economy was able to grow.

Economic instability brought political instability, which led to more economic instability. All elections were held early, and the governments

[1] Mr. Serdengeçti is a former governor of the Central Bank of Turkey. He is currently a senior lecturer at TOBB Economics and Technology University in Ankara and Director of the Stability Institute at TEPAV, Ankara.

that called the elections lost votes, if not the elections. The electorate, given election-year promises that were soon forgotten by policy makers or proved unrealistic, was tired of the economic instability and simply responded on every occasion by voting for the opposition.

All the efforts to stop this vicious circle of instability were unsuccessful. I remember the Central Bank's insistence in the early 1990s on the importance of controlling the growth of monetary aggregates in order to reduce inflation, or the warnings by Treasury officials of the growing unsustainability of public debt.

Similarly, in the case of the banking system, numerous mistakes were made and warnings disregarded:

- Turkey had the worst-possible model of banking supervision and regulation; the Central Bank's off-site authority and the Treasury's on-site supervisory authority were weakened by the real authority on the banking system, which was the minister in charge of the Treasury. Virtually all decisions, whether they were implemented or not, were politically motivated. One example was the practice of granting licenses to newcomers, which increased the number of banks to more than 80. This was at a time when many analysts complained that the balance sheets of all these banks combined did not add up to the balance sheet of one large German bank.
- The efforts to transform this outmoded supervisory and regulatory framework into a modern one went back to 1997. Unfortunately, the establishment of an independent authority had been delayed not only by disagreements over personnel appointments but more importantly by the lack of political will to delegate authority to an independent professional institution.
- The privatization of public sector banks was constantly delayed. This issue was publicly discussed in the early 1980s. At the time, no country behind the Iron Curtain had considered privatization. Ironically, today almost no public sector banks are left in Eastern European countries, whereas Turkey has yet to privatize its public sector banks.
- The untimely opening up of the capital account and lifting of exchange controls in 1989, despite the opposition of the bureaucracy, led the Turkish banking system to simply borrow from abroad and invest in high-yielding public debt, without adequate regard to exchange and interest rate risks, or to maturity mismatches.
- Last but not least, a "clever" decision, which had been taken in April 1994 during one of the financial crises, proved to be fatal.

> The decision was to grant full government guarantees to all bank deposits without upper limit in order to stop a run on bank deposits. The decision was successful in ending a panic, yet it was not sustainable. Unfortunately, in September 1994, the government rejected, it seems, a proposal that deposit guarantees should return to normal and more limited levels, as the maintenance of unlimited guarantees would lead to deepening moral hazard. Not adopting this proposal became a fatal weakness and helped pave the way to the 2001 crisis.

Turning to the economy in general before 2001, an important development took place in 1999. Economic growth was falling due to the negative effects on the Turkish economy from the Russian and Brazilian financial crises, due to political instability after a banking scandal, and due to the effects of the devastating earthquake of August that year.

Politicians were finally persuaded that they had to agree to stabilize the economy. Otherwise they would suffer the consequences not only of even lower growth but also of risking default on the public debt.

This led to the 2000 economic stabilization program supported by the IMF. The program diagnosed price and financial instabilities and fiscal imbalances as the three main issues. It attempted to address them through an exchange-rate-based stabilization approach that would enable two developments. First, incentives for capital inflows and a low-interest-rate environment would be created, which would be crucial for improving the sustainability of public debt; and, second, disinflation would be encouraged, given the strong exchange rate pass-through effect and inflation inertia that had become the primary determinants of inflation in Turkey in the 1990s.

At the start, foreign capital flew in and interest rates came down to levels that had not been seen for almost 15 years. By the end of August 2000, however, a variety of problems developed and intensified. Interest rates, no longer under the control of the Central Bank—itself under the "quasi currency board" rule—started to increase, albeit slowly. Much-publicized debates on structural reforms between the IMF and the government took place in September concerning the reform of public sector banks and incomes policy and created uncertainty. The government was reluctant to tighten fiscal policy despite a deteriorating external current account and the increasingly cloudy environment in international capital markets as Argentina seemed to be heading toward a financial crisis. Many banks were overleveraged and had large open positions in foreign exchange, while the newly independent supervisory authority, after years of delay, had only just become operational. These developments coincided with a political crisis and led to two rounds of speculative attacks on the currency and on weaker banks, in November 2000 and February 2001.

The stabilization program failed, and the currency was devalued and left to float.

As the country found itself in its worst economic crisis, the opportunity for an independent central bank finally emerged. In a floating exchange rate environment, the Central Bank immediately declared that there was nowhere else to go but to adopt a monetary policy of inflation targeting, which would be effective in time as conditions allowed. The Central Bank also adopted a very transparent communications policy to honestly show its determination to fight inflation and affect inflationary expectations, as the only way to reduce inflation.

The new stabilization program—the 2001 program—was announced in May 2001, together with the independence of the Central Bank that had been granted by the parliament. The aims of the 2001 program again were price stability, financial stability, and the restoration of fiscal balances so as to ensure debt sustainability.

The tremendous efforts to revitalize and reform the banking system have been explained in detail in the chapter. But two important points must be highlighted, since they mark the beginning of the painful process of banking reform:

- First, the operations of the public sector banks, under which the Treasury issued government debt securities to cover the public banks' losses and also intervened in the banks' negative capital balances, were followed by the Central Bank making an outright purchase of the debt securities issued by the Treasury, amounting to 14 billion New Turkish Liras (TRY). Moreover, the Central Bank provided these banks with a TRY 7 billion repo facility with short maturities. So, the amount of liquidity provided to these banks by the Central Bank reached TRY 21 billion which is roughly the equivalent of $18.5 billion at April 2001 exchange rates. The Central Bank avoided hyperinflation by mopping up a substantial amount of liquidity from this bank-restructuring operation in a record time.
- Second, the debt-swap operations of the Treasury, which were aimed at reducing the rollover risk of government debt and facilitate a decline in interest rates, on the one hand, and helping banks

> close their large open foreign exchange position, on the other. This operation involved the exchange of TRY 9.3 billion worth of domestic T-bills and longer-dated fixed and floating rate T-bonds for a package of US dollar-indexed bonds and shorter T-bonds. The swap reduced the banks' foreign-exchange open position significantly.

From the very beginning, the 2001 program was under constant fire from some political and business circles and also from the media. Those in charge of it, from the Minister for Economic Affairs, Kemal Derviş, to institutions like the Central Bank and the Treasury, as well as the IMF and the World Bank, were under growing political and market pressure as it became evident that this time the stabilization program was determined to reach its aims. In fact, the program started to deliver positive results as early as 2002 and in the years that followed went on to become a most successful one.

Inflation came down to single digits in 2004 after 34 years of high inflation. Inflation targets were reached for four consecutive years; the public debt to GDP ratio was more than halved between 2001 and 2007; and expected real interest rates, as high as 30 percent in early 2002, came down to 8 percent by early 2006. A currency reform—dropping six zeros off currency denominations—was successfully carried out in 2004 and 2005.

Despite the appreciation of the lira, Turkey improved its international competitiveness and the share of the country's exports in total world exports rose sharply. Meanwhile, the deterioration of trade and current account balances was accompanied by a change in the composition of the capital inflows, from one dominated by hot money inflows from 1989 to 2004 to one dominated by medium- and long-term inflows and foreign direct investment inflows thereafter.

As for the banking system, capital adequacy improved considerably, while the number of banks diminished to about half of their number in 2001. An injection of foreign capital was instrumental in the system's improving health.

The program's biggest success has been in the area of economic growth. From a 4 percent annual average growth rate during the chronic inflation period of 1970–2001, a level lower than in many other emerging market countries, the growth rate rose to an annual average of 7.2 percent from 2002 to 2006.

It's no wonder, as the chapter's authors say, that adverse political developments in 2007 didn't have the same devastating effect on the economy as was the case in 2001.

I wish to conclude my comment by saying that the IMF played a vital role in the recovery of the Turkish economy by collaborating with and supporting the stabilization efforts of successive governments, the Treasury, the Central Bank, and other institutions. This collaboration and support came not only from teams in charge of the stabilization program but also from special teams that worked with the authorities in diverse areas such as helping to implement the inflation-targeting policy of the Central Bank and the currency reform.

5

Tanzania: Reform and Progress, 1995–2007

Robert Sharer[1]

Tanzania's economic performance over the last decade or so has been a major success by any standards. Viewed in narrow terms, real income per capita has increased by almost 50 percent, reversing the declining trend of many years. High inflation, which had destroyed savings and economic incentives, was brought down to single digits and the real level of government expenditures on infrastructure and on essential public services such as education and healthcare has increased sharply. More broadly, the Government has made an important start in the daunting task of reducing Tanzania's pervasive poverty by building a freer, more vibrant, and productive economy. The IMF has played an important part in helping this transformation through its policy advice and technical guidance. These are based on its extensive experience and expertise; its substantial and highly concessional financial support, particularly in the early years of the transformation; its catalytic role and leadership of the broader international donor community; its leading role in initiating and implementing debt relief; and its extensive technical assistance and other support for capacity building.

Tanzania's economic achievements, and the role of the IMF, must be seen in historical context. Julius Nyerere, Chairman of the then sole political party, led the country to independence from British colonial rule in December 1961[29] and he became its first President. Nyerere was venerated by his compatriots and still is, almost a decade after his death in 1999. Known throughout the country as *Mwalimu*—the teacher in Swahili—Nyerere was an inspirational leader, whose vision was of establishing a self-reliant communalist society, a uniquely African brand of Socialism. The vision was set forth in The Arusha Declaration of 1967,

[1] Robert Sharer is an assistant director in the IMF's African Department.

which espoused a society based on *Uhuru* (freedom), *Kujitegemea* (self-reliance), and above all *Ujamaa* (literally familyhood). *Ujamaa* socialism in practice meant state control of the economy and state ownership of all major enterprises. It also meant that the state would seek to foster communalized agriculture (which employed the vast majority of the population) through the establishment of communal *Ujamaa* villages and cooperative societies throughout the country. The agricultural sector was to generate surpluses that would fund the industrialization that Nyerere envisaged as underpinning rapid economic progress that would transform Tanzania from its widespread poverty and underdevelopment.

The Arusha Declaration and its calls for self-reliance and a system of *Ujamaa* socialism, based on Africa's history, culture, and circumstances, became something of a landmark, with influence far beyond Tanzania's borders. It received much international acclaim, particularly in Anglophone Africa and in liberal circles in Europe. Julius Nyerere became a hero to center-left politicians and a highly respected international statesman and spokesman for the continent. Tanzania became one of the first major recipients of aid not only from the Western countries, particularly from Scandinavian countries whose governments admired Nyerere's vision, but also from the World Bank and other international donors.

Unfortunately, reality did not match the dream. Two decades after independence, the policy framework of state intervention and planning led to major economic distortions and inefficiencies. Loss-making state enterprises, subsidies, and budget deficits were financed by printing money, leading to high inflation, a growing black market for foreign exchange, and rising levels of poverty. For some two decades after independence, Tanzania suffered economic stagnation and decline. The growth of the economy did not keep pace with the increase in population and poverty increased. Contact with the IMF during this period was limited and can generally be characterized as a "dialogue of the deaf." The IMF's emphasis on the benefits of market-oriented policies with low inflation did not sit well with the "*Ujamaa*" vision of the Tanzanian authorities. While visiting IMF delegations were treated with traditional Tanzanian hospitality, their advice was ignored and they were often lectured on the evils of Western-style capitalism and the need for the New World Order.

In 1985, President Nyerere, perhaps recognizing the failure of his economic policies, stood down as President. Ali Hassan Mwinyi succeeded him. Subsequently, a start was made in the process of economic reform. Some of the most visible aspects of state economic control were removed—the extensive system of price, production, and distribution controls was scaled back; government control of trade was reduced; and interest rate ceilings were abolished. However, the reforms did not fundamentally change the dominant role of the state. Moreover, financial discipline remained weak. The sole political party continued to dominate Tanzanian politics, with Julius Nyerere remaining in the politically powerful role as its President. There was dialogue with the IMF during this period and the IMF provided some financial support to Tanzania. The Government's antipathy to market-oriented policies remained in place, however, and genuine ownership of the policies the Government set forth was lacking in its Letters of Intent to the IMF. While the most visible negative aspects of state control were scaled back, there was no commitment to a fundamental change in the direction of the economy. The programs supported by the IMF were not effectively implemented.

In 1992, Tanzania amended its constitution to introduce, among other things, multipartyism. In December 1995, in the first multiparty elections, Benjamin Mkapa, the candidate of the Chama Cha Mapinduzi (CCM), or Revolutionary State Party, won a comfortable victory. He inherited a situation where indicators of economic progress and of social well-being were among the lowest in the world and income per capita was stagnant after declining for many years. Infrastructure was poor and generally deteriorating, inflation was high and rising, and there was no effectively functioning financial system to encourage the savings and investments so crucial in a poor economy. The economy was still dominated by large, inefficient, and generally loss-making state enterprises, and the government budget was characterized by a large, inefficient and generally unaccountable civil service.

There was little in Mr. Mkapa's background to suggest that he would be a major economic reformer. Aged 57 at the time, and a former Minister of Science, Technology, and Higher Education, and of Foreign Affairs, Mr. Mkapa was a stalwart of the CCM, which did then, and still does, dominate Tanzania's politics. He was widely perceived as "Nyerere's candidate," beating Jakaya Kikwete,[30] 12 years his junior and widely perceived as the candidate of change and reform. Yet President Mkapa needed no persuasion from the IMF or any other source in determining that Tanzania needed to change its economic direction and policies. Moving carefully, in order to carry the party and public opinion with him, plans were drawn up for the progressive reform of all key sectors of the economy. Beginning in 1996, President Mkapa and the Tanzanian Government initiated a genuine far-reaching and enduring economic reform process, which continues to this day.

This readiness in Tanzania to change economic direction coincided broadly with a period of change in IMF thinking and interaction with low-income countries. The IMF's then Managing Director, Michel Camdessus, was strongly committed to efforts to help low-income countries and was determined to institute lending practices and policies that were designed specifically for the needs and circumstances of these countries. He had been the driving force in the late 1980s in raising some $5 billion from the IMF's member countries to finance a new highly concessional IMF lending facility for low-income countries, the Enhanced Structural Adjustment Facility (ESAF), with an interest rate of 0.5 percent and a term of 10 years with 5.5 years grace. This new facility was well received and heavily used, particularly by African countries. Nevertheless as its use progressed, discussions with African leaders showed that it was viewed as too detailed without adequate attention to help address the key social issue facing the low-income countries of reducing poverty while also promoting growth. It also could be seen as intrusive, with conditionality that was too detailed and far-reaching, going into areas that were beyond the IMF's mandate and expertise, thus tending to undermine genuine ownership of the policies underlying reform programs. An important change in IMF relations with Africa occurred when the ESAF was replaced by the Poverty Reduction and Growth Facility (PRGF) in 1999. Thus, the start of Tanzania's willingness to pursue genuine and far-reaching economic reform and a new direction coincided with efforts by the IMF to adapt its own policies and practices to the needs and circumstances of low-income countries, such as Tanzania. This set the ground for an increasingly close relationship between the IMF and Tanzania that would continue to strengthen and develop in coming years.

Why did President Mkapa and his economic team turn to the IMF? One obvious reason is that the IMF committed, and disbursed, $400 million in highly concessional loans to Tanzania over the following decade in support of its economic reform program. The IMF's financial support is not tied to specific projects or any expenditures and is thus available to support the general growth and development of the economy. Another critical reason is that the IMF played a role as a catalyst for gaining the support of the international community. Multilateral and bilateral donors want to have confidence that the microeconomic policies and projects they are supporting will not be derailed or undermined in their effectiveness by wrong-headed macroeconomic policies leading, among others, to high inflation, as had happened in Tanzania since independence. This is the IMF's core mandate and expertise, so agreeing and implementing an IMF-supported program, and the ongoing support of the IMF, can have a major impact on donor confidence and support. And this is what happened in Tanzania. As the Government implemented these critical macroeconomic policies in their reform program, its credibility grew and total donor support grew sixfold, from $200 million in 1996 to about $1250 million by 2006. The sustained support of the IMF was also important in enhancing the confidence of the private sector and in attracting private-sector investment. There are no miracles in this area, and attracting substantial foreign direct investment (FDI) in a poor country such as Tanzania with a limited domestic market, rudimentary infrastructure, a weak investment climate, and a history of hostility to FDI is a long-term process. The sustained relationship with the IMF, in support of sound government economic policies, has been helpful in moving this process steadily in the right direction. This has been particularly important in enabling the Government's privatization program to proceed in a successful manner.

The direct financial support and the fact that the international donor community very much welcomed a program with the IMF are well known. Less well known but equally important is the IMF's technical and analytic support to countries' macroeconomic and structural policy development and its implementation, as well as to the critical area of capacity building. This is effected through the direct and ongoing dialogue and general interaction with the staff of the IMF's African Department at its Washington headquarters, with the IMF's mission teams that visit Tanzania to discuss developments and prospects, and through the interaction with the IMF's resident representative office in Dar-es-Salaam. It is also effected through the extensive technical assistance provided by visiting teams of experienced experts, through occasional resident experts in specific areas, and more recently through the IMF's Dar-es-Salaam-based Regional Technical Assistance Center (East AFRITAC). This center houses resident experts providing advice and assistance to Tanzania and other countries in the region in the areas of public financial management, tax policy and administration, banking supervision, monetary policy, and statistics. These activities are further bolstered by the numerous programs of the IMF Institute, which runs training programs open to officials nominated by their governments, both in Washington and in Africa. All IMF technical assistance to low-income countries is provided free of charge.

The central objective of President Mkapa's Government was to raise substantially the welfare and living standards of Tanzania's people. This meant raising the level of economic output, complemented by government policies to try to spread the benefits of growth and alleviate poverty. It was recognized that this was very much a long-term goal that would take decades. It required greatly improved infrastructure and public services, as well as human capital through improvements in health and education. Tanzania's experience since independence showed that it also required an appropriate incentive environment for productive private sector activity and investment. Thus, the goals of growth and of poverty alleviation required a productive private sector, complemented by an efficient and effective public sector. In 1995, Tanzania had neither.

Lacking sufficient capital and skills, Tanzania required foreign capital and investment. This was not an externally imposed objective but a fact of life for any poor country like Tanzania. External capital is the most direct route to jump-start economic growth. The two possible sources were substantially enhanced support from the international donor community—the World Bank, African Development Bank, numerous bilateral donors, the IMF—and enhanced private-sector involvement, preferably in the form of FDI, which had helped to lead to such dramatic success in East Asia. However, Tanzania's history and past performance had led to skepticism on the part of the international community, and private sector involvement had been minimal. Thus, a credible overall economic program and clear signs of the government's determination to change course were essential.

A credible overall economic program to foster rapid development must necessarily start with a credible macroeconomic framework. Specifically, this means fiscal, monetary, and external targets and policies that are consistent in balancing the external and domestic demand and supply of goods and services, within a framework that targets low inflation. Lowering inflation was paramount. There is no case of a country successfully sustaining growth and reducing poverty over time without bringing down inflation. This is the IMF's core mandate and its main area of expertise and experience. It is central to its policy advice and to programs supported by use of IMF resources, which in Tanzania was large—over $400 million during 1995–2005. The macroeconomic frameworks agreed with the IMF are implemented and monitored through specific quantitative targets on key economic aggregates, such as the net domestic financing of the Government and the net domestic assets of the banking system or reserve money of the Central Bank, and Tanzania's net international reserves. These targets are designed to ensure that the amount of money created in the economy is consistent with available resources, and that the Government lives broadly within its means, so that there will be enough credit available to the private sector to enable it to increase output and employment.

Tanzania's record in the ten years after 1995 in meeting its policy commitments under IMF-supported programs was excellent. And it worked. Inflation, which had averaged more than 25 percent a year over the period 1976–95, fell steadily, coming down to about 5 percent in the next five years (Figure 5.1). It has since remained at around that level, providing a major boost to economic performance and prospects. It should be underlined that low inflation has to be an important element of any program to reduce poverty, since in practice inflation is a tax that falls disproportionately on the poor.

Fiscal policy, monetary policy, and financial-sector reform are the core of macroeconomic frameworks. Fiscal policy was the most critical in Tanzania because of the dominant role that the state had played in the economy. Fiscal policy had to aim at lowering the absorption of financial resources by the public sector—government and state enterprises—to avoid crowding out productive private sector activity. A policy of privatization addressed the issue of reducing the financial drain of the state enterprises, as discussed later. Nevertheless reducing the amount of financial resources absorbed by Government was problematic because of the clear need to raise the real level of expenditures on critical social and economic outlays, particularly health, education, and infrastructure. The only way to square this circle was for Government to raise its domestic resource mobilization, and also to increase foreign resource

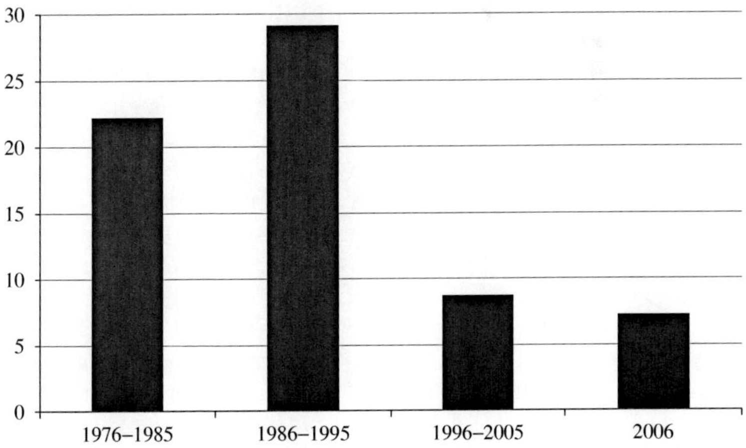

Figure 5.1 Tanzania: Average annual inflation (in percent)

mobilization through the financial support of the international donor community. If successful, this would enable the government to reduce its excessive domestic financing needs while gradually raising the level of real government expenditure. This would be reinforced by efforts to improve the efficiency and allocation of government spending through improved public expenditure management. This really is the core of the whole reform program. The main tools for achieving these goals were a far-reaching revenue reform to broaden the tax base and improve its fairness and efficiency; and public expenditure management reforms to streamline and control expenditure, improve its allocative efficiency, and generally to promote efficient public expenditure and investment decisions and their effective implementation.

And here again, the policy worked. As shown in the Figure 5.2, in the ten-year period beginning in 1998/99[31] (when the tax reform program effectively began), government revenue rose from 10 percent of GDP to about 16 percent. This is a remarkable achievement at a time when the GDP itself was beginning to grow rapidly. Over the same period, because of the authorities' evident resolve and commitment in implementing their reform program, donor budgetary support grew steadily, from about 4 percent of GDP to 12 percent of GDP in 2007/8, or from $350 million to $1 billion. This increase in domestic and foreign resources made possible an increase in total public expenditure in the government budget from about 16 percent of GDP to about 28 percent. This represents an increase of almost 300 percent in the real value of these expenditures, a staggering achievement that has had a huge impact on peoples' lives, including through the sharply increased funding for health and education sectors. At the same time, over this ten-year period, domestic financing of the budget was, broadly, close to zero.[32] This was the major factor in bringing down inflation.

The IMF was very closely involved in these fiscal policy reforms, which were the core of each annual program with the IMF over the period. Tax rates in Tanzania were high, but the tax base was very narrow. The aim of the tax reform, therefore, was to increase revenue mobilization through modernizing and streamlining revenue collection, broadening the tax base by reforming tax practices and policies, and modernizing tax laws. To the extent possible, high tax rates were to be reduced. A further important objective was to make the system fairer and more transparent. The program was initiated with the establishment of the Tanzania Revenue Authority (TRA) in 1997 as a separate entity outside of the direct control of the Ministry of Finance. This enabled it to adopt a management and organizational structure designed for it to meet its objectives, including

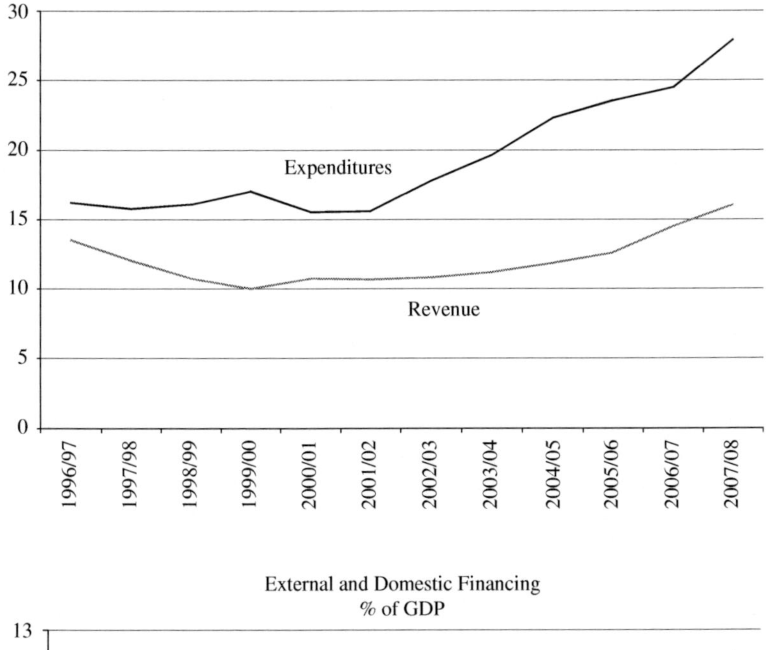

Figure 5.2 Tanzania: Revenue and expenditures (percent of GDP)

pay and conditions geared toward giving employees the incentives to meet newly introduced monthly and annual revenue targets. The IMF provided extensive technical assistance in the establishment and operations of the TRA, bringing in leading technical experts with experience of best practices in this area. In 2003, with the extensive involvement and technical assistance and advice from the IMF, the TRA moved from a departmental structure based on each tax (specifically, an income-tax department and a VAT department) to a functional organizational structure. This enabled the TRA to reallocate its staff to higher yielding tax areas and to improve greatly its auditing and control systems by linking up the databases and information from each department to facilitate an effective auditing function. The first step in this was the formation of the Large Taxpayers Department, which enabled the TRA to focus more audit and review resources on the larger companies. These are standard practice in modern tax systems.

The IMF also provided technical assistance and advice on the reform of individual taxes. Beginning in 2003, there was an extensive review and revision of Tanzania's outdated income-tax law that was designed to remove a variety of loopholes and exemptions and make the law consistent with best practices. In 2004, again with input from the IMF, Tanzania revised its practices for VAT, doubling the turnover threshold for liability to the tax, thus sharply reducing the number of registered small taxpayers and freeing administrative resources for other activities. Concurrently, the Government removed the Stamp Duty and a number of other minor "nuisance taxes" that were administratively costly and yielded only minimal revenue. In 2004, the TRA launched a major reform of the customs administration, again with technical input from the IMF, involving extensive reform of management and administrative practices and policies that were designed to avoid fraud and mismanagement, speed throughput, and greatly enhance auditing.

An important objective of the whole tax reform program was to improve the business environment, promote fairness, and reduce fraud by significantly reducing the level of tax exemptions. Laws were changed to remove the power of ministers to grant discretionary tax exemptions or other favorable treatment. In 2003, the Government introduced a tax-voucher scheme for individuals and organizations exempt from payment of taxes on imports and local purchases, mainly NGOs. With a view to reduce misuse and fraud and make the system transparent, the names of organizations receiving these exemptions are now published. Between 1996 and 2005, the IMF fielded 24 technical assistance missions and visits related to improving tax administration and policy. Conditionality on the implementation of key aspects of the tax reform program was often included in IMF-supported programs. This was not to "impose outsiders' views" but to provide markers to Government that the reforms were proceeding as planned. They also give a clear signal to the donor community of the authorities' resolve.

Clearly, the essential counterpart to the revenue reforms is to improve the efficiency and effective allocation of expenditure within a system that controls total outlays. The latter was achieved in 1996 through the introduction of cash budgeting—a system under which each ministry and agency receives its quarterly budget allocation and has to live within it, come what may. This is something of a sledgehammer approach to the problem of weak discipline and controls that negate fiscal discipline. Obviously, there will be occasions when there are good reasons for a ministry's budget to be exceeded, but under cash budgeting this can only be done through either offsetting cuts elsewhere or by submitting a supplementary budget to parliament—something that the government was always highly reluctant to do. In introducing cash budgeting, the Tanzanians were learning from their neighbors in Uganda, where it was introduced in 1992 with stunning effect. Ugandan president Yoweri Museveni had stated, "inflation is indiscipline—we will not spend money we do not have," and inflation in Uganda had come down from an average of 173 percent in 1987–89 to 6 percent by 1994. Tanzania would achieve the same success.

Cash budgeting has been followed by ongoing efforts to improve public-expenditure management involving a myriad of detailed and time-consuming reforms. The IMF was extensively involved in providing technical assistance in many of these areas, often in partnership with the World Bank and the United Kingdom. The Public Finance Law was rewritten and major changes were introduced into public procurement and the methods of bidding and evaluation of major government contracts. Extensive reforms were introduced into public debt management and a major reform of the civil service was undertaken covering total staffing (which was reduced substantially) pay and conditions (which have improved significantly) and management and organization. This also addressed the issue of fraud and "ghost workers" on the public payroll. An Integrated Financial Management Information System (IFMIS) was implemented, a complex process that has not succeeded in several other African countries. This will increasingly allow government not only to budget and control expenditure effectively but also to track expenditures of ministries to the local level and thus evaluate whether expenditures and services are reaching their intended recipients. The government has also made strong efforts to link budget preparation and outlays to the broad objectives of government policies. These are set out in the Government's Poverty Reduction Strategy Paper—a key government document that reflects a broad public consensus on the broad allocation of public resources. Ministries in Tanzania now make their initial budget proposals under three broad categories: economic welfare, social welfare and poverty reduction, and governance and democracy. An important focus of these reforms has been greater transparency with a view to reducing fraud and corruption.

The other major component of implementing the macroeconomic program was monetary policy and financial sector reform. The monetary policy implemented by the Bank of Tanzania (BoT) aimed at a steady growth of monetary aggregates consistent with a much lower level of inflation. Within this, there was to be sharply increased availability of credit for the private sector to encourage increased economic growth. This required modernization of the BoT, which in the past had operated on the basis of controls and directives. More importantly, it required commercial banks that could effectively perform their basic function of financial intermediation, namely, raising resources from the public (individuals, pension funds, and corporate deposits) and lending them to companies and individuals for investment and productive private sector activity. However, in the 1960s under the policies of *Ujamaa,* Tanzania had nationalized all the commercial banks, and banking remained a state monopoly up to the mid 1990s. It was dominated by the National Bank of Commerce (NBC) for which the great majority of loans and deposits were state enterprises and government. The financial position of most state enterprises was poor and much of the NBC's assets were in fact bad debts, albeit bad debts that were guaranteed by government. A fundamental decision—critical to the success of the reform program—was to move to a fully private commercial banking system. This was to be done by privatizing the NBC and licensing both foreign and domestic private banks. The NBC privatization was facilitated by first hiving off its rural branch network into a separate institution, the National Microfinance Bank (NMB), which would be privatized separately with a view to promoting financial services in rural areas and access to small-scale credit—something that was virtually nonexistent in rural Tanzania. The process of inviting bids for the NBC was initiated in late 1997, and the privatization was completed in 2000.

The privatization of the NMB proved more time consuming. Although badly run and insolvent, its branch network, albeit loss making, was the only vehicle available to promote rural financial development. Drawing up the Invitation to Bid to foster this objective, while bringing in quality management, capital, and experience, was difficult. Moreover, the move toward privatization stirred some political opposition, mainly reflecting vested interests and some political holdovers from the days of state control. In April 2003, parliament rejected the privatization proposal before it. Anyone who doubted President Mkapa's commitment to reform should refer to his traditional May Day speech that followed parliament's action. He decried the continued delays and vowed to resubmit the privatization to parliament. He said, "anyone who thinks the Government should run banks should look at our record in owning them. It is a record of losses and subsidies. The rural areas have not benefited. We must privatize this bank." The NMB was finally privatized in 2005 under a consortium led by Rabo Bank, which has substantial international experience in microfinance and agricultural lending, and included significant private Tanzanian participation.

In 2000, Barclays Bank, which had operated in Tanzania in the 1960s and been nationalized, was licensed to operate in Tanzania. Many others followed it and, by 2007, Tanzania had over 30 private banks. The privatization of the banking system paid off, aided by numerous reforms and incentives introduced by the BoT, as discussed later. In 1997, bank credit to the private sector was only 3.5 percent of GDP, one of the lowest ratios in Africa. Over the next decade, private-sector credit increased by an average of 30 percent each year and was a major factor in the rising growth performance of the economy. By 2003, it had reached 7.6 percent of GDP, and by 2007, it was 14 percent. At the same time, the ratio of nonperforming loans came down from almost 23 percent in 1998 to less than 7 percent by 2007.

The performance of the banking sector was facilitated by numerous detailed reforms designed to facilitate an efficient banking system and conduct of monetary policy. The IMF was at the center of advising the government on the design and implementation of these reforms, both in the course of the frequent missions that negotiated and monitored the programs and through specific targeted technical assistance missions. In the decade under discussion, there were 21 technical assistance visits targeted specifically at monetary policy and financial sector reform. The areas of reform included a new Bank of Tanzania Act and a revised Banking and Financial Institutions Act, introduction of proper prudential and financial regulations and a framework for banking supervision, a regulatory and legal framework for the operation of insurance companies and also for pension funds, introduction of a liberalized domestic money market for Government paper, adoption of new instruments of monetary policy implementation for the Bank of Tanzania, and a new legal and regulatory framework for microfinance. It also included an enhanced legal environment for commercial transactions and the collateralization of loans, development of interbank money and foreign exchange markets, a sharply improved payments and check-clearing system, and introduction and passage of anti–money laundering legislation. This extensive and ongoing financial sector reform program has enabled Tanzania to begin developing a modern financial system that can meet the financial needs of the economy. It has thus been a critical supplement to the successful macroeconomic reforms and improved climate for productive activity and investment.

Another critical area where early action was essential was privatization. There had been three state-owned enterprises (SOEs) at the time of independence. By the late 1980s, in implementing the policies of the Arusha Declaration, they had grown to more than 400, dominating virtually every sector of the economy. The beginnings of reform recognized that these enterprises were a major drain on the budget and the economy. With capacity utilization at around 25 percent, they were highly inefficient. Many built up salary arrears to their employees and tax arrears to the government and were generally unable to service their government-guaranteed debts. Several received direct budgetary subsidies and many had easy access to loans from the state-owned banking system, which could not be serviced or repaid. Thus, they were a major drain on public resources that otherwise could have been used to meet critical social and economic needs.

The privatization program was instituted in the early 1990s, with considerable technical and financial assistance from the World Bank, and the institutional framework—the Parastatal Sector Reform Commission (PSRC) and Loans and Assets Realization Trust (LART) to perform liquidations of bankrupt enterprises and collect the loans and assets of others—was established in 1993. The initial emphasis was more on improving management of major SOEs rather than reliance on the private sector as essential to foster growth. By end-1995, some 50 enterprises had been privatized, but this was mainly through the closure and liquidation of bankrupt companies. In 1996, the Mkapa government announced its decision to divest all SOEs, including the ports, railways, water, electricity, telecommunications, banking, and agriculture. It was recognized that some of these privatizations—particularly the utilities—would not be easy, but the government was determined to redirect its resources and energize the economy.

By 2005, just about all the SOEs were divested. There have been difficulties in some areas. The electricity company remains in state hands and still has financial difficulties. But, overall, privatization has been a major success and has had a dramatic impact on the economy and many industries, including tourism, beverages and tobacco, construction, agricultural processing, transport, and communications, have been transformed for the better.

The IMF has played a vital role in the financing of the reform program, disbursing some $400 million, as noted earlier. However, this understates the importance of the IMF's role. The IMF's rules and practices enable it to act quickly. Therefore, most of this financing was "up-front" at the start of the reform effort. As donors saw the successful implementation of reforms, there was a steady increase in their support, but it was mainly the IMF's support that kick-started the process. The IMF's loans were highly concessional. The IMF, together with the World Bank, implemented the Heavily Indebted Poor Countries Initiative (HIPC) in 1996. Under this initiative, Tanzania had 55 percent of its debts (in net present value terms) to the IMF, World Bank, and Paris Club creditors canceled. Debt-service relief under HIPC totaled $2 billion. Subsequently, in 2006, the IMF and the World Bank implemented the Multilateral Debt Reduction Initiative (MDRI) under which Tanzania's remaining debts to these creditors, totaling $3.7 billion, were canceled.

In conclusion, the case of Tanzania illustrates well the role that the IMF can play in supporting low-income countries in Africa. Tanzania has made enormous progress over the past decade. A stagnating economy has been changed radically. National income is growing rapidly. From an average of about 2.8 percent a year during 1976–95 (stagnant in real per capita terms), it has risen steadily, averaging about 6 percent during 1996–2007 (Figure 5.3). For 2008–9, it is expected to exceed 7 percent. New industries are emerging and old ones have revived. Tanzania now has an emerging vibrant private sector, aided by a sound and rapidly growing financial system. The efficiency and effectiveness of Government has also improved substantially. Major investments are being made to enhance social services, mainly health and education, as well as to improve ailing infrastructure. Substantial gains have been made in almost all indicators of social well-being. Prospects are for this progress to continue.

Looking to the future, much remains to be done. Macroeconomic stability has been achieved, but the economy remains vulnerable to external shocks. The crucial process of mobilization and use of resources for productive purposes must be sustained. In this, Tanzania cannot rely indefinitely on the increased support from the international donor community and on raising ever-increasing domestic revenue. To sustain its success, it will be essential for the country to generate increased

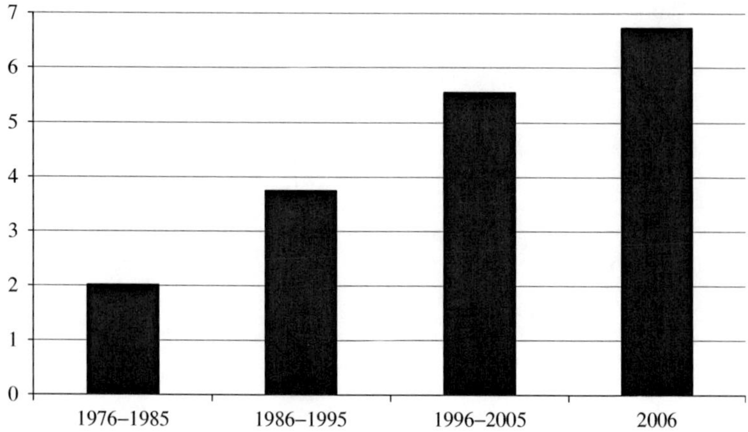

Figure 5.3 Tanzania: Average growth of real GDP, 1976–2006 (in percent)

private sector saving and investment, both foreign and domestic. This will require efforts to improve the business environment, which in turn requires further reform in many areas, including improvement in public sector governance and transparency as well as improving the financial sector, infrastructure, the functioning of the legal system, and the efficiency of public administration and government services, most critically health and education.

And, of course, Tanzania remains a very poor country. Income per capita has increased substantially in the past decade, but at $350 it remains extremely low. Pervasive poverty cannot be abolished quickly; it is a long-term task. This is a matter of arithmetic as much as of economic policy. If Tanzania's economy grows at 7.3 percent, which is the average growth rate of South Korea during 1960–2005, then per capita income[33] would double every 14 years. Thus, by 2035, Tanzania's income per capita would reach about $1500. Clearly, the strong reform efforts of the past decade will need to be sustained for many years to genuinely transform the lives of Tanzania's people. Tanzania has begun this path and has made tremendous gains. It is now in a better position to move to the genuine self-reliance that President Julius Nyerere set out to achieve 50 years ago.

Tanzania—Reforms and Progress, 1995–2007

Gray S. Mgonja[2]

The chapter on "Tanzania—Reforms and Progress, 1995–2007" by Robert Sharer provides a useful insight of the role of the IMF in Tanzania's development process. The thrust of the chapter is to illustrate the positive contribution the IMF made in supporting Tanzania's reforms between 1995 and 2007. The chapter begins by recounting an uneasy relationship between Tanzania and the IMF during the first two decades of Tanzania's independence under the first President Mwalimu, Julius Kambarage Nyerere.

The message from the chapter is that the impressive economic reforms and the rebound of Tanzania's economy from 1995 to 2007 are attributable to three success factors: first, the efforts by the IMF to adapt its policies and practices to the needs and circumstances of low-income countries, such as Tanzania, which began in the late 1980s; second, a political leadership in Tanzania that is committed to reforms; and, third, an international community that became responsive to the role of the IMF in supporting Tanzania.

While the chapter provides a good economic review of Tanzania from the 1960s through 2007, it does not provide a balanced analysis of the reasons for the uneasy relationship between the IMF and Tanzania in the first two decades of Tanzania's independence under President Nyerere. Indeed, one readily infers from the author that some of the reasons that negated the IMF's support in the first two decades of Tanzania's independence had to do with the IMF's unwillingness to adapt its policies and practices to the needs and circumstances of Tanzania at that time.

[2] Mr. Mgonja is Permanent Secretary and Paymaster General in the Tanzanian Ministry of Finance. He was a central figure in the Tanzanian economic reform program.

A historical analysis of Tanzania's circumstances, the IMF's policies, and the Cold War political rivalries would enrich the chapter. The case of Tanzania, as discussed by Robert Sharer, shows that success in reforms depends on the host country's ownership of the reforms and a supportive international community, including the support provided by the multilateral financial institutions.

Tanzania became independent on December 9, 1961, and became a member of the IMF the same year. At independence, President Nyerere inherited a country without a critical mass of educated people to help him run the country. In 1961 Tanzania had only 44 high school graduates. Basic health services were not available to the majority of the people. Given this background, education played an important role in the reforms President Nyerere introduced after independence.

As the author observes, the IMF's emphasis on the benefits of market-oriented policies with low inflation through public expenditure cuts could hardly sit well with the circumstances of Tanzania or any other low-income country. For Tanzania then, President Nyerere saw education as being closely tied to social commitment. The IMF was perceived to have a short-term horizon, which focused on balancing the books, while expecting supply factors in a developing country to adjust in three years. On the contrary, to develop a credible social infrastructure in Tanzania required a longer-term perspective and financing. Thus, reducing social spending to contain inflation, which was a popular prescription by the IMF, was an anathema to President Nyerere. Furthermore, there was hardly any realism in championing Western-style capitalism in Tanzania at the time.

One needs to understand the realities that confronted Tanzania at that time. These were an uneasy relationship with the IMF and a less liberal international environment. The latter was characterized by Cold War rivalries, whereby a developing country such as Tanzania was relevant to a world-power bloc only if it aligned itself with the immediate strategic security and political interests of that power bloc. For the most part, there was nothing in that kind of relationship for the genuine development interests of the developing countries.

The disappointment with the IMF and a hostile international economic order were some of the factors that motivated President Nyerere to build a socialist society whose vision became articulated in the Arusha Declaration of 1967. An understanding of the inflexibility of the IMF's policies then, the pressing issues that Tanzania faced, and the antidevelopment Cold War politics are essential for evaluating Tanzania's efforts in the early years of independence under President Nyerere.

The author observes that reality did not match President Nyerere's dream, citing economic distortions, inefficiencies, loss-making enterprises, subsidies, and budget deficits that were rampant two decades after independence. There is no doubt that Tanzania suffered economic stagnation and decline for some two decades after independence, but such was one of the costs of spending to create a credible social-service infrastructure. Senior Government officials, including this writer, who have later championed successful economic reforms, which the chapter ably discusses, are products of President Nyerere's uncompromising decision to spend on social services during the first two decades of Tanzania's independence.

What is more, Nyerere bequeathed Tanzania a social harmony that has proved and remains an important asset for socioeconomic development. While social harmony in Tanzania does not feature in GDP figures, it is a very important achievement. The author should not be surprised that, while President Nyerere did not score highly on economic management in a narrow sense, he is venerated today as he was then, because what he did in promoting national identity among diverse ethnic groups has contributed to a peaceful environment that has enabled the reform success that the author commends.

It is refreshing to note that the author acknowledges the positive change in the IMF's thinking and interaction with low-income countries as an important factor in the close relationship that has been built since 1996 between the IMF and Tanzania, and indeed other low-income countries. Starting with the initiative of the former IMF Managing Director Michel Camdessus, for concessional lending under the Enhanced Structural Adjustment Facility (ESAF), the IMF's policies and practices have progressively been reformed and designed to address the challenges facing low-income countries. Although the ESAF was still beset with a host of detailed IMF conditions, it offered relatively favorable terms. ESAF embraced a developmental perspective that had been lacking during the first two decades of Africa's independence.

The ESAF was later to be replaced in 1999 by arrangements that were even more favorable under the Poverty Reduction and Growth Facility (PRGF). The PRGF specifically addressed the social and growth challenges that faced low-income countries. The PRGF was not tied and was aligned to support economic growth and development of social services through the National Strategy for Growth and Reduction of Poverty (in the case of Tanzania).

By 1995, the world had freed itself from Cold War politics. President Benjamin William Mkapa, the third President of Tanzania, was quick to capitalize on the enlightened thinking by the IMF and, in relative terms, a favorable international community. He built a development partnership framework with the IMF as an integral part of mobilizing financing for the development of Tanzania. The IMF's enlightened approach included the disbursement of concessional loans to Tanzania in support of the country's economic reform program and continued technical assistance in the far-reaching and enduring reform process, notably in tax administration. The IMF has also been instrumental in Tanzania's effort to mobilize financing from bilateral donors.

Mr. Sharer's analysis acknowledges Tanzania's excellent record in meeting its policy commitments under the PRGF. The review of the reforms, ranging from privatization of state enterprises, which were a major drain on the budget, to reforms in the core macroeconomic framework—fiscal, monetary, and financial sector policies—shows that Tanzania's reforms have paid off. Tax-administration reforms have resulted in Government revenue rising from 10 percent of GDP in 1998/99 to nearly 17 percent in 2007/8. A credible fiscal management, combined with a prudent monetary policy, has reduced inflation from more than 25 percent per annum over the period 1976–95 to an inflation rate of about 5 percent in 2000; and inflation has remained in single digits to date, despite pressures from rising fuel and food prices in the world market.

Parallel reforms in the public service sector have reduced excessive public-service staffing and have introduced better conditions of service and better management and organization. An Integrated Financial Management System to assist in expenditure management and accountability, and a new Public Procurement Legislation, has substantially improved public financial management.

The chapter reviews the IMF's support to Tanzania in several ways. But more important is the role of the IMF in helping to mobilize financing for development. The agreement and implementation of IMF-supported programs provides a seal that has a positive impact on both donor and foreign investor confidence. In addition the IMF, together with the World Bank, promoted the Heavily Indebted Poor Countries Initiative (HIPC) and subsequently the Multilateral Debt Relief Initiative (MDR), both of which have reduced Tanzania's debt burden by a considerable amount.

The contribution of the IMF to the macroeconomic development of Tanzania has been particularly notable from 1997. This is the period during which the Government of Tanzania implemented country-owned and far-reaching policy and structural reforms, with the support of the IMF, the World Bank, the African Development Bank, other financial institutions, and the donor community. The relationship between the IMF and Tanzania has become stronger over the past decade, and is currently at a very high level. Two most important factors explain this positive trend:

- The first is Tanzania's commitment to reform, with enhanced ownership of the reform agenda.
- The second is the IMF's willingness to listen and allow Tanzania to determine policies suitable to Tanzania's circumstances and the IMF responding with adequate support and minimum conditionality. This is a reflection of the IMF's commitment to reform within itself, which was not the case before. For the past three years, Tanzania has prepared its own Letters of Intent outlining the specifics of its policy reform programs. In the past these were prepared by the IMF staff in Washington, and we were asked to sign them.

The results of the changed policy environment are very encouraging. Economic growth has averaged 7 percent a year between 2002 and 2007; inflation is contained at single-digit levels despite external pressures caused by hikes in the prices of imported fuel, food, agricultural inputs, and industrial raw materials. Domestic revenue collection has increased steadily as the tax base has expanded, owing to a very strong tax administration, which has benefited very much from IMF's technical assistance.

In conclusion, I would say that Tanzania, with the support of the IMF and others, has made great strides in economic growth and the expansion of social services. However, for the population of Tanzania, this is just the beginning of a long journey to prosperity. One major challenge is to sustain the gains achieved, and to ensure that they are shared more broadly. The second major challenge is to accelerate growth so as to have a significant dent on poverty reduction. This requires increasing financing for economic infrastructure, which is a prerequisite for accelerated growth. The IMF has a role in this challenge as well.

6
Brazil: Anchoring Policy Credibility in the Midst of Financial Crisis

Lorenzo L. Pérez and Philip R. Gerson[1]

Brazil's negotiations with the IMF in 2002 concerning possible financial support for its economic program took place amid a growing lack of confidence by investors in the course of the country's future economic policies and prospects, and thus in its ability—or even willingness—to service its debt. The victory of the opposition candidate in the presidential elections in October of that year was looking increasingly certain, and investors feared that macroeconomic policies would weaken and that Brazil could default on its financial obligations. As interest rates on Brazilian debt rose to high levels and pressure on the currency mounted, the authorities sought a credible commitment mechanism that would reassure investors that regardless of the election results, macroeconomic policies would continue to aim at financial stability. The authorities saw an economic program supported by the IMF as a key element of this mechanism, especially if the main opposition candidates were prepared to endorse it publicly.

Once the outgoing government of President Fernando Henrique Cardoso formally requested a new program, negotiations were completed very quickly, over the course of about a week in August 2002. This rapid progress was possible for a few reasons. First, because the program sought primarily to convince investors that existing policies would be maintained, it was not necessary to negotiate any dramatic new initiatives. Second, the program intentionally deferred agreement on many details until after the new government would take office late

[1] The authors are Deputy Director, IMF's Middle East and Central Asia Department, and Assistant Director, Office of the Managing Director, respectively. Mr. Pérez is a former IMF mission chief and senior resident representative in Brazil, and Mr. Gerson a former division chief for Brazil.

in 2002, along with much of the financing provided by the IMF. Third, a number of innovations that had been introduced in earlier programs supported by the IMF gave the authorities more policy flexibility. Finally, and most importantly, rapid progress on program negotiations was possible because of the authorities' strong record of performance in delivering on policy commitments and because of the familiarity and trust that had developed between the authorities and the IMF staff team after a number of years of close policy dialogue.[34]

By any objective standard, Brazil's 2002 program must be viewed as a resounding success, both for the country and for the IMF. To be sure, at the end of the program period many challenges remained for Brazil, including most notably that of accelerating growth and improving the country's very inequitable distribution of income. Nevertheless the new government's exemplary implementation of the IMF program allowed Brazil to restore its access to external finance relatively quickly, to control inflation, and to minimize the impact of the financial shock on output. One indication of this strong recovery was the decision by the Standard & Poors rating agency in April 2008 to raise Brazil's long-term sovereign credit rating to the investment grade, the first time in several decades that Brazil had reached that grade.

Stabilization policies, 1993–2002: A mixed record

The decade between the launch of the *Real Plan* in 1994 and the 2002 program supported by the IMF was marked by a series of programs with the IMF that had mixed results in addressing Brazil's underlying weaknesses. While the *Real Plan* had dramatic success in reducing previously very high inflation, the policy mix implemented by the authorities in the remainder of the decade was unbalanced, with excessive reliance on very high interest rates and inadequate attention to tightened fiscal policy to control aggregate demand. Public sector debt grew rapidly. Furthermore, in a vicious circle that both reflected and exacerbated vulnerabilities, an increasing share of the debt was linked to the exchange and overnight interest rates, thus shifting the risks of currency depreciation and of high inflation from bondholders to the government. Rising domestic demand also led to a widening of the external current account deficit, from less than 0.5 percent of GDP in 1994 to more than 4 percent by 1997.

The widening of the fiscal and external current account deficits and the rapid increase of the public sector debt progressively increased the vulnerability of the Brazilian economy to negative external shocks and to sudden changes in investor sentiments. While a significant tightening of monetary policy enabled Brazil to emerge from the Mexican crisis of December 1994 without a significant loss of international reserves, the onset of the Asian crisis in the second half of 1997 proved more troublesome. After large losses of international reserves, the authorities again tightened monetary policy considerably and adopted some fiscal measures. Public-sector debt inched close to 40 percent of GDP, while the shares of variable-interest-rate and foreign-exchange-linked government securities in total domestic debt rose sharply. These developments only increased investor concern about the ability of the economy to withstand further shocks.

Following President Fernando Henrique Cardoso's reelection to a new four-year term in October 1998, the authorities responded to the growing crisis with a renewed sharp increase in interest rates, and with fiscal measures to arrest the growth of public debt relative to GDP. The authorities maintained a crawling peg exchange rate regime and also announced a program of structural reforms to address the major weaknesses in the public finances, strengthen the financial system, continue with the privatization and deregulation efforts, and modernize labor legislation. The program was well received by the international community, and the authorities were successful in obtaining financial support for their program from the IMF, the World Bank, and the Inter-American Development Bank, as well as from a large group of industrial countries.[35] External credit lines to the private sector were closely monitored and foreign banks were encouraged to maintain them.

During the negotiations of this program, the exchange rate regime was the subject of intense discussion. The question was whether in view of market pressures it was better to float the currency, to devalue but maintain the crawling peg, or to continue with the managed float regime. The authorities were adamant about maintaining the managed float, which featured a gradual depreciation of the *real* vis-à-vis the US dollar within a band that was being widened each month. The authorities viewed this regime as the natural trajectory of the *Real Plan* that had introduced a strong currency. They also believed it was essential in order to maintain financial stability and low inflation, and to avoid renewed pressures for indexation of wages and contracts. In the end, IMF management decided to give the authorities the benefit of the doubt and the program was presented with the existing managed float regime, subject to the provision that this policy would be reassessed during program reviews.

While the reaction of the market to the announcement of the program was positive, after setbacks in the implementation of key components in the early stages of the program sentiment soured, with renewed foreign exchange pressures. Delays were experienced in securing congressional approval of the proposed fiscal package, including a revised budget that included important expenditure cuts. In addition, the central bank eased the monetary policy stance prematurely during December 1998, and policy continuity was not helped by a change in central bank governors. At this point, it appears that there was not a clear consensus among the economic authorities in how to proceed.[36] Market concerns heightened about the sustainability of net outflows in the balance of payments in the last few weeks in late 1998. On January 15, in the face of accelerating outflows, the currency was floated and the *real* weakened significantly following the float.

The winter of 1999 was difficult for Brazil and the IMF. The large loss of reserves prior to the floating of the *real* and sharp loss of value of the currency after the floating were viewed by many as a failure of the program supported by the IMF. Following the appointment of Arminio Fraga as the new governor of the central bank in March 1999, understandings on tightening fiscal and monetary policies were reached between Brazil and the IMF that allowed a renegotiation of the program.[37]

The fiscal target for 1999, a primary (that is, excluding spending on interest) balance of the consolidated public sector of 3 percent of GDP, was achieved, as the authorities countered a number of policy setbacks largely outside their control with additional efforts throughout the year. The fiscal effort was improved in 2000 in the context of the beginning of the implementation of the Fiscal Responsibility Law (Figure 6.1).[38] Nevertheless the public sector debt remained broadly stable at close to 50 percent of GDP as the foreign exchange and interest-rate-indexed debt rose (Figure 6.2). The returns on these firm policies were quickly apparent. Instead of contracting in 1999, as expected when the program was revised in March 1999, the economy expanded by almost 1 percent during the year and grew by over 4 percent in 2000 (Figure 6.3).

If the flexibility shown by the IMF on the choice of exchange rate regime under the program ended unhappily, with the eventual abandonment of the crawling peg after a large loss of reserves, other forms of flexibility produced more positive outcomes. The lack of a consistent relationship between changes in monetary aggregates and inflation outcomes in Brazil, at least in the short term, greatly complicated the monitoring of monetary policy under the program. In essence, neither the central bank nor the IMF could be confident that increases in

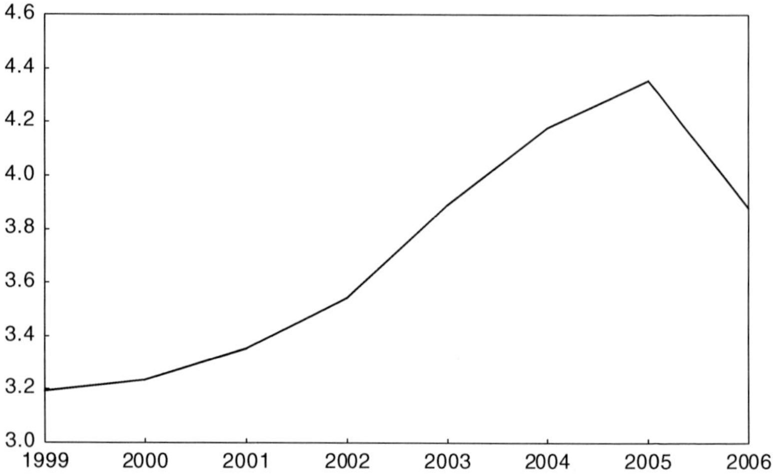

Figure 6.1 Consolidated public sector primary balance (in percent of GDP)

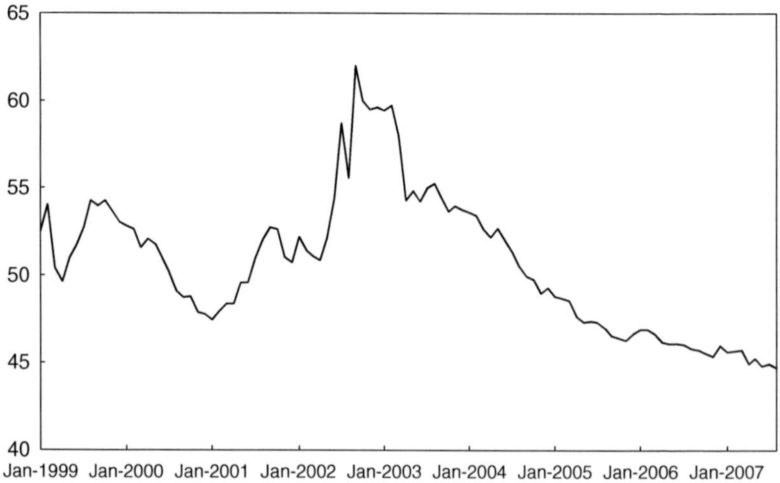

Figure 6.2 Public sector net debt (in percent of GDP)

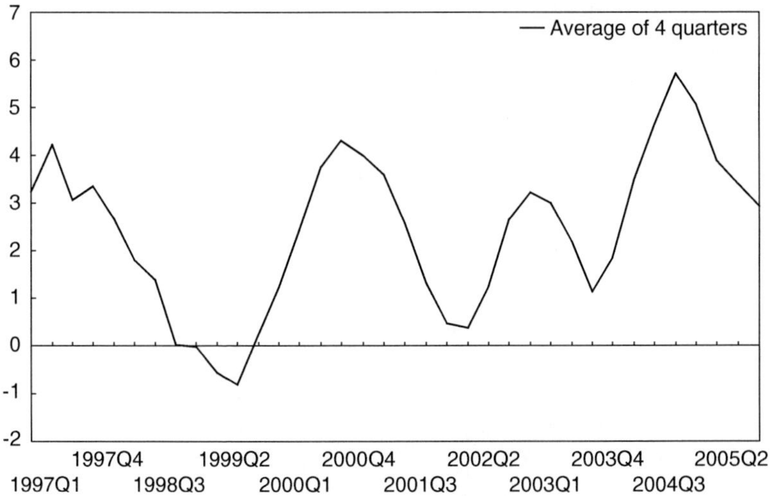

Figure 6.3 Real GDP growth (in percent of GDP)

monetary aggregates presaged a near-term rise in inflationary pressures, nor, conversely, that declines in these aggregates would predictably create scope for a relaxation of policies. In response to these developments, the central bank, in mid-1999 under the leadership of Mr. Fraga, adopted an inflation-targeting regime, which was accommodated in the program through changes in monitoring arrangements. The central bank committed itself to discuss the appropriate policy responses with the IMF staff if consultation bands set around the 12-month inflation targets were breached. These consultation bands and a floor for international reserves became the only monetary policy conditionality of the program, and the central bank credit ceilings were dropped from the program and not included in subsequent ones.

The inflation consultation bands (supplemented with understandings that consultations would also be held if reserve losses passed a certain level) were quite novel at that time. It is to the credit of Mr. Fraga and his colleagues at the central bank that they were willing to offer this arrangement: less confident authorities might have balked at this more transparent discussion of monetary policy with IMF staff. The IMF team of the time, led by Stanley Fischer, then First Deputy Managing Director, and Teresa Ter-Minassian, then Deputy Director of the Western Hemisphere Department, also deserve credit for supporting this approach within the IMF, not an easy thing to do within the review practices of the institution. In the event, the central bank implemented a cautious monetary policy and a fairly clean float in the foreign exchange market. These initiatives and developments were instrumental in strengthening the credibility of the central bank, and in securing a sustained decline in inflationary expectations.

International and domestic developments in 2001 (the final year of the 1998 Stand-by Arrangement) did not prove to be favorable, and Brazil's vulnerability became evident again. The world economy slowed, financial contagion from Argentina spread, progress on the structural reform agenda became more difficult, and a severe drought significantly destabilized the economy (hydroelectric power accounted for over 90 percent of Brazil's energy generation). Access to international capital markets became difficult, the gap between the interest rates the Brazilian government paid and those on comparable debts of the US government (the "spread") rose by close to 200 basis points, and the *real* depreciated by some 20 percent during the first half of the year, pressuring prices (Figure 6.4).

Accordingly, in July 2001, the authorities indicated that they wanted to cancel the existing program and replace it with a new 15-month program that would run until the end of the government's mandate in December 2002. By then, it was clear that investors' assessments of Brazil's situation would take a dramatic turn for the worse without a new program

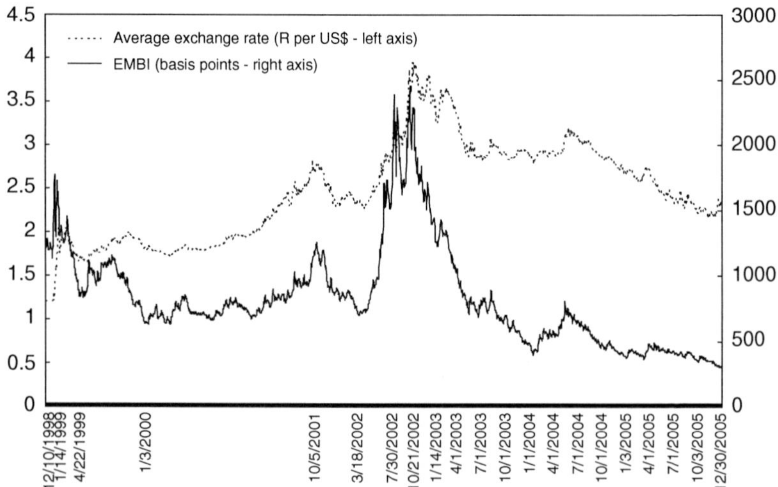

Figure 6.4 EMBIG subindex spread and exchange rate

supported by the IMF.[39] The new program was negotiated quickly and approved by the Executive Board of the IMF in late-August 2001. At that point, the government committed itself to a fiscal primary surplus of 3.35 percent of GDP in 2001 and of 3.5 percent in 2002 in order to halt the rise of the debt/GDP ratio and put it in a downward trend over the medium term. A tight monetary policy stance was part of the program as well as a commitment to the floating exchange rate regime.

The announcement of the August 2001 program did not have the positive effect on investors' assessment of Brazil's economic prospects the authorities and the IMF had hoped for. In addition, global financial conditions took a further turn for the worse after the September 11, 2001 attacks. Brazilian bond spreads started rising further, and the *real* remained under pressure, reaching an all-time low versus the dollar. The Argentine peso devaluation in early 2002 added additional pressure to conditions in the markets for Brazilian bonds, as many investors were forced to sell some of their Brazilian assets to cover their losses on Argentinean ones. Financial market sentiment toward Brazil worsened significantly in mid-2002. Brazilian bond interest rates escalated, and the currency depreciated further. This situation set the stage for the discussions for a new program with the IMF.

The 2002 program: Promoting policy continuity amidst political change

As the 2002 electoral campaign moved into full swing, investors focused increasing attention on political developments. With President Cardoso constitutionally barred from seeking a third term in office, change seemed an inevitable outcome of the election. Jose Serra, the nominee of the president's party, was strongly committed to maintaining the existing macroeconomic framework. Other leading candidates were seen as potentially representing a more dramatic break with past policies. Very early in the year, the strong showing in the polls of Luis Inacio Lula da Silva of the Workers' Party (the "PT") became a concern to market participants. While over a period of years Mr. da Silva's views had moved increasingly toward the center of the Brazilian political spectrum, for many observers—including many investors—the name "Lula" continued to conjure up memories of the left-wing labor leader of his earlier career. As Mr. da Silva's standing in the pools solidified, investors increasingly worried about the risk of an abrupt shift in policies, or even a repudiation of the public debt. It therefore became increasingly difficult to find buyers for Brazilian bonds.

Although Mr. da Silva had been a central figure on the Brazilian political stage for many years, and while PT governments were in place in many states and major cities, it is fair to say that relations between the IMF and the PT were essentially nonexistent at the start of the 2002 campaign. Beginning in early 2002, however, the IMF made its first, tentative steps to reach out to the PT as the IMF's resident representative in Brazil, Rogerio Zandamela, established contacts with the da Silva camp with the help of a journalist friend. Mr. Zandamela was favorably impressed by Mr. da Silva's advisers and reported this to Washington. IMF staff also took the opportunity of a visit by a Brazilian congressional delegation (including members of the PT) to Washington in June 2002 to invite them to lunch to discuss the economic future of Brazil and IMF relations. This lunch was organized by Murilo Portugal, then Brazil's representative at the Executive Board of the IMF. Meetings between members of the opposition and IMF staff were not universally endorsed by the Cardoso team and required courage from those who did support them as there was always a risk that information disclosed in the meetings could be used against the government in the presidential campaign.[40] It is worth noting that these meetings also required some courage on the part of the PT, as some core elements of the party's base still considered contacts with the IMF to be anathema.

During the summer, financial conditions continued to deteriorate. The EMBIG+ spread for Brazilian international bonds shot up to 1200 basis points in June and shortly thereafter to 2400 basis points, a previously unheard of level that essentially closed international capital markets to Brazil and would make a default unavoidable if it persisted for long.

In effect, Brazil was now suffering for policies that had not been implemented by a government that had not yet been elected. While candidate da Silva had carefully avoided any statements that could further roil markets, including openly committing in his widely read "Letter to the Brazilian People" in June to maintain stability-oriented policies, investors were evidently not convinced that President da Silva would avoid the left-wing economic policies he had once espoused. Mr. da Silva himself noted the devastating impact that past episodes of hyperinflation had had on Brazil's poor, and many political analysts observed that a PT government had little to gain from implementing policies that would provoke an immediate financial catastrophe in its first days in office. As if it were needed, the ongoing economic debacle in neighboring Argentina also served as a constant reminder of the potential costs of a financial upheaval. Nevertheless given his persistent lead in the polls, investors continued to price in the likelihood of a da Silva victory and the risk of an abrupt shift in economic policies.

Since the crisis was mainly one of confidence, only an ex post implementation of strong policies would fully assuage investors' fears of policy reversal. To calm markets in the meantime, what was needed was a device to signal investors that Mr. da Silva's commitment to policies aimed at financial stability was genuine.

In July, the Cardoso team raised with the staff the possibility of negotiating another program with large access to IMF resources. The novel feature of this program would be that it would receive the endorsement of all the main presidential candidates before IMF Board approval, and would therefore serve as a means to demonstrate the candidates' commitment to macroeconomic policy continuity. The proposal was that the program would be negotiated with the Cardoso team but that flexibility would be left in setting the 2003 targets to allow the next administration to negotiate them with the IMF.

The proposal of the Cardoso team presented IMF staff and management with a difficult problem. On the one hand, any program that is negotiated by one set of authorities and implemented by another is bound to face questions about its credibility. There was accordingly a significant risk that investors might be unimpressed by the program, with pressure on the currency and debt continuing unabated. And even this outcome assumed that the leading presidential candidates—including Mr. da Silva—signaled agreement with the program. On the other hand, and given the deepening crisis in Argentina, it was impossible to ignore the severe consequences that a default on Brazil's debt would have for other countries in Latin America and elsewhere. Moreover, as dire as the situation in Brazil was at the time, so long as it was possible to reopen international capital markets to Brazil in the near future, the likelihood that the program would be successful was quite high, as the authorities were already following a sound economic policy framework. The setbacks of previous months had been the result of domestic political shocks and of a deteriorating international environment. In fact, a rapid adjustment of the external current account was already taking place by the summer of 2002, led by a rising trade surplus that was reducing the external financing requirements. A renewed IMF endorsement of strong existing fiscal and monetary policies embedded in a new program could start a virtuous circle.

At the end, with available information that a da Silva administration was likely to broadly maintain the existing macroeconomic framework, Horst Köhler and Anne Krueger (who had succeeded Mr. Camdessus and Mr. Fischer as the Managing Director and First Deputy Managing Director of the IMF, respectively) supported the negotiation of a new program to cover the period through end-2003. This occurred during the first week of August in Washington with a Brazilian team led by Vice Minister of Finance Amaury Bier (who by now was well known in the IMF as a reliable interlocutor and tough negotiator) and Ilan Goldfajn, a deputy governor of the central bank and a former staff member of the IMF. Mr. Portugal actively participated in the negotiations to ensure their prompt successful conclusion. On the IMF side, the authors led the IMF team, closely supervised by Anne Krueger; Claudio Loser, Director of the Western Hemisphere Department; and Timothy Geithner, head of the Policy Development and Review Department.

While the general macroeconomic policy framework was already in place, IMF representatives argued for an increase in the primary fiscal surplus to 4½ percent of GDP compared with the existing target for 2002–03 of 3¾ percent of GDP. The higher primary fiscal surplus would result in a more robust debt sustainability scenario. Moreover, the IMF staff felt that its attainment would not have been that difficult given there was likely to be overperformance on the fiscal target in 2002 to around 4 percent. However, Mr.Bier and his team were not willing to consider a higher fiscal surplus target because the 3¾ percent of GDP had just been announced in mid-year (from 3½ percent previously) and had become politically acceptable in the presidential campaign. They feared that presidential candidates would refuse to endorse a higher target. At the end, the IMF staff agreed, and convinced IMF management to accept the Brazilian proposal with the understanding that the target for 2003 would be at least 3¾ percent of GDP, and would be reassessed during the reviews of the program in 2003.

As part of the new program, the authorities committed themselves to continue to implement the inflation-targeting framework with a flexible exchange rate policy. Despite several shocks and the upper bands under the program-monitoring framework being exceeded a number of times, the inflation-targeting regime had acquired considerable credibility. The procedures for consultation with IMF staff and the Board were maintained in the event that inflation deviated from the specified path that aimed at an end-2003 inflation of 4 percent.[41] Agreement on the foreign exchange intervention policy of the central bank was more complicated to achieve. IMF staff recognized that the closing of the international capital market for Brazil made it appropriate for the central bank to intervene in the foreign exchange market in the short run. In the period leading up to the 2002 program, the central bank intervened actively in the foreign exchange and external debt markets to alleviate pressures on the currency. The central bank used a policy of preannounced interventions in the spot foreign exchange market and foreign exchange repurchase (repo) transactions. The question was how low should the international reserve target of the central bank be set to give flexibility to the central bank to address the current very difficult situation, while ensuring that a minimum reserve level was protected. Missing the international reserve target of the new program would have been particularly damaging to investor expectations. For this reason, the reserve floor was significantly reduced, with the program calling for consultations if the accumulated intervention level reached a prespecified amount in a given period. Overall, the program terms were probably more flexible than was typical in other large, roughly contemporaneous IMF programs.

The new program could not be ambitious in the area of structural reform on the eve of a change in government. It contained commitments to advance the fiscal reform agenda, for example converting a federal cascading tax into a value-added tax in a revenue-neutral manner. A constitutional amendment that was prerequisite for a new central bank law would continue to be sought. But there was a recognition that a fuller structural adjustment agenda would be up to the next government after the elections, and was—at least in the short run—not as relevant to the concerns of investors as was the maintenance of strong fiscal and monetary policies.

The amount of financing that the IMF would provide to Brazil was a very strategic variable. The level of access to IMF credit is usually determined at the end of the program negotiations and depends on the strength of the program and the situation facing the country. Based on consultations with market participants and key shareholders of the IMF, Mr. Geithner argued that this was an area where the IMF could provide a positive shock, by offering a level of financing that would exceed investor expectations and signal a high level of IMF confidence in the implementation prospects of the program. At the end, Mr Köhler decided to recommend to the IMF Board access to IMF resources of $30 billion, or 752 percent of Brazil's IMF quota, going well beyond the normal financing limits of the IMF and making this the largest program ever financed by the IMF. At the same time, the quarterly disbursements of the financing were back-loaded to 2003 to ensure that the bulk of the financing would be provided only after evidence of good program implementation by the new government. This was intended not only to protect the IMF's resources but just as importantly to enhance the credibility of the program by giving a new government a strong financial incentive to implement it. It would also, of course, reduce the extent to which the IMF's resources could be used to "bail out" investors who choose to pull their money out of Brazil before the new government took office.

As envisaged, prior to the approval of the program on September 6, 2002, the various presidential candidates publicly endorsed the targets of the new program in general terms. Investor sentiment, however, did not improve immediately. Indeed, there was considerable skepticism during the 2002 Annual Meetings of the IMF and the World Bank in late September about whether Brazil would be able to overcome its financial problems and avoid a debt default. Some market participants who followed Brazil closely, like Michael Dooley, at that time with Deutsche Bank, felt that the central bank was going to run out of reserves at any time, and that the program would not be able to succeed. The bond spread peaked at about 2500 basis points around the time of the first round of presidential elections in early October (newly issued bonded debt carried a maximum one year maturity), and the *real*/US dollar rate hovered close to R$4 per US dollar just prior to the election of Mr. da Silva in the second round of the presidential election on October 27.

Nevertheless, after a difficult start, investor confidence was gradually restored in Brazil. The appointment by President-elect da Silva of a strong economic team was an important contributor in this regard. His appointment of his campaign director, Antonio Palocci, who had developed a very positive relationship with investors, was welcomed by the financial community, as was his choice to head the central bank, Henrique Meirelles. Not only did Mr. Meirelles come with extensive experience in the private financial sector, he had also been newly elected to congress as a member of the opposition PSDB. His appointment by Mr. da Silva was therefore a strong indication of the new president's willingness to reach across party lines to deal with Brazil's difficult economic situation. In addition, President da Silva continued to commit himself to stability-based economic policies even as he pledged a renewed focus on social issues. The announcement of an increase in the primary surplus target—from 3¾ percent of GDP to 4¼ percent of GDP—shortly after the new government took office demonstrated that this commitment went beyond mere words. An easing of interest rates in the United States was also beneficial for Brazil.

All of these factors, along with the contribution to liquidity and credibility that came from the IMF-supported program, drove a steady improvement in market conditions that led to a stabilization and then recovery of the exchange rate and a decline in spreads on Brazilian debt. As early as April 2003 Brazil regained access to international capital markets, and by mid-2004 spreads had fallen to about 500 basis points. Indeed, the speed of the recovery in market conditions took the IMF somewhat by surprise, with, for example, the authorities recognizing before the IMF staff the scope that existed to begin unwinding the large increase in exchange-rate-linked debt that had occurred in the period leading up to the election, when investors were generally unwilling to bear the risk of a large depreciation of the exchange rate.

Performance under the program was exemplary, with all program reviews completed on time and all performance criteria satisfied. Fiscal policy remained strong, with significant overperformance on primary fiscal surplus targets. The central bank continued to implement a tight monetary policy that aimed in particular at ensuring that the large depreciation of the *real* that had occurred in the period before the election did not provoke significant second-round inflationary effects. In addition, Governor Meirelles maintained the practice of Mr. Fraga of appointing economists with solid professional credentials to the board of directors of the central bank. There were also changes in the IMF team. In late 2002, Anoop Singh became Director of the Western Hemisphere Department and Jorge Marquez-Ruarte took over as mission chief. By September 2003, financial pressures had abated so much that the authorities decided to treat the program as precautionary. That is, while they would continue to comply with the program, they would not make the final drawing under it, which would have been expected to occur just prior to the program's expiration at end-December 2003.

The 2002 program was followed by a successor precautionary arrangement that provided a gradual transition out of IMF programs and featured yet another innovation in the form of an adjustor that would allow a limited decrease in the primary surplus target should the government undertake specific types of social spending. Strong market conditions and the continued implementation of sound economic policies allowed Brazil to repay all of its outstanding obligations to the IMF by December 2005, ahead of schedule. Since then, international reserves and the exchange rate have continued to strengthen, and growth has improved. Maintaining this positive growth momentum and making further progress in improving social conditions remain challenges for Brazil, but ones that are now faced with much more solid economic fundamentals than in many years.

Conclusion

The experience of Brazil shows that it takes time to overcome deep-rooted economic structural weaknesses such as the type of fiscal and monetary problems that the country faced in the 1990s and first years of the new century. It also demonstrates that these weaknesses can make countries vulnerable to domestic and external shocks even if they are implementing sound policies. There is no "magic formula" of policies that can quickly resolve deep-seated and long-standing economic problems, and no substitute for sound policies, faithfully and at times even courageously implemented.

The success of Brazil in avoiding financial collapses at various times during 1998–2003 shows that the IMF can play a very valuable role in providing policy advice and, when needed, financial support. IMF endorsement is also valuable in fostering more sober investor assessments provided this endorsement is grounded on sound analysis and on realistic political assumptions. In retrospect, the strict implementation of a sound fiscal responsibility law, the introduction of a flexible exchange rate regime, and the adoption of inflation targeting have proven to be the main pillars of Brazil's macroeconomic stability and its success in achieving better rates of economic growth. While the credit for these achievements belongs to the authorities, IMF management and staff were actively involved in the policy discussions and the technical assistance that contributed to the adoption of these policies.

The record of Brazil highlights the importance that authorities have ownership of their economic policies, be sufficiently ambitious in addressing economic problems and shocks with policies subject to their control, and establish a good track record in delivering on their policy commitments in programs. Only in these circumstances can the IMF and the international community at large be in a position to maintain their support for authorities' programs when unexpected shocks require significant adjustments to planned policies. The IMF for its part needs to be ready to take risks and be flexible if circumstances warrant. This is most likely to happen if the country authorities and IMF staff invest the time to have candid and open policy discussions on a sustained basis and get to know each other well. In turn, this underscores the importance of maintaining close and cooperative surveillance discussions during good times, to enable the IMF and country authorities to agree quickly on an effective response—which could include program involvement—when times turn more difficult.

Brazil: Anchoring Policy Credibility in the Midst of Financial Crisis

Arminio Fraga[2]

Lorenzo L. Pérez and Philip Gerson have done an excellent job in reviewing Brazil's experience with the IMF during the difficult period from 1998–2003, focusing mainly on the 2002 program. I am in general agreement with their discussion, so my comments consist largely of my personal summary views of those years, with special emphasis on the four years I headed the Central Bank.

Let me start with a bit of background: the years covered here included a number of global crises (Russia/Long-Term Capital Management in 1998; and the NASDAQ crash, the global slowdown, and Argentina in 2001) as well as our own crises in January 1999, the Fall of 2001, and last three quarters of 2002. During the four years I was in government, we had about six quarters of offense time, starting in the last quarter of 1999 and lasting until the beginning of 2001. The rest of the time we were constantly under pressure, mostly playing defense. Despite the hard times, we had the benefit of working as an extremely cohesive economic team under the leadership of President Cardoso. In the brief discussion below I will leave out most names, because every important strategic decision was taken by the team, an informal entity of a dozen or so people that operated together beautifully under severe pressure during this difficult period. This team developed over the years a strong degree of trust with the IMF, a relationship that would prove to be invaluable to us. I will also leave out the names of the IMF people involved in our programs, but I would like to stress that they put their reputations on the line for us and we are most grateful for that.

[2] Mr. Fraga is currently Founding Partner, Gávea Investimentos. From 1999 to 2002, he was President of the Central Bank of Brazil.

It is also worth mentioning here that I had the privilege of having with me at the Central Bank a number of superbly gifted colleagues, and that we were given during those four years complete operational independence to pursue our goals.

I was called at home in the United States on Saturday morning January 30, 1999, to take the head job at the Central Bank. During the month of February, while I waited for confirmation hearings in the Senate, I worked as an adviser to Pedro Malan, the Finance Minister. In that capacity I flew to Washington, DC, with Deputy Finance Minister Amaury Bier to start a discussion on the inevitable redesign of our IMF program. We mentioned to our interlocutors that we were serious about the fiscal adjustment that President Cardoso had announced before the elections of 1998, and that we intended to stay with a floating exchange-rate regime, anchored by an inflation-targeting commitment.

At that point we felt this was the best choice for Brazil, but nevertheless not an easy one to implement. The main risk we were facing was that inflation would climb and bring the return of indexation. In March 1999 we announced that we were going to adopt inflation targeting through a series of steps. Our first announcement was that we would strive to bring inflation down do single-digit annualized rates by the last quarter of 1999. We also announced that we would put in place a full-fledged inflation-targeting system by the end of June, including specific targets for 1999 and 2000.[42] The IMF played a key role here in helping us avoid an overshooting of the exchange rate with a financing package that was large enough to cover our short-term balance of payment needs under realistic assumptions. An important detail was that the Technical Memorandum of Understanding (TMU) we signed with the IMF allowed us to use the reserves that were furnished by the program, a novel step that was noticed by market participants and helped stabilize the foreign exchange market. The IMF also provided us with support in learning from other central banks that had adopted inflation targeting. This networking was of crucial importance to us at the time and in the years that followed. Finally, there was substantial pressure coming from within the official sector for us to take a more aggressive stance in our dealings with our creditors (called Private Sector Involvement at the time), but we felt strongly this was not necessary and would have been counterproductive. The IMF played a key role in helping us avoid this mistake.

As we now know, things worked out rather well. We tightened macroeconomic policies and never had to use much of our reserves for intervention to support the *real*. Inflation came down quickly, and growth ended up in the plus for the year, five percentage points higher than the consensus forecasts of early 1999. In June we announced the formal inflation targets and amended the TMU as described by Pérez and Gerson. Inflation expectations converged fairly quickly to the target path we announced, and growth picked up substantially in 2000.

Fast-forward now to mid-2001. At that time the US economy was slowing and markets were in turmoil. I had been asked by the IMF to chair a group to review the IMF's Monetary and Exchange Affairs Department and was in Washington, DC, when market conditions got bad enough that we felt a new program with the IMF would be useful to avoid another round of sentiment over-shooting. I asked to be excused by the group I was chairing to join my colleagues in Brazil in a discussion that was followed by a meeting with IMF staff and the Managing Director that got the ball rolling toward a new agreement. Here I have a slight disagreement with Pérez and Gerson, as Figure 6.4 indicates; the program actually had a very positive impact on markets, and that improvement lasted until it became clear in early April 2002 that the government's candidate was not doing well on the polls. Only then did all hell break loose!

This brings us to the last of our three programs, the one designed to deal with the confidence crisis of 2002. As we approached the (northern) summer of 2002 it was abundantly clear to us that we were facing a tremendous challenge, one that went beyond our ability to manage the standard macroeconomic policy levers. The fear being priced into the markets was related not to our policies but to expectations of future policies under the next government. We felt that the only way out would be for the main candidates to commit to sound macroeconomic policies. In order to encourage the candidates to publicly commit to sound policies, we provided them with our assessment of the situation they were likely to face if elected, not a pretty sight! But we also made it clear to them that we thought the panic was unjustified and driven by expectations that the next president would run irresponsible macro policies.

We approached the IMF to ask whether it would agree to do a new and substantial program if the main candidates indicated that sound policies would be maintained. Simultaneously we approached the main candidates and told them that if they committed to sound policies they would receive the support of the IMF. Little by little they started to change their posture and to make their revised views public. A key factor in this crucial change was the indication that a substantial credit line from the IMF would be made available, in back-loaded fashion as mentioned by Pérez and Gerson. By early September it was becoming clear that Lula da Silva was the leading contender and that he would not commit economic suicide if elected. The IMF in bold fashion approved the program, and soon markets began to calm down. The stock market in Brazil fell for a couple of weeks after the agreement was signed, but went straight up from there, climbing over 300 percent in dollar terms over the following 15 months!

I agree with the conclusions drawn by Pérez and Gerson: there are no magic policy formulas for countries. What is required is the consistent implementation of sound policies over time. That said, often the destinies of countries depend crucially on the right decisions being taken at the right time. Often these decisions entail substantial amounts of risk and may not be undertaken because of political difficulties. Here the IMF can play a key role in supporting sound policies so as to improve the odds of success and, as a result, increasing the odds of getting things done right. Such was the case in Brazil.

7

Uruguay 2002–3: Recovery from Economic Contagion

Steven Seelig and Gilbert Terrier[1]

In early 2002, Uruguay faced a classic case of financial contagion. A traumatic economic crisis in its neighbor, Argentina, triggered withdrawals of deposits from Uruguayan banks that gradually crippled the country's banking system and caused other severe economic problems. Within seven months, withdrawals by Argentine citizens of their deposits in Uruguayan banks and fears of Uruguayan citizens that their savings were no longer safe caused bank deposits to fall by half, an unprecedented amount in recent international experience. The Uruguayan peso was floated by mid-year, which, in the context of rapidly depleting foreign reserves, led to a sharp depreciation. As a result, bank and corporate balance sheets, in which foreign currency liabilities were high, deteriorated sharply, and the value of the stock of predominantly foreign currency-denominated public debt doubled in domestic currency terms. In turn, this raised questions about the government's ability to honor its obligations. Economic activity contracted by over 10 percent, and unemployment soared to nearly 20 percent.

This severe crisis hit an economy that had been performing relatively well, though it did have areas of vulnerability that had, until then, proven to be manageable. In the early 2000s, Uruguay was a middle-income country with a relatively high per capita income for Latin America, at around $6000. During the 1990s, its economy had registered rates of growth above the historical average but, in 1999, the country

[1] Mr. Seelig is an advisor in the IMF's Monetary and Capital Markets Department. He previously served with the U.S. Federal Deposit Insurance Corporation. Mr. Terrier is Assistant Director in the IMF's Western Hemisphere Department. He has served as IMF resident representative in Argentina and as a mission chief for Chile, Peru, and Uruguay. The authors are grateful for comments and inputs from Andreas Bauer and Monica de Bollé.

entered into a recession. With a bloated public sector, the economy remained highly dependent on activity in the tourism and banking sectors. Uruguay was a regional financial center with a reputation for stability and safety, and total bank deposits were high by regional standards, at the equivalent of 85 percent of GDP at end-2001. Over 40 percent of these deposits were held by nonresidents, mainly Argentines.

Over time, however, the Uruguayan economy had become vulnerable to a number of influences. Persistent fiscal deficits (equivalent to 2–2½ percent of GDP) had led to substantial borrowing by the public sector. Although Uruguay had secured investment-grade status on its public debt, which stood at 43 percent of GDP at end-2001, virtually all of this debt was dollar denominated, leaving it exposed to a sharp depreciation of the peso. The operations of banks were also highly dollarized: at the end of 2001, 93 percent of deposits and 70 percent of loans were denominated in foreign currencies (mainly US dollars), as a consequence of high inflation episodes in Uruguay's economic history. Furthermore, a large share of bank lending in foreign currency was extended to borrowers with no dollar earnings. Finally, the financial positions of the two large state banks, Banco de la República Oriental del Uruguay (BROU) and Banco Hipotecario del Uruguay (BHU), which together accounted for one-third of total bank deposits, were weak.

At the early stages of Uruguay's financial turbulences, a strategy to prevent a full-blown crisis meant above all halting the fear-induced run on bank deposits. Any continuing withdrawals by cash-strapped Argentines, who were prohibited from drawing on their deposits at home because of a tight deposit freeze, would have to be handled in an orderly manner. However, halting the deposit run proved difficult in practice and took several months of increasingly more determined efforts. Early measures to stabilize the situation were overwhelmed by a series of negative economic news from both Uruguay and Argentina.

While the government was anxious to avoid breaching contracts and trust with depositors, the virtually total loss of foreign reserves by mid-year made the situation precarious. Only a comprehensive package of measures adopted in August 2002 and supported by the IMF with large new loans stopped the run and enabled the subsequent rehabilitation of the banking system. However, there were more policy challenges facing the authorities. The government needed to adopt tough fiscal adjustment measures in order to produce broad balance in the overall public sector accounts. This was necessary to stop adding to the public debt, which had ballooned because of the sharp depreciation of the currency and the costs of salvaging the banking system, and to service the debt after the adoption of a comprehensive restructuring.

Eventually, the sustainability of the high debt burden was resolved in a unique way. Early options that were explored included the possibility of a comprehensive restructuring, with a significant "haircut." However, Uruguay did not wish to pursue such a reduction in the principal amount of the debt owed because it wanted to preserve its historically excellent standing in international capital markets. The government instead adopted a voluntary approach that extended maturities at very favorable precrisis terms, thus yielding substantial debt-service relief. To succeed, this approach required evidence of a much-improved capacity to service the debt, which was demonstrated through Uruguay's large fiscal effort.

Overall, Uruguay's strategy to overcome its financial crisis was successful. Six years after the crisis, stability has been reestablished, and the economy has been experiencing strong and steady economic growth with much reduced unemployment levels for several years in a row. In addition, the country has regained access to international capital markets and repaid all its debt to the IMF ahead of time.

The banking crisis

The 2002 financial crisis developed according to a sequence which, with the benefit of hindsight, can be seen as composed of three phases leading to the adoption by the government in August 2002 of a comprehensive package of policy measures that stopped the run on deposits and began the rehabilitation of badly weakened banks. These phases were, of course, not apparent at the time and it took the adoption of several packages of increasingly stronger policy measures to resolve the situation.

The first phase

Faced with a deep financial crisis, on December 3, 2001, Argentina froze most deposits in its banking system and subsequently redenominated all foreign currency loans and deposits into domestic currency, which led to a wave of panic among depositors. In the following weeks, the country announced that it was defaulting on its debt, and the Argentine peso, long set at parity with the US dollar, was sharply devalued. In Uruguay, depositors seemed to agree—initially at least—with the authorities' position that the country's longstanding commitment to the rule of law and compliance with contracts offered strong assurances that their savings would remain safe.

In January 2002, however, some Argentine residents started withdrawing their deposits from the Uruguayan subsidiary of a large Argentine bank, Banco Galicia. Such withdrawals remained isolated from the rest of the Uruguayan banking system, and the takeover of this bank by the regulators in February led to only limited deposit withdrawals from other Uruguayan banks. However, serious corporate governance problems also emerged at a large domestic bank, Banco Comercial. A shareholder of the bank had left the country after embezzling an amount of money broadly equivalent to the capital of the bank, and when the authorities approached the foreign shareholders for a recapitalization of the bank, they initially refused to do so.[43] In addition, confidence was shaken in February by the decision of a bond-rating agency to downgrade the Uruguayan sovereign debt from its investment grade level.

In an effort to help salvage Uruguay's investment-grade status and bolster confidence, the government announced a package of fiscal measures. In January, in the wake of the devaluation of the Argentine peso, the Uruguayan central bank had already broadened the exchange rate crawling band, which allowed for greater exchange rate flexibility and a faster rate of depreciation of the Uruguayan peso. In support of these policies, and to help buttress a weakening situation, in early March 2002, the IMF approved a 24-month Stand-By Arrangement for Uruguay, totaling almost $0.7 billion.

The second phase

The government's policy reactions and the announcement of the new IMF arrangement provided some relief, which quickly proved to be temporary, as domestic confidence deteriorated further in the second half of April. After the freeze on deposits was further tightened in Argentina, both nonresidents and residents intensified the withdrawal of deposits from Uruguayan banks. Banks at first used their liquid assets to finance the outflows. However, domestically owned banks did not have access to dollar funding from abroad and, as a result, had to rely increasingly on support from the central bank to finance the outflows. In April, local private banks were faced with an increasingly tight liquidity position. Problems mounted at a second large Uruguayan bank, associated with its high exposure to Argentina, and then spread to a third and a fourth bank.

Despite reassurances from the authorities, domestic depositors grew increasingly concerned that the Uruguayan government would also impose a general freeze on deposits, as had been done in Argentina. The state-owned bank BROU, which had so far been relatively unaffected by the run, began to experience significant drains and mounting difficulties in meeting deposit withdrawals. As a result, market confidence sagged, the exchange rate weakened to the edge of the crawling band, the interest cost on government bonds in international capital markets rose sharply, and other ratings agencies marked the Uruguay debt down to subinvestment grade. With a sharp contraction of activity in neighboring Argentina, Uruguay's GDP fell by 11 percent during the first half of 2002.

The third phase

Although the Uruguayan authorities fully implemented the policies agreed with the IMF, new waves of deposit outflows, primarily by resident depositors, began in late June. In turn, these outflows led to additional foreign reserves losses. The severe liquidity pressures and the drop in international reserves resulting from attempts to support ailing domestically owned banks led the authorities, at the urging of the IMF, to float the currency at end-June. During this period and in the ensuing weeks, discussions continued with the IMF on the best policy response to the crisis and the financing needs. At the time, the law governing the central bank strictly limited its ability to provide financial support to the banking system. As the assistance that the central bank could provide soon became insufficient, in June 2002 the authorities created a US dollar facility, the Fund for Fortifying the System of Banks (FFSB) to meet projected liquidity needs. In June, the IMF arrangement was increased by $1.5 billion, and the schedule of disbursements accelerated to allow for immediate access to $0.5 billion, which was allocated to the facility. As the crisis deepened, these resources were used up within a period of ten days, and additional financing, which had been expected to be provided by other multilateral institutions and the government, failed to materialize.

The period from late June to July was pivotal, as it rapidly became evident that, to stem the deposit outflows and restore confidence, more financing was needed along with additional measures to limit the outflows without paralyzing the payments system. The decision to float the currency had led to a sharp depreciation of the Uruguayan peso, of close to 50 percent against the US dollar. As a result, the debt-to-GDP ratio more than doubled from its level at the end of 2001, to close to 100 percent of GDP. In turn, this raised doubts among creditors about the government's debt-servicing capacity, at a time when gross foreign reserves were rapidly running out, falling from $3.1 billion at end-2001 to $0.6 billion at the end of July 2002. By then, gross reserves were only slightly above the short-term reserve liabilities of the central bank, leaving it with virtually no ability to support distressed banks.

On July 30, after bank deposits had fallen by half since the beginning of the year, the central bank took the dramatic step of closing all banks for a week-long "bank holiday." The declaration of the bank holiday stretched Uruguay's social and political fabric to its limits. Some episodes of looting and protests broke out, but they remained largely isolated, and it became clear that a dramatic turnaround was needed to prevent broader social unrest and a full-blown institutional crisis.

Crisis resolution

During the bank holiday, there were intensive high-level contacts between the authorities, the IMF, and the US Treasury to work out a comprehensive solution to the crisis. The authorities and IMF officials worked feverishly to develop and put in place a strategy. There were initially large differences of views on important aspects of the strategy, although there was also agreement that the key objectives of the strategy should be to safeguard the payments system, reestablish confidence in the banking system, and lay the basis for economic recovery. A critical component of the strategy was to decide how much liquidity would be available upfront to meet the demand for withdrawals.

Given the limited available resources, IMF staff considered a freeze on term deposits at domestic banks, which would be exchanged for medium-term securities. In that option, the scarce resources available would have been used upfront to protect the payments system. It is fair to say that IMF staff was very hesitant about providing more funding to Uruguay, at a time when abundant resources had already been provided and the crisis was deepening further. The Uruguayan authorities had a different position. They were of the view that any bank restructuring would have to be coupled with more abundant upfront liquidity, which they thought should be provided by the IMF. They also argued forcefully that deposits at public Uruguayan banks were covered by a guarantee embedded in the constitution and, thus, that any default in repaying these deposits would, in the eyes of the public, be tantamount to a default on public debt obligations. In the end, the Uruguayan authorities were able to secure the support of the US government and of other major shareholders of the IMF for the provision of a large amount of liquidity, in the context of an augmentation of the IMF program, approved in August. The agreed upon plan included a compulsory lengthening of the maturity of term deposits at public banks.

In early August, the authorities announced this strategy to the general public, and the IMF gave its commitment to provide financial resources upfront. The total amount available under the Stand-By Arrangement was increased by another \$0.5 billion and the schedule of disbursements was accelerated. Financing from the IMF made it possible to create the Fund for the Stability of the Banking System (FSBS), which was endowed with sufficient resources to fully back all dollar sight-and-savings deposits at core Uruguayan banks. This fund was endowed with \$1.5 billion in resources, expected to be sufficient to assure depositors that their deposits were safe. An amount of \$0.8 billion was immediately disbursed by the IMF, which was entirely used to capitalize the FSBS. The World Bank and the Inter-American Development Bank committed additional amounts of \$0.5 billion and \$0.2 billion, respectively. The US government also provided a one-week bridge loan to ensure that sufficient financial resources were available upon the reopening of the banks.

This time, the available liquidity was sufficient to restore confidence and stem the deposit outflows. The key elements of the government's strategy were embedded in a law approved on August 4. Quite remarkably, it only took 48 hours for the Uruguayan government to secure approval of this law by congress—a clear sign of the authorities' strong determination. In addition, Alejandro Atchugarry, a well-regarded senator who had been appointed Finance Minister only two weeks earlier, played a critical role in the adoption of the law. His leadership and exceptional negotiating skills were instrumental in mobilizing a majority in congress to ensure the prompt approval of the law by the two chambers. The main elements of the program were as follows:

- *No restrictions on access to all sight and savings deposits of banks.* This condition was critical to ensuring the working of the payments system. In practice, no restrictions were placed on all peso deposits, as well as all foreign currency current account and savings deposits, in both private and public banks.[44] The total of such deposits stood at \$2.7 billion.
- *All foreign banks left free from any restrictions.* The policy on liquidity support continued to require that foreign bank branches and subsidiaries would seek to finance their liquidity requirements entirely by themselves and/or through borrowing from their parent companies. In return, the government was committed not to apply to them any restrictions or administrative measures on the conduct of their banking businesses.

- *Compulsory lengthening of the maturities of US dollar time deposits with the two public banks BROU and BHU.* As these deposits ($2.2 billion in total) matured, they were to be extended by a period of up to three years: 25 percent would be repaid after one year, 35 percent after two years, and the remaining 40 percent after three years. Depositors could exchange their deposits at any time with government-guaranteed bank bonds or certificates of deposit, or use them to cancel debts at face value. All dollar deposits at the BHU were transferred to BROU, in exchange for a BHU note guaranteed by the government.
- *Closure, restructuring, and sale of the four domestic private banks.* These banks, which had become insolvent, were taken over by regulators and not reopened. They were to be restructured and time deposit holders at these banks to be repaid from the liquidation proceeds.

While liquidity assistance from the FSBS was aimed at restoring confidence, there was no way of measuring ex-ante its likely success. The authorities and the IMF expected that substantial withdrawals would follow the lifting of the long bank holiday. On Tuesday, August 6, however, when BROU and other banks reopened, the Uruguayan population showed a remarkable degree of discipline, and deposit outflows were significantly less than feared. Orderly lines formed outside the banks with depositors waiting patiently for their turn. This was the first reassuring sign that the situation might eventually turn around. Part of the deposits paid out, especially to Uruguayan residents, flowed back into the system, primarily to public and foreign banks. After a few weeks, deposits stabilized and, slowly, a system-wide net reflow of deposits began.

In total, in response to the banking crisis, the Uruguayan authorities had provided $2.4 billion to the financial sector in various forms of liquidity support (that is, directly from the central bank, and from the FFSB, and the FSBS). This was equivalent to about 20 percent of the country's GDP in 2002. Since then, the government has recovered only a fraction of this total.

Exiting from the banking crisis

In addition to providing liquidity, a comprehensive resolution and restructuring of insolvent domestic banks was required to stabilize the banking system and return it to viability. At the same time, depositors needed reassurances that they would not bear all of the costs of the bank resolution. These considerations led to lengthy discussions among stakeholders, including the government, shareholders, depositors and other bank creditors, bank borrowers, and the powerful bank employees union, on a strategy to resolve the banking crisis.

Throughout the fall of 2002, discussions were held with the IMF to explore available alternatives. This led, in late December, to the passage of legislation that allowed the authorities to move forward with an innovative resolution approach. In January 2003, the government placed three of the four suspended private banks into liquidation. With technical assistance from the IMF, a new bank, Nuevo Banco Comercial (NBC) was created in February 2003, with the government as the sole shareholder. NBC purchased the good assets from the liquidations of the three banks and simultaneously issued certificates of deposit to pay for the assets. This was a key innovation for the Uruguayan authorities, as it avoided the need to put up cash that the government did not have at that time. The certificates of deposits were distributed to the depositors and creditors of the three banks in liquidation. In addition, the government used the share of deposits that it received as a creditor of the failed banks to provide coverage against loss to depositors up to $100,000. In March 2003, NBC opened for business, in full compliance with prudential norms.[45] In line with the original plan and commitments under the IMF program, the government sold the bank in 2005 to private investors at a profit over its original capital investment.

Important steps were also taken to rehabilitate the ailing public banks. Foreign currency deposits from the insolvent state mortgage bank BHU were transferred to the state commercial bank BROU in return for a government-guaranteed note. In addition, as noted, the maturities of time deposits at BROU were compulsorily lengthened over a period of three years, even though the return of confidence later allowed this bank to fully free up these deposits ahead of schedule, by April 2005. BROU itself was recapitalized by the government through the transfer of nonperforming loans to a trust and the loans were replaced with government-guaranteed notes. In addition, the internal controls of the bank were significantly strengthened.

Since the crisis, the Superintendency of Banks has, under the skilled management of Superintendent Fernando Barrán, made significant strides in improving bank supervision. With assistance from the IMF and the Inter-American Development Bank, new regulations designed to address risk-management concerns and foreign-exchange risks have been issued, training has been strengthened, and the number of supervisory staff has been increased. Perhaps equally important has been the increase in transparency and in the availability of public information on the banking sector. Finally, the banking crisis highlighted the need for a deposit-protection scheme. A formal limited deposit-insurance scheme was introduced by presidential decree in 2005 as a response to problems in a small cooperative bank. Draft legislation has been prepared, giving the deposit insurer the full range of bank resolution powers found in other countries.

Restructuring the public debt

Although Uruguay's public debt situation was characterized by a relatively high debt level going into the crisis, there were no acute concerns about the government's ability to honor its debt servicing obligations until the banking crisis became particularly severe. As the currency depreciated and the debt-to-GDP ratio surged, however, it became evident that both liquidity and solvency issues needed to be addressed.

Negotiations between the IMF and the authorities on a strategy to restore debt sustainability took several months to finalize. As indicated above, the Uruguayan authorities wished to avoid at all cost any aggressive debt-restructuring strategy that would have involved principal reductions. They were committed to preserving the impeccable track record of Uruguay, one of the few Latin American countries that had never defaulted on its sovereign debt in its entire history.

Discussions eventually converged toward an agreed upon macroeconomic scenario to underpin the debt-sustainability analysis, including the medium-term path of the fiscal primary surplus (the fiscal balance before interest payments). Differences of views on the path of the economic recovery and the projected rate of growth of the economy over the medium term were also gradually reconciled. IMF staff cautioned that the projections should not assume overly optimistic primary surpluses, given Uruguay's past experience in that area (during the 1990s, the primary balance had been at, or near, equilibrium). Agreement was finally reached on a fiscal primary surplus of 3 percent of GDP in 2003, which would rise to close to 3½ percent by 2006 and 4 percent over the medium term.

The authorities gradually recognized the value of a broad-encompassing approach to deal with the debt issue. They assumed strong ownership of a debt operation in which holders of Uruguayan bonds would be offered to swap their existing bonds for new, longer maturity, instruments with broadly the same face value and coupons as the old bonds. Given that most of these bonds had been issued when Uruguay enjoyed investment grade status, they carried very low interest rates. And, given the interest rate conditions prevailing in the market in early 2003, at the time of the exchange, this implied some net present-value reduction. This strategy, which centered around a voluntary exchange, provided very significant relief in amortization payments in the years following the exchange, and IMF staff supported the authorities' proposal.

The debt exchange offer was launched in April 2003, covering virtually all of Uruguay's debt to private creditors. A high participation rate of creditors was critical to achieve sufficient cash flow relief and fully eliminate any residual fiscal and balance of payments financing needs during 2003–5. To that effect, the authorities announced that they were committed to complete the offer only if total participation exceeded 90 percent. To minimize nonparticipation, the authorities warned that, if the exchange was successful but if they ever became unable to meet all debt-service obligations, they would service the new debt in preference to the old.

Mobilizing creditors to participate in the exchange was a daunting challenge. Sovereign bonds were held widely among both retail and institutional investors in Uruguay itself, Latin America, United States, Europe, and Japan. However, when the offer closed on May 29, after a short extension of the exchange period, the participation rate reached the exceptionally high level of 93 percent. Near-universal participation by domestic retail bondholders demonstrated that brokers, banks, and other intermediaries were able to mobilize a widely dispersed retail base. Holders exchanging the external bonds were asked to approve special clauses (exit consents) limiting the liquidity of the old bonds and reducing the ability of the holders of these bonds to enforce debt service payments.

As a result of the debt exchange, principal repayments on medium- and long-term debt due in 2003–7 were reduced from $2.1 billion to $0.3 billion. The financing needs of the public sector were also cut to less than $0.4 billion a year in 2003–4, an amount that could be easily financed through disbursements from international financial institutions and placements in the domestic financial market. In net-present-value terms (measured on the basis of interest rates prevailing at the time of the exchange), Uruguay's debt was reduced by around 20 percent.

A striking characteristic of the Uruguayan debt restructuring is that it did not provoke a second round of banking distress. In some other countries, public debt restructuring had destructive effects on banks' balance sheets. However, in Uruguay, the banking system had little exposure to public debt (at end-2001, bank holdings of government debt amounted to less than 3 percent of their total assets). Furthermore, the authorities' emphasis on maintaining cooperative relations with their creditors, together with their willingness to avoid debt principal reductions, helped solidify confidence. In that respect, discussions with investors in key financial centers in early 2003 involving Central Bank President Julio de Brun, Ministry of Finance Chief Macroeconomic Adviser Isaac Alfie, and Financial Representative Carlos Steneri played a critical role in assuaging concerns in the financial community.

Macroeconomic policies

The successful resolution of the banking and fiscal problems restored confidence and set the stage for an impressive economic recovery. After registering a drop of 11 percent in 2002, real GDP has been growing at an annual rate of 7 percent since then. While initially the recovery was driven by net exports, helped by buoyant agricultural commodity prices and the recovery of the Argentine economy, growth has become more broad based, with a strong contribution from domestic demand, including private investment. Unemployment fell from a peak of 19.8 percent in November 2002 to 9 percent at end-2007. Gross official reserves have surged from less than $0.8 billion at end-2002 to $3.8 billion at end-December 2007. In nominal terms, the peso has been appreciating against the US dollar, while still remaining almost 50 percent more depreciated than at its precrisis level (Table 7.1).

After the success of the debt exchange, the authorities were of the view that it was critical to adhere firmly to sound macroeconomic policies to ensure a return to debt sustainability. In the fiscal area, this was expected to require both enhanced revenue efforts and continued expenditure restraint. The IMF-supported program envisaged that the authorities would be able to maintain large average primary surpluses over the medium term, which seemed a tall order since it required dramatic improvements over the past record. Demonstrating the determination of the Uruguayan government, fiscal developments have been broadly in line with the demanding targets, as the primary surpluses averaged 3.7 percent of GDP over the 2003–7 period. In addition, as the government regained access to financial markets, it was able to repay all its debt to the IMF well ahead of schedule (the last repayment took place in December 2006). Debt management also improved, including through the issuance of longer-term instruments in indexed units in domestic currency.

Table 7.1 Selected economic indicators

	1990–2000 (average)	2001	2002	2003	2004	2005	2006	2007
				(Percentage change)				
Real GDP	1.8	−3.4	−11.0	2.2	11.8	6.6	7.0	7.0
GDP (US$ billions)	17.3	18.6	12.1	11.2	13.3	16.7	19.3	23.0
CPI inflation (e.o.p.)	21.9	4.4	25.9	10.2	7.6	4.9	6.4	8.5
Unemployment rate	10.2	15.3	16.9	16.9	13.1	12.1	9.1	9.1
				(Percent of GDP, unless otherwise indicated)				
Broad money (US$ millions)*	8,418.8	9,778.8	6,150.4	6,949.2	7,573.4	8,288.5	9,221.0	10,558.0
Credit to the private sector (constant exch. rate, percent change)	28.9	−3.8	−17.6	−23.9	−11.2	2.7	9.1	15.5
Public sector:								
Primary balance	0.0	−1.2	0.1	2.7	3.9	4.1	3.9	3.4
Overall balance	−2.2	−4.2	−4.5	−3.2	−2.2	−0.7	−0.6	−0.3
Public sector debt*	24.6	43.2	95.5	110.4	96.9	75.2	66.2	61.7
External current account balance	−1.2	−2.8	3.2	−0.5	0.3	0.0	−2.4	−0.8
Foreign direct investment	0.7	1.7	1.5	3.6	2.4	4.3	7.1	3.8
Gross Official Reserves (US$ millions)	2,149.1	3,099.0	772.0	2,087.0	2,512.0	3,438.4	3,090.6	4,096.0
In months of imports of goods and services	6.5	10.0	3.4	6.6	6.5	7.1	5.5	6.0
In percent of short-term debt plus nonresid. deposit*	27.3	57.2	16.7	51.2	55.4	75.8	101.5	129.8
Real effective exchange rate (percentage depreciation—e.o.p.)	7.1	−5.4	−20.3	−13.2	8.7	12.4	−4.9	.

*The average for the 1990s covers the period 1995–2000.

As noted, the authorities also strengthened the banking system, by disposing of the assets of liquidated banks and restructuring the public banks. As a result, bank deposits recovered from \$6.2 billion at end-2002 to \$10.6 billion at end-2007, only slightly above the precrisis level. However, nonresident deposits did not return fully, as they amounted to \$1.7 billion in November 2007, compared with \$6.5 billion at end-2001.

Questions about the crisis resolution

Useful insights into crisis prevention and resolution may be gained from the 2002 Uruguayan crisis. At the same time, it should be recognized that, for some aspects of crisis resolution, it may be difficult to provide definitive answers, particularly for those in which country specifics play a critical role. This is, for instance, the case for assessing the optimal sequencing in the adoption of measures aimed at addressing bank deposit runs and those dealing with debt restructuring.

Could the magnitude of the crisis have been smaller if the IMF had provided more resources upfront? Given the depth of the turmoil in Argentina and the large size of Argentine resident deposits in Uruguay, contagion was bound to spread from one country to the other. Initially, the run on deposits was driven by nonresident withdrawals, and it seemed that banks would be able to accommodate it. Subsequently, however, when the bank run spread to resident depositors, a critical issue for the IMF was how much financial support it should provide, and when. In hindsight, it appears reasonable to say that the initial support in March 2002 was insufficient. More upfront financing would have helped limit bank deposit outflows, particularly if it had been accompanied by a package of strong policies to build confidence.

Was the total financial assistance provided by the IMF too large? By all standards, the financial support eventually provided by the IMF to Uruguay was very large. IMF financing was equivalent to close to 650 percent of Uruguay's quota and almost 20 percent of its 2004 GDP, in relative terms one of the largest ever IMF-lending operations. The IMF became by far the largest of Uruguay's creditors. Assuming full use of the IMF loan, debt-service obligations to the IMF were projected to peak at 7½ percent of GDP in 2006, equivalent to 30 percent of exports of goods and services and close to half of Uruguay's external debt service. These numbers entailed considerable risks to the IMF. However, a clear lesson from the Uruguayan bank deposit run is that such runs can only be stopped by making abundant liquidity available to reestablish confidence among depositors. In that respect, the August 2002 measures, which included a comprehensive set of policies and large financial support, successfully ended the hemorrhaging of deposits.

Could the timing for the change in exchange rate regime have been better? In June 2002, foreign reserves were almost fully depleted and any attempt to sustain the crawling peg regime was no longer a viable alternative. The severe liquidity losses prompted the floating of the currency. In a dollarized environment, the sharp depreciation of the currency magnified bank problems, as depositors rushed to convert their dollar deposits into cash dollars, which resulted in immediate losses of central bank reserves. The increase in IMF loans in June 2002 was clearly insufficient to back a significant portion of dollar deposits. However, at that time the authorities were unwilling to consider tougher measures to stop the run on deposits, such as the compulsory lengthening of the maturities of certain deposits in public banks. They wanted at all costs to signal that their crisis resolution strategy would differ substantially from that followed by Argentina, which had adopted a broad freeze on deposits. With hindsight, shifting to a floating regime would have been less disruptive in early August, once the comprehensive strategy to deal with the bank run adopted after the bank holiday was in place.

Should the banking and debt problems have been handled simultaneously in mid-2002? Given the low level of domestic bank exposure to Uruguayan sovereign debt, there was probably little to gain from addressing the banking and debt issues simultaneously, unless a more aggressive debt restructuring than the one that was ultimately implemented was considered. Therefore, it does not seem that an attempt to handle the banking crisis and the debt problems together would have been better than the approach chosen. Obviously, an earlier debt exchange by, say, mid-2002 would have provided immediate debt relief, at a time when foreign exchange was scarce. However, conditions at that time were probably too turbulent to formulate and implement the type of voluntary operation that was later launched. Moreover, given the extent and urgency of the banking problems, there probably would not have been enough time to conduct informal consultations with private investors, nor would investors have had confidence in a positive outcome of the banking crisis, which was critical for them to evaluate the proposed debt exchange.

Was the debt strategy ambitious enough? It has sometimes been argued that conditions in August 2002 may have allowed the adoption of an aggressive debt stock relief operation. In light of the substantial increase in the debt-to-GDP ratio and the cash flow difficulties associated with the loss in reserves, it is however doubtful that investors would have been willing to accept deeper debt relief. In addition, getting domestic retail investors to participate was viewed as critical to a high participation rate, and asking for principal reductions would have run a considerable risk of the exchange offer failing. In turn, this could have reignited a run on banks and likely led Uruguay to suspend payments, generating more adverse economic consequences. In any case, such an approach was not considered by the Uruguayan authorities, for whom it was of great importance to respect their contractual obligations with creditors. In agreement with their creditors, the authorities considered that Uruguay faced a liquidity, not a solvency, crisis. Therefore, emphasis was placed on improving the cash flow profile, not on seeking a reduction in the principal of the debt. Ex-post, given the favorable global environment for emerging market economies of recent years, the debt exchange seems to have been sufficient to restore medium-term viability. The debt-to-GDP ratio has declined from above 100 percent of GDP in 2003 to 62 percent in 2007, and an aggressive debt liability management has helped lower debt service payments at manageable levels throughout the medium term. The debt exchange has also given the authorities additional time to implement key economic reforms.

Should the IMF have been more aggressive in pushing for improvements in bank supervision prior to the crisis? At the outset of the crisis, bank supervision was weak and the financial position of public banks fragile. In addition, Uruguay's role as a regional financial center meant that the banking sector was vulnerable, as a large part of the system was engaged in recycling foreign capital in the domestic market and was thereby exposed to liquidity shocks originating from abroad. The IMF, in the context of both program monitoring and surveillance, had raised concerns over these issues and encouraged the authorities to address them by strengthening bank supervision and building a large cushion of international reserves. Still, the IMF could have been considerably more forceful in urging the authorities to take action in the context of the financial programs it supported during the 1990s.

Have sufficient efforts been made in recent years to address the high degree of dollarization of the banking system via prudential measures? The crisis has shown that large amounts of dollar lending to domestic entities with no earnings in dollars had compounded bank difficulties, particularly after the devaluation of the peso. Hence, some of the damage to the financial system and the impact of a crisis on the economy could have been mitigated if these weaknesses had been properly addressed before the crisis. In recent years, the authorities have taken some steps to enhance dedollarization (that is, increase the share of peso operations in the total assets and liabilities of banks), by introducing lower reserve requirements on peso deposits, higher deposit insurance premiums and lower coverage for dollar deposits, and higher capital charges for loans in foreign currency to unhedged borrowers. However, given the persistence of dollarization in the banking system, more could possibly be done. In addition, until long-run inflationary expectations are markedly reduced, Uruguayans may continue to wish to hold dollar deposits as a hedge against inflation.

Conclusion

Uruguay suffered an economic ordeal in 2002/3 that was triggered by traumatic economic events in neighboring Argentina. The crisis of confidence in its banking system and the run on deposits was of such virulence that initial attempts by the authorities and the IMF to overcome them were continuously overwhelmed by fresh bad news. The authorities showed great determination to preserve Uruguay's reputation as a safe regional banking center and maintain trust with depositors and foreign investors that contracts would not be broken, spending very large sums of public resources to demonstrate that. Thus, administrative measures to lengthen by fiat the maturity of some time deposits in order to save public funds were only taken as a last resort in August 2002, when there were no reasonable alternatives. This determination was understood and honored by the public in recovering confidence in the banking system, and by foreign investors in Uruguayan bonds when they agreed to a voluntary debt relief operation. Uruguay's determined policies have been rewarded with strong and steady economic growth since 2003.

The successes of Uruguay's policy in recent years, in the context of buoyant global financial markets, have enabled the country to fully repay its large loans from the IMF within a period of only half a year after the last drawing from the IMF loan was made. Uruguay's public debt stock remains relatively high, at around 60 percent of GDP, leaving little room for policy slippages. However, the debt-to-GDP ratio is projected to decline further over the medium term, to about 40 percent of GDP by 2012, and debt liability management has helped lower debt service ratios to more manageable levels. A key challenge will be to sustain medium-term policies that maintain fiscal primary surpluses of close to 4 percent of GDP. This, together with decisive steps to address banking weaknesses and further reduce the degree of dollarization, will be key to maintaining macroeconomic stability and growth. In that respect, the Uruguayan crisis has also shown that countries should always try and take advantage of favorable times to implement policies aimed at reducing existing vulnerabilities.

The Uruguayan crisis and its resolution also provided valuable lessons for the IMF. First, the experience showed that, even in a crisis context, there is room to develop and adopt innovative solutions. Hence, exploring rigorously alternative policy options, even under severe pressures like a deposit run and the prospects of insolvency, is critically important. Second, the Uruguayan case also illustrated the importance of incorporating specific local circumstances in the design of policy responses. Several elements of the bank resolution and debt strategy were tailored to Uruguay's specific context and may not necessarily have worked elsewhere. All along, the authorities and IMF staff were engaged in a constant dialogue that never stopped, even during the most difficult moments.

At the end of the day, it is accepted, even by some original skeptics, that the IMF-supported program in Uruguay was a success. One of the critical factors contributing to the rapid turnaround in Uruguay was the commitment of the authorities. This commitment, combined with having the right people in the right jobs, contributed greatly to Uruguay's rapid recovery from the crisis. In addition, another positive element was the determination of the authorities to make progress through building a political consensus. When compared to some other countries, there was very little political criticism, or obstructionism, once decisions were taken. While the consensus process followed by the authorities may have delayed some decision making, in the long run it contributed to the success of the program.

Uruguay's close relationship with the IMF was highlighted by Finance Minister Danilo Astori at the time of the repayment of the debt to the IMF, in November 2006. At that time, the minister emphasized that Uruguay would continue to maintain a friendly relationship with the IMF, an institution of which Uruguay was one of the founding members. On that occasion, he also stressed that the government would press ahead with the implementation of the program agreed with the IMF, given that this was the country's program. In retrospect, this may be the best recognition that the IMF can receive from the authorities of one of its member countries.

Uruguay 2002–3: Recovery from Economic Contagion

Carlos Steneri[2]

One of the ultimate challenges in economic policy making is to deal simultaneously with a bank run and a sovereign debt crisis. Uruguay faced such a challenge in 2002–03, with a crisis of unusual intensity that originated from regional contagion. The issues that it raised for policy makers at the time were either new or of a very large magnitude. Naturally, this resulted in significant differences of views on the diagnosis of the problems and the best policy responses. Looking back, the resolution process of Uruguay's 2002–3 crisis is, in many respects, a textbook case and invaluable lessons can be learned from the crisis and its resolution.

A first lesson for policy makers is that, for bad or good, policy ownership always needs to rest with the country. It is their society that is faced with the full impact of the crisis, in all its dimensions. In the end, economic policy measures have a broad impact, well beyond their immediate effects, and touch upon the fundamental determinants of societies, such as the social fabric, institutions, and cultural values. The leadership of the country needs to take all these aspects into account when deciding on the policy response. Let me be quite explicit on this aspect. The most important differences between the Uruguayan authorities and the IMF in the search for a way out of the crisis were not around numbers, but were instead often related to these fundamental social determinants.

Policies can be successful only if they are crafted in such a way that they fully take into account the specifics of each country. In Uruguay, a core cultural value, embedded for generations in its society, is a deep

[2] Mr. Steneri is Financial Agent of the Government of Uruguay in the United States and Director of the Management Unit at the Ministry of Finance.

commitment to fully comply with the rule of law. Any shift away from compliance with existing contracts would, in the Uruguayan context, be tantamount to institutional weakening, with adverse spillovers to the entire economy and the social fabric. At the most difficult times of Uruguay's history, the political system and civil society, including trade unions, have always provided strong support for continued adherence to the rule of law. At these moments, there were periods of expectant silence and call for patience within the Uruguayan society, which looked to and trusted its representatives to work out the best solution for the country. This was again demonstrated in 2002, when Congress approved in less than 48 hours a critical law to resolve the banking crisis and reschedule time deposits with public banks.

This Uruguayan consensus has, without doubt, been a source of great strength in our discussions with the IMF. In many ways, the quality of the policies adopted by a country in times of crisis reflects the cohesiveness of its society and the strength of its political system. For a small country like Uruguay, social cohesiveness and respect for the rule of law have been the cornerstones that have enabled us to successfully overcome challenges which, at the time, seemed insurmountable. These factors have also given us some moral backing to make our case before the international community.

This explains why Uruguay did not want to resolve the run on banks through a general freeze on deposits and to, subsequently, unilaterally default on debt payments as suggested by the IMF. It is true that such policies were advocated at the height of the crisis, when it seemed that the international community would not be willing to provide additional financial support to Uruguay. However, these recommendations would have run counter to Uruguay's deep-seated commitment to the rule of law and compliance with its contractual agreements.

With respect to the banking crisis, a second lesson is that it is unwise to fight a run on deposits with limited upfront liquidity. Such an approach is not only wasteful in terms of the use of scarce foreign exchange reserves but it also runs the risk of paralyzing the payments system. In retrospect, the original program from the IMF did not provide sufficient upfront liquidity and was thus doomed to be unsuccessful. Uruguay adopted a tight fiscal adjustment program and, as suggested by the IMF, let its currency float, but this was done at a suboptimal time—without sufficient liquidity to restructure the banking system to stop the run and preserve the highly dollarized payments system. Larger upfront financing would have helped limit bank deposit outflows. It was only after the authorities secured the support of the US Treasury and other large shareholders of the IMF that the strategy was modified to provide enough upfront liquidity to protect the payments system and create the conditions for an orderly bank restructuring.

During the debt problem resolution, extended discussions led to financial costs that could have been avoided, at a time when scarce reserves were needed for the banking crisis. It took several months to complete the debt exchange, in part because the IMF did not initially agree with the strategy pursued by the Uruguayan authorities. In fact, delays in reaching an agreement on the approach at some point put the whole strategy at risk, given that bank runs temporarily resurfaced in January 2003.

More flexibility and speed is needed in the negotiations of IMF-supported programs. Within the IMF, this would imply changes in work practices, regarding in particular program approval processes and conditionality. During the negotiations, we sometimes felt that staff was placed in a straitjacket by the IMF's management and its Executive Board. However, it is difficult to elucidate who had the final responsibility in this type of symbiotic decision process but, certainly, the cumbersome decision process led to protracted discussions, excessive delays, and suboptimal results. In the current context, it is therefore critical for the authorities of a country under stress to establish very close contacts with key members of the Executive Board (G-7 countries, particularly) to design the program according to the needs of the country.

A third lesson is to strengthen the role of the IMF in a financially interdependent world, where contagion is bound to happen from time to time. The Uruguayan crisis was intimately tied to the 1998 Russian debt default, the 1999 Brazilian crisis, and the 2001–2 Argentinean crisis. These links highlight the importance of introducing a new international financial architecture, in which the IMF has a significant role. It would be inefficient, and even dangerous, not to have an international institution endowed with sufficient resources to assist countries during international financial crises.

In that respect, neither the IMF's Articles of Agreement nor the modest size of its capital appear well adapted to the challenges of today's world. In the present economic and financial world, imbalances in one part of the world can generate adverse ripple effects on a whole host of other countries. Emerging countries can potentially suffer the most in times of crisis, with the risk that the benefits of reform efforts which took years to implement could be rapidly erased. This is perhaps one of the most important pending subjects that the international community has to deal with today.

In all, much can be learned by all parties involved from episodes of crisis resolution. There is no doubt that, today, both Uruguay and the IMF are better prepared to assess not only the risks but also the benefits associated with the implementation of sound policies. A challenge is to learn how to minimize the risks taken to ensure the best policy outcome. It is fair to say that, in the end, the IMF fully backed the policies that had been agreed upon with the authorities. Once agreement had been reached, both partners worked closely on a program that involved significant risks for the IMF in terms of prestige, with exceptionally high cash disbursements and a voluntary debt swap that required skilled design and careful implementation to be successful.

The rewards from such decisions have not taken long to materialize. Bank deposits began to reflow in October 2002, as an orderly restructuring of the banking system was being implemented. Most importantly, GDP started growing at an accelerated pace, initially pushed by exports, and it has continued to grow rapidly in recent years. Similarly, Uruguay has been able to regain access to international capital markets, and it is quite remarkable that, just five months after the finalization of the debt swap, it successfully issued in the international market a $300 million bond denominated in domestic currency.

Finally, as a society, Uruguay has demonstrated full ownership of its program, transcending the particularities of who was in government. The new government, which took over in March 2005 with a center-left agenda, did not significantly alter the program that had been agreed with the previous administration. The fiscal stance has not only been maintained but also somewhat reinforced, bank consolidation has continued, and debt contracts have continued to be fully honored. The success of the policies in place can also be measured by Uruguay's ability to repay in advance the full amount owed to the IMF and the emergency loans extended by the Inter-American Development Bank and the World Bank.

Part II Preventing Financial Crises and Promoting Monetary Cooperation

8
Opening the Economic Books of Governments and of the IMF

Timely and reliable economic and financial information is vital to good economic policy making, to good decision making by businesses and individuals, and to the efficient functioning of markets.

As recently as the mid-1990s, the IMF was a largely closed and secretive institution. Now, a decade later, it publishes virtually everything worth knowing about its work. This is the first story told in this chapter.

Most of the financial crises in emerging market countries in the 1990s revealed serious deficiencies in data vital to policy makers and markets, contributing significantly to the buildup of conditions leading to the crises. A decade later, and with the help of the IMF, much-improved transparency in data and in economic governing practices is in place in many countries. This is the second story told in this chapter.

The IMF steps out of the shadows

Thomas Dawson II[1]

The IMF's external relations strategy in its first 40 years or so can be illustrated by a story, possibly apocryphal. One of the early Managing Directors met for the first time with the first-ever adviser for external relations. The adviser asked, "what shall I tell the press?" The Managing Director leaned back in his chair, stroked his chin and thought briefly before answering, "you will tell them nothing."

In short, the IMF's external relations strategy, if there really was one, was to stay out of the news. While never really a successful strategy, the costs were not apparent in the early decades.

[1] Mr. Dawson is a former director of the IMF's External Relations Department. He previously served as IMF Executive Director for the United States.

Curiously, from the beginning the IMF was required by its Articles of Agreement to prepare an annual report. Tellingly, however, it was not required to be made public! This was a far cry from the narrative and numbers-laden public document that evolved in later years. Possibly the most sought-after IMF "publication" for many years was the "Blue Sheet," a daily news summary prepared for staff with a closely guarded distribution, but nonetheless eagerly sought by outsiders familiar with it.

For most of its existence, the IMF's approach to external relations and transparency was strongly supported, and matched, by most of its members. This is not to say, of course, that the IMF was always out of the news. IMF loans were big news, and often controversial, especially in borrowing countries. However, the expectation was that any explanation of what was going on should come from the borrowing member government. And in many, if not almost all, cases the government was not interested in highlighting, or even explaining, the role of the IMF. The case of the United Kingdom in 1976 is illustrative. Great public attention was focused on the seemingly collapsing economy, and the UK government's decision to request a loan from the IMF was big news, and controversial. So much so that the visiting IMF mission actually suggested to the UK authorities that the mission meet with the press! The authorities rejected the idea out of hand. This is a far cry from present practice, where in most cases visiting IMF missions meet with the media.

However, it is important to note that, to this day, member governments can exercise wide control over the IMF staff's activities in a country as well as over public statements about the member. The annual surveillance reports on a country (an assessment of a country's economic policies and performance) can only be published with the member's consent. If staff wishes to visit a country they must first obtain permission of the Executive Director representing that country. Staff members visiting a country are also prohibited from meeting with the media without permission of the authorities. Similar constraints can exist on in-country contacts with parliaments, and nongovernmental organizations.

Until recent years, member countries almost without exception exercised this control. While in the present era of transparency few members exercise this right, some do and the present level, indeed existence, of greater openness and transparency exists at the suffrage of the membership. This is important in understanding the culture of the institution as well as the limits and pressures on the staff in dealing with the public.

An appreciation of the important role of the IMF's Executive Board is also critical to gaining an understanding of the IMF and how it operates, especially in its contacts with the outside world. The Board generally meets three times a week, approving loans, reviewing economic policies and performance of members, assessing global and regional economic conditions, and dealing with the administrative matters of the organization. While at times the image of the institution is one of a lack of accountability, IMF staff members often feel they are micromanaged by the Executive Board (and through them by the member countries) in matters great and small. For their part, the Executive Board and member countries rather understandably view much of this as proper oversight and good governance. However, as the era of openness, transparency, and instant communication developed, this too often makes the work of "explaining" what the IMF is up to difficult, to say the least. It is not surprising that until recent years one of the words most associated with "IMF" in media "searches" was "secrecy."

It was only in 1980, some 35 years after the IMF's foundation, that the External Relations Department was established. While recognition of the need for some external relations component certainly was shown in setting up the new Department, the extent of external relations activities was limited and reactive, if not simply defensive. This reflected the continuing belief, indeed culture, at the IMF that it was a specialized financial institution accountable to its shareholders rather narrowly defined (specifically, finance ministries and central banks). There was even resistance to reaching out when requested by member countries! An example: when the US Congress was considering legislation for a quota increase in the early 1980s, the US Treasury approached the IMF about hosting a dinner for interested Members of Congress. Only with great reluctance did IMF Management agree, thinking that it was not the IMF's role to help make the case! Ironically, in later years the tables were often turned with the US Treasury restricting and closely monitoring IMF contact with Capitol Hill. This led to the Congress passing legislation assuring access to information from the IMF. Other governments similarly wanted, and some to this day still want, to maintain control over contacts with their parliaments.

Contacts with the media, even at headquarters, were also highly circumscribed. Most staff members were simply prohibited from talking with the press and, even as recently as the early 1990s, IMF staff dealing with the media were not allowed to be quoted by name or institutional affiliation, being only identified as "a monetary source." When lapses occurred, staff could expect to be reprimanded and the consequences could be severe. The privilege of speaking on the record was generally reserved for the Managing Director.

The establishment of the External Relations Department, though important symbolically, did not mark a fundamental change in the IMF's approach to the outside world. It was recognition of the need to deal with the outside but there was not yet a commitment to engage proactively with outside actors. Real transparency in terms of the details of IMF-supported programs and data dissemination were to wait until the mid–late 1990s. However, public demand for more information about the IMF certainly took off in the 1980s and the IMF did respond. An important factor initially was the need for legislative support for quota increases and amendments to the Articles of Agreement. This was especially true in the case of the United States. But the demand for more transparency soon became broader, challenging an institution that once thought that establishing an external relations department would go a long way toward solving the "problem."

Early support for greater openness (transparency was not yet really a concept) came from (a few) governments, (a few) parliaments, media, and academics, as well as nongovernmental organizations (NGOs).

The IMF, especially the staff, found itself in a curious position in this growing debate. The culture of the institution was traditionally closed and secretive, not unlike most of the central banks and finance ministries which were its direct stakeholders and provided many of its staff. At the same time, the institution did not lack self-confidence, and many felt strongly that if only the institution would respond to criticisms all would be well. In a highly structured and disciplined organization like the IMF, though, change was likely to occur only from the top, with the broad support of the membership. And the membership was split.

Much of the early push for greater openness came from a few developed countries: the United States, France, the United Kingdom, and Canada. In a sense this was not surprising since their parliaments were active in questioning the institution's activities. But what was surprising was that, at least until the mid-1990s, a number of European governments were actively opposed to increased transparency. The Scandinavians and Dutch were prominent in this regard, taking the view that the IMF was a monetary institution which was accountable to central banks and finance ministries. Interestingly, US NGOs played a role in energizing their international counterparts, especially in Europe, to gain support of governments for the opening process.

Opposition to increased openness came from a number of developing countries (and to a lesser degree still does) for a variety of reasons. The conflict is most interesting, and difficult, in country-lending programs.

It is, and should be, the responsibility of the borrowing country to explain its own policies and not the IMF's job. This is, of course, what "ownership" is all about. Ultimately, for the country and the IMF the common objective should be to achieve the definition of a successful program advanced by Stanley Fischer (former First Deputy Managing Director): "when no one calls it an IMF program."

Too often, some countries' opposition to openness has seemed to reflect a lack of commitment to the underlying program (including the terms of the loan agreement) or even the principle of openness in, for example, simply publishing the analysis of individual countries' policies and performance. On the other hand, country authorities should have a better understanding of their own circumstances and considerable deference should be given to their analysis and preferences in terms of an external relations strategy. Brazil is a perfect example. It meets Mr. Fischer's definition: a country that has had clear country "ownership," especially in recent IMF-supported programs and enjoyed great success while limiting IMF external relations activities and public commentary to the minimum required.

As experience with transparency grew, attitudes among members changed. Developed country "laggards" came on board as they faced, and accommodated, demands for openness in their domestic institutions and adopted a consistent position at the IMF. While this was also true for developing countries, there was a more interesting factor promoting increased transparency: competition! As developing countries sought to attract international capital, investors naturally valued transparency. Countries that adopted the IMF's data standards (discussed elsewhere in this chapter) or published IMF reports thus had an advantage in the competition for capital and investors. The early "publishers" were soon joined by many others and, as noted later, the large majority of IMF members, developed and developing, now publish the surveillance reports.

Openness, of course, was not just an issue with the finance ministries and central banks who have traditionally been the de facto "owners" of the IMF. Parliamentarians were and often are kept at a distance by their own governments when dealing with the IMF. In parliamentary systems, party discipline can "allow" governments to manage the relationship without substantive contact between the IMF and the parliament. However, good governance and "ownership" calls for more involvement of legislatures in countries' dealings with the IMF, especially with more legislative bodies gaining a formal oversight or authorizing role in the relationship. Increasingly, parliamentarians are interlocutors of IMF missions and the experience is generally positive. However, such activities are by no means universal and continuing parliamentary hostility or skepticism toward the IMF is not helped by the lack of contact.

For much of the IMF's history, "openness" was thought of in terms of the media. From the beginning the media has always been "interested" in the IMF. However, media interest in the institution tends to be specialized and also limited except in times of crisis. However, traditional IMF secrecy clearly contributed to the institution's problems, with the implicit message seeming to be that there was something to hide. The Asian financial crisis prompted one of the greatest changes in the IMF's external relations strategy in the area of media relations. In late 1999, a regular, generally biweekly, series of on-the-record press briefings was established. To the extent possible, and as allowed by authorities, IMF missions began to engage with the media. Recent Managing Directors have also been quite active in working with the media. The effect of the commitment to openness is shown by the fact that the IMF/secrecy word association referred to earlier is no longer a serious issue.

Among outside actors, academics (mostly economists) have always had the greatest degree of access to the institution, given the "research" nature of much of the IMF's work. Increased transparency certainly has occurred in this area and has benefited the academic community, especially in analyzing IMF-supported programs and conducting research.

NGOs started expressing interest in IMF issues in the late 1980s and early 1990s, largely in the area of the environment. Broader concerns such as poverty alleviation and the impact of IMF-supported programs on the poor came to the fore later. Once again, the membership was split, but support for NGO contacts and outreach was sufficient to allow Management and staff to engage with NGOs. The relationship was never an easy one, but the principle of access has been established and at least the distrust sowed by secrecy has been lessened.

Until the mid–late 1990s, the supply of details of IMF-supported programs or economic and financial data on members was limited, to say the least. Indeed, borrowing countries were often none too interested in the dissemination of such information. The control members exercised over releasing information on their own economy made this rather easy. Change, at least as seen in retrospect, began to appear in the 1990s. Public Information Notices and press releases reporting on IMF actions and Board discussions started the ball rolling.

The cases of Switzerland and Korea provided interesting examples of transparency before the word become either a buzzword or a principle. Switzerland joined the IMF only in 1992, after a national referendum. When it came time for the first Swiss surveillance consultation, the Swiss authorities published the report for all to see. They did so in good faith and believed it to be appropriate in the name of transparency. Unfortunately it was a clear violation of the existing rules on confidentiality of IMF documents. They were obliged to apologize to the IMF for this breach. Few would have thought that less than ten years later such publication would become the norm.

Similarly, in early 1998, the contents of much of the tentative agreement with Korea concerning IMF crisis support were leaked to the press. It was greeted with shock by many inside and outside the IMF, but the effect was, in fact, to increase understanding and confidence in the markets and by the public in the seriousness of the authorities' program. Again, few anticipated that just a few years later publication of all documentation related to IMF-supported programs would essentially be required.

The experience of the Asian financial crisis finally tipped the balance in favor of a level of transparency that few would have imagined conceivable. In the area of publication of IMF documents, what began as a trial program of publishing a few countries' surveillance reports has evolved to a situation where virtually all documents relating to IMF loans and 80 percent of surveillance reports are public. Likewise, all staff papers on general policy issues are published after they are considered by the Executive Board. Indeed many documents are published prior to Board discussion (such as the Board's Agenda) and publication includes budget and other "internal" matters as well. Publishing, of course, is now increasingly electronic and the IMF's Web site (www.imf.org) has an irreplaceable role in the transparency effort.

In the area of media relations, the best evidence of the transparency revolution is that the press makes few complaints about "secrecy" and lack of access. Parliamentarians and IMF staff in many countries have regular contacts and the IMF has an active program of seminars with parliamentarians in a wide range of countries. Many NGOs still have complaints about the IMF but access is well established and the differences revolve mainly around policy issues.

Transparency, of course, is not simply a matter of opening up the books. Important also is the ability to analyze and evaluate IMF activities. Interested outsiders can and have used increased transparency to make their own, presumably also better-informed, judgments about IMF performance. Most international institutions have established evaluation offices to provide an independent yet also official contribution to transparency and good governance.

After several years during which independent evaluations were commissioned by the Executive Board from outside experts, the IMF's Independent Evaluation Office (IEO) was established in 2001. The IEO operates at arms length from the Executive Board, is independent of IMF management and staff, and is free to select the topics it evaluates and with full access to all relevant information. Earlier attempts to institutionalize an evaluation office foundered on a lack of consensus among members and a reluctance by IMF management on the need for a permanent office. With energetic leadership, a policy of open consultation, and public outreach, the IEO has quickly established a reputation for the independence and generally high quality of its analyses. This view was confirmed by an external evaluation in 2006 of the IEO's work to date.

While transparency is very much in the eye of the beholder and there is no universally agreed upon measure, outside observers do credit the IMF with an "above average" performance. For example, in a 2006 report, One World Trust, a UK-based organization, ranked the IMF third in transparency out of the ten surveyed international organizations. Informal contacts with media and academic observers have also yielded similar feedback.

The IMF has come a long ways from the policy of "You will tell them nothing." Indeed, recent Managing Directors have been strong advocates of transparency, often pushing the Board and staff to be more proactive. The gains seem irreversible but the formal governance structure remains and is a reminder that ultimately the IMF is an organization controlled by its member countries that control its destiny.

The growth of economic transparency and the IMF

By Charles Enoch[2]

Good decision making, whether by policy makers or market participants, requires transparency of information. This in turn requires good data, and a clear understanding as to how the information in the data

[2] Mr. Enoch is Deputy Director of the IMF's Statistics Department and a former deputy director of the IMF's Monetary and Financial Systems Department. The author is grateful for comments from Zdravko Balyosov and Claudia Dziobek.

will be used. With the growth of financial markets, and the associated risks in such markets, good data and clarity of policy objectives have increasingly been seen to be important. The IMF has had a central role in recent advances in both these areas.

Traditionally, central banks, and financial authorities more widely, have hidden behind a thick curtain of secrecy. It was argued, at least until the past decade, that management of markets would be most effective if the authorities could work behind the scenes to determine the best policies and then launch these on to the outside world. Thus interest rate changes or changes in regulations should be held very close, since only by surprising the market would they have an impact. Similarly, the financial conditions of the banks should be a secret, so that the authorities would be able to address any problems before they became public and confidence was undermined. And official figures, such as those on reserves, could be restricted or massaged, on the argument that the public should focus on what the authorities regarded as the underlying position, and not be confused about random variation. If a small country had just had bought a Boeing plane, for example, it would distort the picture if the entire cost of the plane were reflected in the reserves figures for a month, so there would be a case for smoothing the picture, for instance by borrowing reserves over the end of the reporting cycle, so the plane-induced fall in reserves should not cause concern that there was a loss of confidence in the country's currency.

A number of factors worked to counter this view, particularly from the early 1990s. Most broadly, there was rapid growth in private markets, and a growing belief that markets—if given full information—would know best how to react. Second, there was a corresponding decline in trust that policy makers would on their own make the right decisions—either because they were self-interested, or because things were getting too complicated. US pressures for "prompt corrective action" were a reflection of distrust at the response of the US banking regulators to the problems of the savings and loans industry. In New Zealand, the framework for banking supervision was amended so that banking soundness was essentially to be protected by requiring the provision of information to the general public rather than the traditional model where regulators are tasked to initiate supervisory action based on banks' confidential reporting to them; the emphasis on public disclosure of information has become widely accepted, and underlies one of the three "pillars" of the Basel II framework for banking supervision that is being adopted as the general standard for supervision worldwide.

Transparency in data

In 1994 the international financial community experienced what IMF Managing Director Michel Camdessus termed "the first crisis of the twenty-first century" when Mexico went into financial crisis as market operators decided to withdraw massive amounts of funds from the country. The "tequila effect" of capital withdrawals spread through much of the continent as market participants feared that if a crisis could hit Mexico it could hit elsewhere. The crisis prompted detailed analyses of the causes.[46] Among the main findings was that data had not been available to analyze developments properly, leading to delays in recognizing emerging problems and then heavy reaction in the markets once the problems had finally been sighted. Similarly, there were no recognized standards for data, nor for the assessment and supervision of the financial institutions that were the major players in Mexico as well as other emerging markets.

The Asian financial crisis served to accelerate the recognition of the need for transparency in data. As the crisis unfolded from mid-1997, it became apparent that even senior policy makers had been in the dark owing to officially driven distortions of critical financial information. Most spectacularly, the Thai finance minister believed in the summer of 1997 that his country had over $30 billion of foreign exchange reserves. As the need to access these reserves built up, however, it became apparent that nearly all these reserves had already been committed, and that less than $1 billion was available for foreign exchange market intervention. The collapse of the exchange rate, and the concomitant failure of many of the country's financial institutions, soon followed.

Among the initiatives launched by the IMF in response to the developments in Latin America, Asia, and elsewhere was the development of a standard for the dissemination of macroeconomic data, which became known as the Special Data Dissemination Standard (SDDS), begun in 1996. This was to be a voluntary standard, which was considered appropriate particularly for countries participating in international financial markets or with aspirations to do so. Those countries that subscribed to the SDDS committed themselves to disseminate specified sets of macroeconomic data (including national accounts, and price, external, fiscal, and monetary data) with given minimum levels of coverage, periodicity, and timeliness.[47] Countries also had to disseminate details of their data ("metadata"), so that observers could see how the data were generated. The metadata were posted on the IMF's Web site and were hyperlinked to the national Web pages with the macroeconomic data. The creation of this standard provided a framework for many industrial countries to overhaul their dissemination of statistics, and for statistical development in emerging markets that had not yet reached the specified requirements. At the outset, as monitoring of dissemination practices began in 2000, 47 countries were subscribers to the SDDS, including nearly all industrial countries, as well as transition countries in central Europe and emerging markets in Latin America and South East Asia. At the time quite a number of these countries (particularly some of the small European countries) were not in practice disseminating data in line with their obligations, within a few months there was close to full observance.[48]

This standard has been periodically reviewed by the IMF and, while there is a reluctance to "raise the bar" on subscribers, there have been modifications since its introduction. Most significantly, SDDS subscribers now also have to disseminate the "reserves template"—a table containing around 30 subcomponents of international reserves which, if reported properly, severely limits the possibility of distortions in the reporting of a country's reserves position.[49] A number of countries were initially extremely nervous about disseminating this information in full, in particular because of concern that, for instance, the identification of a central bank's forward position in the foreign exchange markets might enable market counterparts to trade against it. Thus a lag of one month and minimum frequency of dissemination of one month was agreed for the standard, even though some countries disseminate these data more frequently and more rapidly. In practice, fears that disseminating the template would enable markets to trade against the central banks have not been realized, and this is no longer seen as a major issue.

Meanwhile, the IMF became involved in developing other standards, and in working with other bodies developing standards, to provide a comprehensive suite of standards for financial markets. The IMF itself developed both a fiscal and a monetary and financial transparency code. The Basel Committee set out the Basel Core Principles of Banking Supervision, and the International Organization of Securities Commissions (IOSCO) set out a code for securities firms. Similarly codes of behavior were established for payments systems and securities settlement. The World Bank set out standards for accounting and auditing, corporate governance, and insolvency. Finally, the Financial Action Task Force (FATF)[50] set out a code for best practices for Anti-Money Laundering and Combating the Financing of Terrorism. All these, however, differed from the SDDS in that, while the SDDS was voluntary and not expected to be immediately relevant to all countries, it needed to be observed in full once a country did subscribe. All the other standards were considered potentially applicable to all countries, but it was recognized that few countries could meet all their components, at least at the outset.

Once these standards were developed, the IMF—and, for most of the standards, the World Bank—became involved in explaining the standards to the professional community and the wider public, in providing technical assistance to countries so that they could achieve them, and in assessing observance of the standards. Joint IMF/World Bank teams traveled to major financial centers between 2000 and 2002 to explain the role of the new standards, and to solicit feedback as to how they could be made more useful. A new IMF/World Bank product, the Report on the Observance of Standards and Codes (ROSC) was developed, to summarize the results of the assessments. While publication of these Reports was, and is, voluntary, more than two-thirds have been published. They can be found on the IMF's Web site, as well as often on the domestic Web sites of the assessed country. The financial sector standards have been assessed through the IMF/World Bank's Financial Sector Assessment Program (FSAP). As of end-January 2008, 645 ROSCs for a total of 129 countries have been published. FSAPs have been published for 78 countries.[51]

Of the various standards, market practitioners have indicated that the SDDS is probably the one at which they look at most closely. Studies[52] have indeed shown that a subscription to the SDDS tends to lower a country's borrowing costs by roughly half a percentage point—hence meeting the requirements of the standard has a substantial, and lucrative, impact on a country's return from its involvement in international financial markets. The SDDS is likely also to have led to a decline in countries' attempts to manipulate markets. South Africa, for instance, at one point had distorted its external position in order to support its exchange rate by a large, undisclosed, and unsustainable involvement in the forward markets. Careful economic management over several years was required to reverse this position, so that by the time the underlying position was disclosed through publication of the reserves template there was no potentially damaging shock to the markets.

While the SDDS makes an important contribution in its own right, it has from the outset been subject to the observation that specifications on timeliness and periodicity of data do not necessarily guarantee the quality of the data. Indeed, in their efforts to meet the timeliness and periodicity requirements, countries might compromise the quality of the data. The IMF's assessment of the data of SDDS subscribers, as conducted in the "data ROSC," therefore does not only look at dissemination practices but also at a whole range of other aspects of the data, set out in the IMF's "Data Quality Assessment Framework (DQAF)." In addition to dissemination practices, this looks also at, for instance, the institutional framework underpinning the data: Do the officials producing the data have professional independence? Are statistical agencies sufficiently resourced? Are there safeguards against governmental influence on the data? The DQAF assesses the methodologies used in producing the data, and the statistical processes in checking and revising the data; it assesses also whether the data meet the needs of the users. Teams undertaking a data ROSC typically send a questionnaire to a range of users to solicit feedback as to how they regard the data. While such contact between statistical agencies and users has long been established practice in some countries, in many others it has been a novelty.

The data ROSC program has had an important effect in improving a country's data. Those countries innovating most rapidly have indeed been keen also to obtain "updates" out of concern that results posted on their Web sites from earlier data ROSCs may have become obsolete and give an inaccurate picture of the actual state of their data. European transition countries have been among those most active in this regard; while most of these began the 1990s with no history of dissemination of data as understood in a market economy, several now have among the most complete observance of the best practices set out in the DQAF. Hungary has had four updates since its first data ROSC in 2000, although this is exceptional, and very few countries have had more than one update or reassessment. Data ROSCs (including reassessments and updates) peaked at 18 in fiscal year 2004, but budget pressures at the IMF have led to a decline since then: only 11 data ROSCs were conducted in FY 2007, and there are now plans to start charging countries for future ROSCs. As the process matures, there is talk that it may be possible, at least in part, to start outsourcing ROSCs, or that private institutions (perhaps including rating agencies) might themselves start producing ROSCs.

As of end-January 2008, 64 countries were subscribing to the SDDS.[53] These include all industrial countries except New Zealand.[54] They also include many of the other countries in Europe, and the major countries in Latin America, South East Asia, and North Africa. Many other countries are working with the IMF to meet the requirements of the SDDS, with up to 20 new countries possibly subscribing by 2010. Among these may be virtually all the remaining countries in Europe, as well as the first countries (apart from South Africa) in sub-Saharan Africa. Especially in the latter cases, SDDS subscription is seen as an important element of their moves toward accessing international markets. With investors particularly leery of involvement in this region, the transparency afforded by SDDS subscription may be particularly useful in increasing the availability, and decreasing the cost, of market access.

For those countries not yet able to subscribe to the SDDS, the IMF and the World Bank established in 1998 a General Data Dissemination System (GDDS). Participation involves countries setting out their statistical methods (metadata) for specified categories of macroeconomic and sociodemographic data, meeting certain recommendations as to timeliness and periodicity of dissemination (generally not as rigorous as those of the SDDS), and committing to use the framework for statistical development. Data ROSCs for countries participating in the GDDS follow the GDDS requirements. Substantial technical assistance has been provided by the IMF and the World Bank, frequently together with bilateral donors such as the UK Department for International Development (DFID), particularly in Africa. China became a GDDS participant in 2003, amid considerable publicity, and has used the framework to achieve fundamental improvements in its economic statistics. And although the Middle East region has been clearly lagging in its involvement in SDDS/GDDS, there has recently been a significant increase in interest. Work on improving the Middle East countries' data is among the most intensive activities in which the IMF is currently involved in these countries.

The various data initiatives have had a wide impact. Macroeconomic data in many countries are available now on a more timely and frequent basis than earlier, and meet generally accepted levels of coverage. Statistical agencies have become more central to the policy-making nexus, as the need for statistical independence and resources is recognized. Statistics laws in a number of countries have been passed to remedy identified deficiencies. There is a wider recognition of best-practice methodologies and many countries are making efforts to attain them. One hundred and seventy-one countries are now reporting their balance of payments data to the IMF on the basis of the most up-to-date balance of payments manual (the fifth edition of the *Balance of Payments Manual*).[55] Many countries have development plans to move toward the new best standard for fiscal data (as set out in the IMF's *Government Fiscal Statistics Manual* 2001). Policy makers and those affected by them now have a more robust basis for decision making than at the start of the last decade.

Transparency in the policy framework

While developments in the 1990s had shown the problems that had arisen in part because of the lack of reliable data, they also led to disillusion with traditional monetary frameworks. New Zealand had moved to a regime of directly targeting inflation in 1989, following disillusion with its earlier exchange rate target. Following their problems with the European Exchange Rate Mechanism in 1992, Sweden and the United Kingdom, too, moved to inflation targeting (IT). Unlike traditional monetary regimes, where trends in monetary aggregates or the exchange rate are clearly visible as triggers for policy action, with IT future developments in inflation will prompt policy action. This in turn depends on expectations of the paths of the factors that determine inflation. An IT regime depends critically on having reliable and credible data, sound forecasting techniques, and a credible set of rules as to how the authorities will implement the regime. Such a regime is thus most effective when there is transparency both as to the data and the authorities' policy objectives and procedures.

Across many emerging markets, the financial crises of the 1990s led to disenchantment with traditional monetary policy and with the institutions responsible for them, and a search for an alternative. Many looked with interest at the possibility of adopting IT. Stanley Fischer, at the time the IMF's First Deputy Managing Director, was prominent in advocating and facilitating such a switch. Brazil was the first major emerging market economy where the usual quantitative-based IMF program was complemented with an IT framework for monetary policy action. Many other countries soon followed.

IT brings together a number of helpful characteristics in the present environment. With central banks having been given operational independence in many countries, the various elements of transparency, in particular the need to preset targets, provide an obvious way to meet the accountability requirements that are essential for this independence. The forward-looking aspect of the framework necessitates efforts on data production and forecasting tools, and so strengthens the forces for making monetary authorities more professional.

Full-fledged IT may not be straightforward for an emerging or developing country to implement. The IMF has been to the fore in giving assistance in this area. The introduction of IT has been an important part of the technical assistance provided to member countries by the Monetary, Research, and Statistics Departments of the IMF.[56] In many cases this has involved a series of visits to the country, not only to develop a research and forecasting capability but also to guide changes in the processes—internal and external—for setting and communicating monetary policy. Such assistance frequently has involved collaboration between IMF staff and officials from central banks that have already adopted IT. The Bank of Canada and the Czech National Bank have been among those most prominent in supplying expertise in this regard. Assistance has ranged from initially explaining the basic concepts and their advantages, then through technical elements such as data and forecasting, and finally to practice run-throughs. In Romania, for instance, with IMF assistance, the central bank ran through two complete trial quarterly IT cycles before the framework was formally adopted as the basis for policy making.

Conclusion

One of the most enduring contributions that the IMF has made to the international financial system in the past decade or so has been through fostering the enhancement of transparency in economic developments and policy formulation. The former has included the IMF's involvement in setting and monitoring of best-practice data standards; the latter has been in supporting and facilitating the widespread adoption of the IT framework for monetary policy formulation. Together these initiatives are likely to have significantly enhanced the quality and depth of financial market development and management, and to have assisted in an extended period of growth and stability.

Opening the Economic Books of Governments and of the IMF

Martin Parkinson[3]

The push for enhanced transparency, including the adoption of internationally recognized standards, has been among the most persistent trends in international economic governance over the last decade. While the importance of greater openness and the adoption of standards and codes gained momentum with the increasing integration of financial markets during the 1990s, the capital market turmoil caused by the 1997 Asian financial market crisis provided the key impetus for the significant improvements in public disclosure of economic data and of the content of policy discussions between the IMF and its members that has occurred over the last decade.

In the immediate aftermath of the 1997 crisis, and particularly the revelations that published foreign exchange data was misleading, both the private sector and the international community placed high priority on improving information flows between potential borrowers and lenders. This took a range of forms: a push for greater transparency in the IMF's views of member country policies and of its own operations, including the advice it was providing to members; and in demands for better national level data—more comprehensive in scope and definition, more frequent and more timely.

These two sections of the chapter provide a range of useful insights into how those pressures unfolded. Dawson describes the significant progress made in the public dissemination of IMF activities that has

[3] Mr. Parkinson was appointed Secretary of the Australian Department of Climate Change in 2007. Between 2001 and 2006 he was Deputy Secretary in the Treasury, and Australia's representative on the International Monetary and Financial Committee and the Joint Bank–Fund Development Committee, and a deputy of the G-20. From 1997 to 2000 he was a staff member in the IMF's Policy Development and Review Department.

brought us to the situation where the vast majority of IMF documents become publicly available. Enoch discusses in detail the development and use of the first disclosure and dissemination standard, the Special Data Dissemination Standard (SDDS) and the development and use of Reports on the Observance of Standards and Codes (ROSCs).

Both describe an impressive degree of progress in casting the searchlight of transparency into areas that were previously subject to limited public scrutiny and accountability. The two authors leave the clear conclusion that they view enhanced openness and the widespread adoption of internationally recognized standards and codes as two of the IMF's success stories.

While both issues are indeed successes for the IMF, in that almost all IMF reports on members policies and programs are now published and that considerably more and better data is (to varying degrees) now available from all IMF members, neither author makes an assessment of whether these initiatives have been successful in the broader sense of improving the functioning of the international financial system. Using this metric, I suspect the judgment would be more a case of "well done, but this is still a work in progress."

The rationale for greater transparency in economic data and decision making was straightforward: if the goals and instruments of policy were known publicly, market participants could assess information on potential borrowers in ways that would result in better investment and lending decisions. Adoption of common internationally accepted standards would provide a common metric for this information, and thereby make an important contribution to the better working of markets and the strengthening of the international financial and monetary system.[57]

As such, ROSCs have their antecedents in the conclusions of the G-22 Working Group on Transparency and Accountability (October 1998), one of three such working groups established in response to the Asian financial crisis. The G-22 proposed the IMF prepare a "Transparency Report" that summarized the degree to which an economy met internationally recognized standards, a proposition echoed by the G-7 finance ministers who, in October 1998, called on the IMF to "publish in a timely and systematic way the results of its surveillance of the degree to which each of its member countries meets internationally recognized codes and standards of transparency and disclosure in the form of a Transparency Report."

While this may seem uncontroversial now, at the time these calls led to much soul-searching within the IMF and among its members.

As Dawson notes, for much of its history the IMF took much the same attitude to public disclosure of information as did its members—that important economic issues were best discussed and debated in secrecy, and that disclosure, including of data, risked creating confusion rather than contributing clarity. When combined with the IMF Executive Board's generally consensus-oriented approach to decision making, the result was to make the IMF appear reluctant to embrace transparency.

In fact, there were legitimate concerns that the IMF would not be able to reconcile its traditional role of candid (and confidential) policy adviser with greater transparency. Some member countries and executive directors and staff believed that by releasing to the world its views on a member's policies or an assessment on the adherence to a set of standards, the IMF would be creating an incentive for the member to avoid revealing its own concerns, and data, to the institution, thereby undermining the capacity of the IMF to conduct its core function—surveillance over the global monetary system.

While these concerns were overblown, the IMF was right to be wary. The regular reviews of surveillance have spent considerable time assessing whether publication of Article IV and other reports have eroded the IMF staff's willingness to make hard calls or have led to members withholding information. Thankfully, such fears have not eventuated—the IMF has not only maintained its own integrity, I believe, it has also benefited from the contestability of ideas spurred on by greater transparency.

The IMF was on stronger ground in being concerned about the way in which its conclusions might be presented and interpreted, particularly the ROSCs which, it was feared, might lack the capacity of Article IV staff reports and program reviews to present detailed and carefully balanced assessments of the entire suite of policies being pursued.

All countries would have some areas where improvement could be made given the breadth of standards proposed for assessment. It was agreed that it would be important to place the member's current position relative to each standard in context, discussing progress identifying areas where further improvement is important, and understanding the authorities' intentions and plans to improve transparency practices and the observance of standards.

How the markets might then interpret such information was also a matter of much discussion. Would a country starting from a low level of adherence to international standards but moving rapidly to implement them be a greater or lesser credit risk than a country with national standards closer to international benchmarks but which was making no attempt to improve them further?

The result was that it took a considerable time to build widespread support for moves to improve transparency, whether through publication of staff reports and program documentation or Executive Board assessments (the Public Information Notices, or PINs) and ROSCs. Significant effort was invested in confidence-building measures in all these areas to assuage the concerns of member countries and certain members of the Executive Board.

For those of us working on these initiatives, what was never in question was the belief that more information would contribute to better functioning markets, reducing the likelihood that private participants might be uninformed or misled and rewarding national authorities following good practices. With hindsight, though, and notwithstanding evidence that borrowing costs are influenced by whether a country has subscribed to the SDDS, it is not yet clear to me that markets have utilized the increased information in the way anticipated.

Perhaps insufficient recognition was given to the fact that some standards were aimed at improving the quality of substantive actions (for example, accounting standards) while others were aimed at improving disclosure and how information was disseminated (for example, the fiscal and monetary policy transparency standards, the SDDS), with the latter group premised on the assumption that improved disclosure would allow market participants to make their own assessments of the underlying policies.

One of the key aims of establishing the SDDS was to encourage greater transparency in reporting economic developments, thereby gradually changing countries attitudes toward the release of data, broadening the availability of statistics to the public, and fostering closer cooperation between producers and users of statistics. The experience with the SDDS, and with the reporting on observance of standards more generally through the ROSCs, highlights that while an increase in the observance of standards can contribute to better policies and help reduce borrowing costs, greater disclosure alone will not necessarily provide market participants and economic policy-makers with deep insights into emerging vulnerabilities.

The expectation was that the market participants would quickly become aware of the quality limitations of a data by recourse to the country's metadata, and would complement statistics with sound economic analysis and broader conceptual thinking.

Instead, meeting disclosure standards has at times been misinterpreted as a reflection of the quality of the underlying data. Some chose not to investigate the quality of the metadata, instead treating observance of the dissemination standard as a mark of broader good practice—observance of the SDDS and other disclosure standards was interpreted as the IMF's seal of approval on the underlying data—a situation which has prompted the welcome creation and use of the IMF's Data Quality Assessment Framework.

It was also anticipated that market participants themselves might quickly begin to prepare ROSCs for commercial gain—notwithstanding occasional flurries of interest this has yet to eventuate. It may be that the ROSC is an example of a classic public good, but even if it is the IMF needs to regularly assure itself that market participants find the presentation of the information, and the information itself, meets their needs.

Because meeting standards of timeliness reveals nothing about the country's conduct of macroeconomic policy or its mix of macro and structural policies, relying on adherence to disclosure and transparency standards, and their presentation through the ROSCs, can never substitute for a careful assessment of underlying economic policies.

But combining assessments of adherence to a wide range of standards with greater transparency in views on policy through the release of IMF staff reports and Executive Board deliberations has been a valuable breakthrough in improving the information available to market participants. Notwithstanding the progress made to date, ongoing efforts will be required to heighten users' understanding and encourage a demand for higher quality, appropriately timely and sufficiently comprehensive, data and assessments of policy. And, since the present level of openness and transparency exists at the gift of the membership, it will be critical to be alert to the potential for backsliding.

9

Strengthening Financial Sectors and Preventing Crises

Tomás J. Baliño[1]

In the latter part of the 1990s, several emerging market economies, particularly in East Asia, had serious crises whose effects were felt worldwide. Large capital outflows were accompanied by major financial and economic distress in the region in a mutually reinforcing process. The problems spread across borders, as banks and other investors in developed countries fled from emerging markets. Deprived of funding, banks and other financial intermediaries in East Asia cut down credits and in some cases (for example, Indonesia) banks faced runs and many had to be closed down. This resulted in sharp devaluations, major falls in output, high unemployment, and large fiscal costs. Major financial markets also suffered, as fears spread about the exposure of various international banks to distressed emerging markets.

These crises differed from earlier ones in that they reflected a disequilibrium of stocks (a portfolio reshuffling) that affected the flows that impact the capital account of the balance of payments, rather than the flows that affect the current account. Furthermore, the countries that suffered the crisis most acutely—Indonesia, Korea, and Thailand—had maintained generally prudent fiscal and monetary policies. Analysts focused on the role of the financial sector and of rigid exchange rates in those countries in triggering the crises, amplifying their effects, and transmitting the problem across borders.

[1] Tomás Baliño is Deputy Director of the IMF's Monetary and Financial Systems Department. The author wishes to acknowledge the helpful contributions of Martin Cihak and Mark Swinburne in providing information about the state of the program and on recent developments in European countries, as well as their valuable comments.

Poor lending practices and lax supervision and regulation were identified as major contributors to the crises. Thus, practically at the same time that the international community sought to contain and resolve the crises, the search for an explanation of what went wrong and how to prevent future crises began in earnest. What was the problem: globalization or inadequate preconditions to make it work? Analysts and policy makers called for reforms of the international financial architecture, in order to make financial systems more resilient to shocks. This required both improving prudential supervision and regulation (that is, supervision and regulation aimed at preserving the stability of financial systems) and disclosing more information, so that market participants could better price risk and punish excessive risk taking. Exchange rate management also came up as an issue for debate. The pegged exchange rates of Asian countries prior to the crises encouraged unhedged borrowing. For instance, some Korean banks had relied on short-term borrowing abroad to finance a substantial part of their lending. Moreover, the level of reserves that central banks held proved insufficient to cope with a reversal of the capital inflows.[58] More flexible exchange rate regimes and higher reserve levels have helped many emerging markets maintain financial stability since the Asian crises. IMF publications have discussed this development, as well as the lack of long-term effectiveness of controls on capital flows.[59] Moreover, a recent review of IMF exchange rate policy advice by the IMF's Independent Evaluation Office (IEO) noted that in cases where that advice was provided it favored more exchange rate flexibility.[60]

The cross-border aspects of the crises made it obvious that action was needed, not only at the national level but also internationally. Also, the close links between various segments of financial systems (such as insurance and banking) suggested that the financial sector had to be looked at as a whole. This differed from the approach countries have traditionally taken to regulate and supervise the financial sector. Notwithstanding the increasing globalization of financial flows and institutions, prudential supervision and regulation was—and remains—a matter reserved to nation-states, as part of their sovereign powers, although these national supervisors often meet in international committees or associations, to exchange information and coordinate their action. In addition, the traditional model split regulation and supervision responsibilities among various authorities, each covering one segment of the financial sector (for example, one agency would supervise banks, and another insurance).

The crises strengthened the call for internationally accepted standards to be observed by the various segments of the financial sector. These standards sought to ensure that financial systems followed some common principles that would make them sounder.

The role of the Bretton Woods institutions

The members of the IMF and the World Bank felt that these agencies had a major role to play in improving crisis prevention. The crises had highlighted the fact that financial sector distress in one country could quickly lead to macroeconomic instability that would often spill over to other nations. Thus, helping members preserve financial sector stability was a key concern of the IMF. Moreover, a well-functioning financial system can help in mobilizing and allocating savings, thus contributing to economic development—a key concern of the World Bank. Also, both institutions had valuable expertise. For many years they had been working with their members to improve the functioning of financial systems all over the world. In particular, in the 1960s, the IMF had begun a program of technical cooperation to help newly independent states set up central banks. That work continued and its scope broadened over the years. It was greatly expanded in the early 1990s, when, first, countries in Central and Eastern Europe and, later, those in the former Soviet Union decided to adopt market-orientated reforms. At that point, the IMF organized a collaborative effort with a large number of central banks and supervisory agencies to assist those countries adapt their financial systems and financial sector authorities, so that they could meet the needs of the transforming economies. The World Bank also set up programs to help in that direction.

Since both the IMF and the World Bank were interested in strengthening the international financial structure—including the financial sectors of each of their members—coordinated action seemed appropriate. Thus, the two institutions decided to launch a joint program, the Financial Sector Assessment Program (FSAP) in 1999. After a one-year pilot phase, which comprised 12 countries, the Executive Boards of the IMF and the World Bank decided to make the program permanent and open to all their membership. Several reasons supported the inclusion of advanced economies, even though the crises of the 1990s had originated in emerging markets and developing countries. First, all countries can benefit from a rigorous and independent review of the functioning of their financial institutions, particularly if done by their peers—as is the case of the FSAP. Second, developed countries have also suffered financial sector crises at various points in history. Third, many financial institutions with headquarters in developed countries have important operations abroad and thereby the potential to affect other countries' economies. Thus, it is of interest to the whole international community to be informed about the soundness of the financial sector and supervisory arrangements in those countries. Fourth, the size of financial systems in developed countries implies that even small improvements can have a payoff that exceeds the cost of an evaluation like the FSAP. Fifth, having developed countries subject themselves to FSAP evaluations takes away the stigma that could be attached to participation in the program if it was open only to countries deemed likely to be vulnerable. Finally, if the program is supposed to inform IMF surveillance—which is mandatory for the whole membership—it would be awkward to exclude any one category of countries.

The IMF and the World Bank designed the program as a cooperative effort involving their whole membership. But although the IMF or the World Bank may encourage a country to participate, the member has to volunteer to be assessed.[61] The cooperative nature of the FSAP goes way beyond the cooperation between the Bretton Woods institutions and the member being assessed. On the assessment side, many other organizations participate. Other international bodies (such as the Basel Committee)[62] have issued most of the standards assessed in the FSAP. Moreover, the assessment teams have routinely included outside experts, most of whom are staff released by their parent central bank or supervisory agencies for a specific assignment. This arrangement has provided extremely valuable up-to-date expertise, while preserving full IMF/World Bank accountability for the program.

The FSAP seeks to assess the stability and degree of development of a country's financial sector, to identify vulnerabilities and shortcomings and to suggest ways to address them. It is not intended—nor could it be—to pass judgment on the soundness of individual financial institutions. Its findings are intended to (a) help national authorities improve the country's financial system; (b) inform the rest of the IMF/World Bank membership of significant issues; and (c) if the report is published, to help market participants make more informed decisions. The results are integrated with the macroeconomic analysis the IMF staff regularly undertakes, and are summarized in a paper submitted to the IMF Executive Board, typically to conclude the regular surveillance discussions with the member. Indeed, this integration with the rest of the macroeconomy is one of the major advantages of the program.

What is done in an FSAP and how?

Once the IMF and the World Bank jointly agree to a country's request for an FSAP, a team is assembled to carry out the work.[63] The team leader discusses with the member the scope and the detailed modalities. The scope depends on what the staffs of the IMF and the World Bank believe is appropriate to get a clear picture of the financial sector's stability and development needs, while taking into account the authorities' preferences. As regards the modalities, in addition to the desk work done from Washington, at least one visit to the country takes place. The desk work includes the analysis of data and answers to questionnaires filled by the country authorities.

The fieldwork is crucial. The team meets with senior officials (typically ministers and the heads of the central bank and of major supervisory and/regulatory agencies) and with market participants (such as banks and securities companies). The team follows a clear diagnostic structure that relies on quantitative and qualitative tools, as depicted in Box 9.1.

The financial sector indicators include data on asset quality, equity, liquidity, profitability, indebtedness of the corporate and household sectors, and any other information that the FSAP team may deem useful to analyze actual or potential vulnerabilities of a particular system, and its resilience to shocks. Getting the appropriate information is not easy. Data definitions are often inconsistent across countries and across time, making comparisons difficult. Moreover, financial positions can change very rapidly, making information obsolete. Thus, teams need to complement balance sheet information with market data and discussions with market participants.

Stress tests and sensitivity analysis are key analytical tools. They test how the system would react to various shocks, such as an increase in

Box 9.1 FSAP methodology

A. Quantitative tools

- Financial sector indicators
- Stress tests and vulnerability analysis

B. Qualitative tools

- Standards and codes
- Setup for crisis prevention and management

interest rates, a devaluation of the currency or a recession. The shocks are calibrated to be large but not implausible; they are not predictions. The tests focus on macroeconomic events to which the whole financial system is exposed. Thus, they differ from other tests that financial institutions routinely do, which often assume that a shock affects only a particular institution.

The FSAP team works closely with the national authorities and financial institutions in the design and execution of the tests, and assesses the plausibility of the results, which are then presented in FSAP documents in a way that preserves the confidentiality of individual institutions' data.

The qualitative analysis evaluates the institutional setup: is it geared to prevent systemic distress, and if a crisis occurs is it able to resolve it with minimal disruption and cost? The analysis of observance of standards and codes, and the peer review of regulations and practices are key pieces of the qualitative analysis. Those standards and codes comprise general principles that specialized bodies—such as the Basel Committee on Banking Supervision—have adopted and the IMF and World Bank Boards have endorsed (Table 9.1). They help in the diagnostic and serve as benchmarks of the quality of supervisory practices and the institutional setup. The staffs of the IMF and the World Bank, in consultation with the authorities of the country involved, decide which assessments would be most effective to carry out in a given FSAP, since assessing all of them in every case would be too costly for both the country and the assessor team.

Those norms cover a broad set of issues. For instance, the 25 Core Principles for Effective Banking Supervision "are globally agreed minimum standards for banking regulation and supervision, covering a wide range of aspects including areas such as licensing, ownership of banks, bank capital adequacy, risk management, consolidated supervision, ways to deal with problematic situations in banks, and the division of tasks and responsibilities between home and host authorities."[64] To facilitate the assessment—and make it as objective and consistent across countries as possible—the IMF, the World Bank, and other national and international bodies have jointly developed assessment methodologies that complement the principles. However, highly skilled assessors are still required. Different national circumstances mean that a "cookie-cutter" approach to the assessment would be disastrous.[65] The task of the assessors is not to tick off boxes indicating the degree of compliance, but to understand how well the design and implementation of a system meets the objectives of the standard or code being assessed. Thus, they

Table 9.1 Standards covered in FSAPs

Banking supervision	Basel Committee's *Core Principles for Effective Banking Supervision* (BCP)
Securities	International Organization of Securities Commissions' (IOSCO) *Objectives and Principles for Securities Regulation*
Insurance	International Association of Insurance Supervisors' (IAIS) *Insurance Supervisory Principles*
Payments and securities	Committee on Payments and Settlements Systems (CPSS)
Settlement systems	*Core Principles for Systemically Important Payments Systems* and CPSS-IOSCO Joint Task Force's *Recommendations for Securities Settlement Systems*
	Anti–money laundering and combating the Financing of Terrorism Financial Action Task Force's (FATF's) *40 + 8 Recommendations*
Corporate governance	OECD's *Principles of Corporate Governance*
Accounting	International Accounting Standards Board's *International Accounting Standards (IAS)*
Auditing	International Federation of Accountants' *International Standards on Auditing*
Transparency	International Monetary Fund's *Code of Good Practices on Transparency in Monetary and Financial Policies*

need to exercise judgment in deciding, first, how a particular principle applies to a given system and, second, whether the arrangements in place meet the objectives of the principle.

The FSAP team obtains inputs from many sources to assess the observance of standards and the overall soundness of the system. It collects data and holds meetings with the local authorities and market participants. Sometimes it also visits supervisory authorities in third countries if, because of links between financial institutions in both countries, they have information useful for the FSAP. The team looks not only at what regulations say but also how they are implemented. Moreover, while a different standard or code applies to each segment of the financial system (that is, the BCP for banking, the IOSCO standard for securities, and so on), the experts work together to integrate those separate analyses into a complete view. This is particularly important given the financial linkages between the segments.

The FSAP team discusses its preliminary assessment with the authorities and with IMF and World Bank staff members in Washington. In particular, to facilitate the integration of the financial sector analysis with the rest of the economy in this process, the team works closely with the IMF staff in charge of analyzing the macroeconomic situation of the country.

The team produces several documents. A Financial Sector Stability Assessment (FSSA), which includes reports on the observance of standards and codes (ROSCs), is included in the documents that are presented to the IMF Board, usually as part of the regular surveillance discussion but sometimes as part of a review of a loan to the country. Moreover, the main conclusions are also woven into the staff report that discusses the overall macroeconomic situation. In addition, some documents are provided to the authorities only (a detailed assessment of observance of each standard and code included in that particular FSAP, and an aide-mémoire with the team's analysis and broad evaluation). The IMF and the World Bank welcome the publication of most of the documents, but national authorities make the final decision.[66] More and more countries are choosing to publish FSAP documents.[67]

Results of the program

The program has succeeded in attracting the interest of the members of the IMF and the World Bank and in making a strong contribution both to the policy debate and to the implementation of policies on financial sector issues. Although participation is voluntary, 111 initial evaluations and 27 updates had been completed as of end-2007. Since this number includes two monetary unions, a total of 123 jurisdictions have been covered at least once, since the Central African Economic and Monetary Community (CEMAC) comprises six countries and the Eastern Caribbean Currency Union (ECCU) six countries and two British territories (Table 9.2). In addition, a number of other countries have initial FSAPs or updates in process or have indicated their interest in participating. Table 9.2 also shows that participation runs across the whole gamut of economic and financial development, although with differences among regions. In Europe and the Western Hemisphere, most countries have been assessed, while participation falls off in Asia and Africa. Moreover, some major financial systems, like those of the United States and China have yet to be evaluated. Some of these

Table 9.2 Participation in initial FSAP assessments and updates[a]

(As of end-December 2007)		
Albania	Iran[b]	Sierra Leone
Algeria	Ireland[b]*	Singapore
Armenia*	Israel	Slovak Republic*
Australia	Italy	Slovenia*
Austria	Jamaica	South Africa[b]*
Azerbaijan	Japan	Spain
Bahrain	Jordan	Sri Lanka*
Bangladesh	Kazakhstan[b]*	Sudan
Barbados	Kenya	Sweden
Belarus	Korea	Switzerland*
Belgium	Kuwait	Tanzania
Bolivia	Kyrgyz Republic*	Trinidad and Tobago
Bosnia and Herzegovina	Latvia	Tunisia*
Botswana	Lebanon[b]*	Turkey
Brazil	Lithuania	Uganda*
Bulgaria	Luxembourg	Ukraine
Cameroon[b]	Macedonia, FYR	United Arab Emirates*
Canada[b]	Madagascar	United Kingdom
CEMAC[c]	Malta	Uruguay
Chile	Mauritania	Yemen
Colombia[b]*	Mauritius*	Zambia
Costa Rica	Mexico*	
Croatia	Moldova	
Czech Republic	Morocco	
Denmark	Mozambique	
Dominican Republic	Namibia	
ECCU[d]	Netherlands	
Ecuador	New Zealand	
Egypt*	Nicaragua	
El Salvador[b]*	Nigeria	
Estonia[b]	Norway	
Finland	Oman	
France	Pakistan	
Gabon	Paraguay	
Georgia*	Peru*	
Germany	Philippines	
Ghana*	Poland*	
Greece	Portugal	
Guatemala*	Qatar	
Guyana	Romania	
Honduras	Russia	
Hong Kong SAR	Rwanda	
Hungary[b]**	Saudi Arabia	
Iceland*	Senegal*	
India[b]	Serbia	

Source: IMF.

*One update; **two updates; [a]As defined as when the IMF Board has discussed the FSSA; [b]The initial assessment was a part of the pilot program; [c]The Central African Economic and Monetary Community (CEMAC) comprises Cameroon, Central African Republic, Chad, Congo, Equatorial Guinea, and Gabon; [d]The Eastern Caribbean Currency Union (ECCU) comprises six IMF members: Antigua and Barbuda, Dominica, Grenada, St. Kitts and Nevis, St. Lucia, St. Vincent and the Grenadines, and two British territories, Anguilla and Montserrat.

differences are going to be reduced once the IMF and the World Bank complete ongoing evaluations and carry out evaluations for those countries that have already committed to participate in 2008 and 2009.[68] These differences in participation mostly reflect differences in the timing of members' decision to volunteer for an FSAP evaluation, since the IMF has been keen to assess all major financial systems and to have a balanced regional distribution.

The report of the IEO (2006) is probably the most comprehensive analysis of the program's impact. To carry out its assessment, the IEO interviewed country authorities, standard setters, and various other sources; collected information both in Washington and overseas; and carried out analytical work. As regards the program's influence on members' policy debate, the IEO noted:

- the greatest impact was on within-government dialogue and in supporting the authorities' position vis à vis the legislature;
- the authorities highly valued having an independent, external assessment of their country's financial system;
- the impact on the policy debate included also advanced economies, where officials particularly valued the FSAP's ability to raise issues that are highly sensitive domestically; and
- the authorities particularly welcomed the interaction with the FSAP team.

While the report notes that the use of the FSAP in public debate had been limited, it finds exceptions to that, of which the most notable at the time was the FSSA discussion of the "three-pillar system" in Germany (described in Box 9.3). However, some later FSAPs, like the one for Spain, also prompted significant public discussion.

The IEO study also recognized the FSAP's important role in improving the assessment of financial sector risks. For instance, following their participation in an FSAP, several countries began to do stress tests on their financial systems, extended them beyond banking, or refined their stress-testing methodologies. This contribution of the FSAP was evident not only in developing countries but also in developed and emerging market economies.

Countries have implemented many reforms following FSAP evaluations. The IEO report classifies them into the following categories: (1) changes in financial legislation or regulations (such as banking laws), (2) changes in the institutional arrangements (for example, moving insurance supervision from a ministry to an independent supervisor, as in Ireland), (3) acceleration of broader financial sector reforms (for example, reform of the payments system, as in Mexico), and (4) introduction of new products or practices in financial stability (for example, financial stability reports, changes in stress testing methodologies). To illustrate this point, Boxes 9.2, 9.3, and 9.4 summarize three FSAP cases (Mexico, Germany, and Tanzania). Moreover, countries that have volunteered for an FSAP or plan to do so (such as Thailand) often undertake reforms in the run-up to the evaluation.

The FSAP's impact goes beyond the financial sector. The program highlights those conclusions that have macroeconomic relevance. These can cover many issues. For instance, a weak, poorly supervised financial system can jeopardize an economy's successful integration with the rest of the world. Combining the financial sector analysis with the rest of the economic analysis of a country is not easy. The linkages

Box 9.2 Mexico: A timely FSAP

A new administration took office in Mexico in December 2000, and the incoming authorities wished to vigorously reform the financial system and its regulation and supervision, to strengthen it and prevent future crises. They wanted to discuss their plans and get additional inputs from independent sources; they requested an FSAP.

There was a momentum for reform: Mexico's financial system was coming out of a serious crisis, which started with the devaluation of the peso in December 1994. Owing to the crisis, a large number of banks had had to be closed or taken over by the deposit insurance scheme. The direct fiscal cost of the crisis was estimated at more than 19 percent of GDP as of mid-1999, which does not include the economic cost of the associated sharp drop in GDP.* Thus, strengthening the system and preventing future crises were key objectives of the authorities, which underpinned their request for the FSAP.

Diagnostic work and implementation of reforms were quick. After intensive discussions in Mexico City in March 2001, the team presented its preliminary recommendations. In April, Congress passed a package of legislation that allowed the reform to proceed, enhancing supervisory practices, allowing additional banking operations, restricting bank lending to connected borrowers, strengthening corporate governance, and facilitating the development of mutual funds. Mexico continued to improve the functioning of its financial system, in line with the recommendations of the FSAP. The IMF followed up on this progress. Each year, the Article IV consultation reports identified the measures taken, and the IMF Executive Board provided comments and encouragement to the authorities.

In 2006, the authorities requested an FSAP update, to review the progress made and suggest areas for further improvement. The update confirmed the notable achievements made since the initial FSAP, which included

- more effective banking supervision and securities regulation, leading to stronger observance of standards. This included the move to risk-based banking supervision, enhanced transparency, stronger legal powers of the regulator, and better market infrastructure.
- removal of significant payments system shortcomings, such as the elimination of uncollateralized central bank lending, and improvement of the legal and oversight frameworks.
- state-of-the-art regulation and supervision of insurance.
- increased competition among private managers of pension funds.
- improved functioning of the housing finance market.
- better procedures to deal with problem or insolvent banks.
- preparation of legislation to improve anti-money laundering practices.

While the FSAP team suggested measures to make further progress, what was done between 2001 and 2006 adds up to an impressive record of reform. The strong commitment and determination of the authorities were essential for the success. The FSAP helped in providing a sounding board for their plans and suggestions that identified areas for improvement and facilitated the implementation of the reforms. Follow-up during the Article IV process provided further inputs and the encouragement and recognition of the international community to the authorities' efforts.

*Hoelscher, David, Marc Quintyn, and others, 2003, *Managing Systemic Banking Crises*, IMF Occasional Paper No. 224 (Washington: International Monetary Fund).

Box 9.3 Germany—The FSAP in an industrial country

Germany's FSAP illustrates how the FSAP—and indeed the IMF—can contribute to policy debate in an industrial country. It also shows how the results of the FSAP can be integrated into macroeconomic policy discussions and be followed up through time.

The assessment took place in 2003. As is normally the case, the team covered not only issues common to all financial systems but also some specific to the country. Two were particularly highlighted in Germany: the light supervision of reinsurance and the three-pillar banking system.

While Germany was not alone in having a light supervision of reinsurers, the fact that it is the home for some of the largest reinsurers warranted strengthening that supervision.

The three-pillar banking system divides banks into three segments that differ both in ownership and purpose: public sector banks, cooperatives, and commercial banks. It also includes mutual support mechanisms for pillar members. To help make the system more efficient, the FSAP recommended allowing institutions in all the segments to decide on their capital composition—including incorporating private capital, and to remove barriers to competition, such as the regional principle which sets limits on territorial expansion of some types of banks.

The German authorities found the FSAP helpful. In particular, they welcomed the IMF's support for strengthening the regulation and supervision of reinsurers. But it was the discussion of the three-pillar system that attracted most public interest. The system has a long tradition in Germany but various factors—including the procompetition stance of the European Commission (EC)—made a critical examination highly topical. Even before the team completed its work, several press reports argued in favor of or against modifying the system. This attention continued throughout the period the FSAP was being carried out and even after. Also, IMF staff was invited to participate in some of those public discussions.

The IMF policy dialogue with the German authorities on financial sector issues continued after the FSAP. All the staff reports prepared for the subsequent Article IV consultations reported on financial sector discussions and on the implementation of the FSAP recommendations.

The authorities took several actions in line with the FSAP. One was to pass legislation to strengthen the supervisory authority's power to regulate and supervise insurance companies. Another was to regularly present stress-test results in the Financial Stability Report. Also, some relaxation of the three-pillar system took place—such as allowing a private buyer of Sparkasse Berlin to keep the "Sparkasse" name (previously reserved exclusively to public sector entities) and incorporating private capital into some Landesbanken. Moreover, there have been some openings to private capital investment in traditionally state-owned banks—like the announced public offering of HSH Nordbank. This process has been helped by the phasing out of the state guarantees on state-banks' borrowing, in compliance with an EC finding that such guarantee impeded competition. Still, some impediments to efficiency criticized in the FSAP remain—like the regional principle and constraints on the incorporation of private capital to the banks structured as cooperatives or state-owned institutions.

Box 9.4 Tanzania: An FSAP focused on developmental issues

While stability is a prerequisite for development, Tanzania's FSAP illustrates how the program can help countries deal with other developmental issues and how it can be integrated with the IMF's financial support and technical cooperation program, as well as with the assistance that the World Bank and other donors provide.

The World Bank and IMF team visited Tanzania in 2003 and its conclusions were integrated not only with the overall economic diagnosis but also with the program of financial support that the IMF had agreed with the member. The recommendations included

- reviewing legislation to facilitate the use of land as collateral,
- reviewing unduly constraining regulations on credit extension and loopholes on offshore exposures,
- moving to risk-based supervision,
- phasing out government lending to the private sector,
- strengthening microfinance institutions,
- creating a credit registry to facilitate the assessment of creditworthiness, and
- improving the management of system liquidity.

The IMF and World Bank staff also helped develop an action plan that fleshed out the FSAP prescriptions, and both institutions supported implementation with technical cooperation. Moreover, while the World Bank provided loans to finance-related financial sector projects, the authorities included some key elements of the reform in their commitments in the financial support program they agreed with the IMF.

between that sector and the rest of the economy are often hard to draw in a very precise way. In particular, rapid financial innovation makes estimation difficult.

Given the importance of the financial sector for economic policy, the IMF has been devoting more attention to it in its regular surveillance discussions with member countries. Thus, many of the tools used in FSAPs, as well as staff with expertise in financial sector issues, have been included in the regular surveillance consultations with member countries. The documents prepared for the 2007 consultation with Israel (which are available on the IMF Web site) provide a good example of what can be done.

In addition to its impact on individual countries, the FSAP has also made important contributions at the multilateral level, both at the Bretton Woods institutions and beyond. The information gathered by the teams feed into the IMF's regional and global analyses, such as regional economic reports and, most importantly in the *Global Financial Stability Report* (GFSR) and the *World Economic Outlook* (WEO), two well-established biannual publications. These last two documents provide the basis for the discussions of the world economic situation that take place at the Annual and Spring ministerial meetings of the IMF. In particular, the GFSR draws insights from both the analyses of major financial markets—which transactions go far beyond the country where the market is located—and that coming from aggregating the analyses of individual countries and regions. Much of the latter information comes from the FSAP. The World Bank's analysis of development issues also benefits from the insights gained from this program.

The insights from the FSAP also impact other international organizations, in particular those that set financial-sector standards. Most of these organizations set the standard but do not carry out assessments themselves. As noted earlier, practically all FSAPs include standards assessments, which have fostered better observance of those norms.[69] The endorsement of standards and codes by the

Executive Boards of the IMF and the World Bank has also facilitated acceptance by countries that are not represented in the organizations that drafted some of those norms.

In addition, the IMF and the World Bank also influence the contents of the standards and of the assessment methodologies. The staffs of the two institutions routinely participate in the discussions that lead to the adoption or reform of financial sector standards. They have brought to these discussions their experience in assessing observance, frequently distilled in special studies prepared by the staffs of the IMF and the World Bank, which also identify common shortcomings in financial systems—such as a lack of independence and resources of supervisors, and insufficient disclosure of information. Moreover, staffs from national central banks and supervisors—some of which are also members of standard setters—participate in FSAP teams, thereby acquiring first-hand knowledge of practices and issues in other systems. Through all this work, the IMF and the World Bank have helped standard-setters in improving and disseminating their principles and norms.

The IMF and the World Bank have also published a handbook on financial-sector assessment, to disseminate information on key issues and sound practices on the topic.[70] This should help member countries in carrying out self-assessments as well as give guidance on policy issues related to the financial sector.

The IMF has hosted conferences on financial stability and workshops on stress testing and other technical issues, and its staff participates in similar activities hosted by other international organizations—like the Financial Stability Forum,[71] national authorities, and private organizations. In addition, there are many informal exchanges of views among experts in the IMF, the World Bank, and other supervisory agencies, including many that sit in standard-setting bodies. Staff members also write papers on their experience and on analytical issues regarding financial sector stability.

All these activities help to disseminate knowledge among the membership and facilitate the exchange of views on policies and techniques that can enhance financial stability. This is particularly important given the fast-changing financial landscape, where new instruments and institutions constantly appear in the market.

It is important to keep in mind what the FSAP cannot do. While it can identify risks and vulnerabilities to the system, it cannot assess the health of any individual institution. It was never an objective of the program to do the latter and FSAP teams lack the mandate, resources, and legal powers to obtain and process the information that would allow such assessments.[72] It can—and it does—assess whether the supervisory authority has systems in place to make it possible for it to discharge its duties in assessing the health of an individual institution.

Ways to strengthen the IMF's contribution to preventing financial crises

The crises of the 1990s illustrated two points: that weak financial systems can trigger and amplify a crisis, even in countries with otherwise prudent economic policies, and that financial crises cross borders easily. Thus, joining efforts at the national and international level and paying more attention to the financial sector seemed the way to go. To do its part, the IMF has added new tools to help the international community in preventing financial crises. In particular, the joint IMF/World Bank FSAP has been a key component of these efforts. It has helped members to identify potential vulnerabilities and upgrade their financial systems and their prudential regulation to make those systems more resilient. As part of its efforts to strengthen multilateral surveillance, the IMF has strengthened its dialogue with market participants, and has revamped its biannual *Global Financial Stability Report* to facilitate the exchange of views among members about risks to stability.

Despite all the progress made since the 1990s, the financial turmoil of 2007/08 that originated in the US subprime mortgage market makes it evident that crisis prevention must be an ongoing effort in all countries, including in particular in large industrial countries. Constant financial innovation has benefits but also brings up new forms of risk, which are often difficult to assess even by sophisticated analysts. Thus, both market participants and policy makers need to keep up with this process, in particular by updating their methods and practices on risk management and supervision, so as to ensure that the system has the capacity to price risk properly and the capacity to bear it without unduly endangering systemic stability.

Furthermore, there is an important asymmetry in today's financial world. The power to regulate and supervise financial institutions is vested in national authorities, while ever more financial sector transactions transcend national borders or are carried out by multinational institutions. Moreover, strong competition in a globalized financial market makes it difficult—and of limited effectiveness—for any individual supervisor to act if others do not.

In this environment, the IMF can make an even more substantial contribution to the prevention and management of financial crises, drawing on the unique resources it can bring to the table. In particular, these include a practically universal membership, a legal mandate to visit and hold regular consultations with all its members, experience in working cooperatively with many parties, and a vast experience in dealing with financial sector issues in member countries. In addition, its expertise in integrating financial sector issues with the macroeconomic aspects allows the IMF to provide a unique perspective on these matters. Specifically, the IMF can bring out in its publications, and policy discussions, the linkages between the financial sector and the macro economy. Thus, it can help in addressing them by working on both sides of the problem. It can use both its bilateral and multilateral surveillance dialogues (including the newly developed multilateral consultations) to help countries devise policies that deal with macroeconomic imbalances. And it can work with other organizations and forums, like the Financial Stability Forum and standard setters, to review regulations and supervisory techniques to make financial systems more resilient. It can organize conferences, workshops, and informal meetings and participate in similar activities organized by others, helping both in creating new knowledge and disseminating available information on ways to enhance financial stability and efficiency, and in crisis management.

The IMF has been doing all or most of these things under its medium-term strategy, but the pace should be accelerated and the focus sharpened on the two areas where the institution has a comparative advantage: the linkage between the financial sector and the macro economy, and the integration of the work being done by different agencies and forums all over the world. But the IMF cannot do this on its own: it needs strong support from its membership, both politically and in terms of resources.

Strengthening Financial Sectors and Preventing Crises

José Viñals[2]

This clear and concise chapter by Tomás J. Baliño gives an accurate idea of the important role that the IMF has played in recent years to strengthen the financial sector of its members and thus prevent crises. As the author indicates, the work of the IMF in this domain improved significantly after the Asian Crisis of the late 1990s, and took the form of the so-called FSAPs. His chapter very neatly describes and analyzes the methodology, principles, and likely impact of FSAPs, taking into account also the experience to date.

As purported by economic principles and widely corroborated by experience, a sound and efficient financial system is key to achieve sustained economic growth and to minimize the intensity of cyclical fluctuations. As far as growth is concerned, a soundly functioning financial system, which efficiently performs its role of intermediating between savers and investors, helps achieve a better allocation of resources in the overall economy and ultimately fosters total factor productivity and growth. As for cyclical fluctuations, a solid financial system is by definition less crisis prone. On the one hand, it reduces the likelihood and potential costs associated with financial shocks and, on the other, it helps reduce the overall economic costs arising from real shocks insofar as it acts as a buffer.

The FSAP program, jointly launched by the IMF and the World Bank in 1999, is a most important initiative aimed at identifying potential financial vulnerabilities and preventing financial crises. We can all benefit from the initiative: the country undergoing the FSAP, the IMF, and other countries. For the country concerned, regardless of

[2] Mr. Viñals is Deputy Governor of the Bank of Spain. He holds a Ph.D. in economics from Harvard University and has taught at Stanford University.

whether it is a developing nation, an emerging market economy, or an advanced economy, the main benefit of the FSAP is that it provides a comprehensive, independent, and objective external assessment of its financial system performed by a high-quality team of professionals with unique expertise on the subject. In addition, as I had the opportunity to observe during the FSAP that the IMF carried out for Spain in 2005–6, the exercise gives the domestic institutions participating in it a strong incentive to develop and improve methods and tools for assessing financial system soundness, which remain useful long after the FSAP is completed. Another important benefit arises from the interactions triggered among the different domestic agencies taking part in the exercise, and between them and the IMF's team. It also helps raise questions that were never asked before, contemplating solutions that were not envisaged beforehand, stimulating public discussion on key financial issues, and obtaining external support and encouragement to take the appropriate policy measures to enhance the solidity of the domestic financial system.

From the IMF's viewpoint, the most significant benefit to be derived from FSAPs, as also acknowledged by Baliño, is that they provide for a more thoroughgoing analysis of the economy of the individual country insofar as financial and real issues are better brought together. In practice, this requires that the results of FSAPs be adequately integrated into the traditional Article IVs that the IMF routinely carries out as part of its bilateral surveillance. However, it must be acknowledged that this integration is not always easy, since FSAPs may not be updated frequently enough to take into account changes of potential importance in the financial system.

So far, I have simply commented on the benefits to be had from FSAPs from the standpoint of bilateral surveillance. However, as the current turmoil in international financial markets vividly demonstrates, FSAPs can be highly valuable too regarding surveillance at the multilateral or global level, with clear benefits for the whole membership. Indeed, as the author indicates, the rich information collected by FSAPs, when suitably added up, can be a powerful vehicle for the identification of risks to the global economy and thus for the prevention of financial crises. In this regard, it may be advisable that when FSAPs are carried out in systemic countries, attention be paid not only to assessing the soundness of the domestic financial sector but also to examining through suitably designed stress-tests how domestic problems may impact on other countries in order to better grasp the possible risks to the global financial system. In turn, the design of stress tests of advanced countries too should take into account how financial problems originating outside can affect their own financial sectors. Beyond this, other potential innovations—such as devoting special attention to systemic countries in the FSAPs or performing more frequent updates of FSAPs—may be limited in these cases by the voluntary nature of the program, by the need to preserve even-handedness in the IMF's affairs and by the limited resources available to pursue these activities within the institution.

I fully share Baliño's view that improving the IMF's surveillance is a key priority for the institution, in respect of both bilateral and global surveillance. Indeed, the globalization of financial markets is a key element of today's financial landscape, and as the current turmoil shows, financial problems can spread rapidly from one country to other parts of the world, causing a lot of trouble for the global economy. The introduction of the FSAP program was the most significant step in enhancing the capacity of the IMF to help prevent financial crises. Moreover, the recent launching of the medium-term strategy by the IMF, and its declared goals of putting financial issues at the center of the institution's work and of improving global financial surveillance are also of paramount importance. Let us hope that the IMF can achieve these objectives in the near future, as this will lead to a sounder and safer international financial system from which all—advanced, emerging, and developing countries alike—will benefit. Tomás Baliño's excellent chapter on the role of the IMF in Strengthening Financial Sectors and Preventing Crises makes a strong case for this endeavor.

10
The IMF Staff's View of the World: The *World Economic Outlook*

Graham Hacche[1]

> *While there are competitors, the comprehensiveness of the Fund analysis tends to make the WEO and ICMR indispensable to anyone interested in an objective and detailed perspective on the global economy and the increasing interdependence among its components.*
>
> —John Crow, Ricardo Arriazu, and Niels Thygesen, *External Evaluation of IMF Surveillance: Report of Group of Independent Experts*[73]

Origins and roles of the *World Economic Outlook* (*WEO*)

For almost three decades, the *WEO* has been a flagship publication of the IMF, gaining the attention of policy makers, economists, and media commentators for its analysis and projections of world economic developments and its assessments and advice on economic policies around the globe. The *WEO* was first published in 1980. At that time the IMF published relatively little, and the then Managing Director, Jacques de Larosière, referred to the *WEO*'s publication, in a preface, as an experiment. It was evidently judged a success, as publication became an annual event, in the spring of the northern hemisphere, until 1984,

[1] The author, currently Deputy Director of the IMF's External Relations Department, was formerly Assistant Director of the Research Department, and headed its division responsible for producing the *WEO* during 1995–99. He wishes to thank, without implicating, Charles Collyns, David Hawley, Flemming Larsen, Michael Mussa, and David Robinson for comments on an earlier draft. Work for the chapter was begun when the author was visiting Nuffield College, Oxford during 2006–7, on a sabbatical from the IMF.

when autumn updates were introduced. Five years later, the autumn updates became full reports, and subsequently "Interim Assessments" also appeared at times of economic crisis. In 2007, regular summer and winter updates of *WEO* projections began to be released, so that *WEO* projections are now published every quarter.

In his preface to the first published *WEO*, Mr. de Larosière stated that the report was being issued "in the name of the staff." Prefaces to subsequent *WEO*s have continued to note that "both projections and policy considerations are those of the IMF staff and should not be attributed to Executive Directors or to their national authorities." This independence from political influence has enabled IMF staff to establish the credibility and standing of the *WEO*. These have also depended, of course, on the quality of the *WEO*'s analysis. But the *WEO* is more than the product of an independent think tank: the *WEO*'s standing is also based on the role of the IMF as the world's central monetary institution and the *WEO*'s role in the IMF's surveillance operations. The IMF's Articles of Agreement call for the institution to conduct both country-level or "bilateral" surveillance over each member country's compliance with its obligations and global or "multilateral" surveillance, which includes the responsibility to "oversee the international monetary system in order to ensure its effective operation" as "a framework that facilitates the exchange of goods, services and capital among countries, and that sustains economic growth." As an internal report, the *WEO* was one of the main instruments of global surveillance since before its external publication began. It provided the basis for discussions and assessments by the IMF's Executive Board of the global economic situation and outlook, and of countries' policies in a global context.

Thus it was as a report for Executive Board discussion that the first, unpublished, *WEO* was produced by the IMF's Research Department in 1969. During the 1970s, the *WEO* became an integral part of the work of the IMF and a regular item on the Board's agenda. Its projections became determined in a process involving country economists in the IMF's area departments as well as the Research Department. Its country coverage broadened from the seven major industrial countries to the world as a whole. And its subject matter expanded from the presentation of projections to the discussion of policy issues and related analytical questions, which drew on the expertise of economists throughout the IMF's staff. Also, beginning in the mid-1970s, the preparation and Board discussion of the *WEO* report were timed to be in advance of meetings of the Interim Committee of finance ministers and central bank governors representing the IMF's member countries, and the

WEO became a regular item on the Committee's agenda. In fact, the *WEO* has for many years usually been at the top of the agenda for the meetings of both the Interim Committee and its successor since 1999, the International Monetary and Financial Committee (IMFC).

The *WEO*'s value and standing benefit not only from its role in the IMF's surveillance operations but also from the process by which it is produced. In this *WEO* process, projections for the world economy are built up from projections for individual countries formulated by experts on the IMF's 185 member countries in the IMF's area departments. Those projections are based partly on assumptions for global variables (like real exchange rates, assumed constant, and the price of oil) set by the Research Department on the basis of the latest information, and partly on the assumption that countries' policies will be maintained on established paths—as indicated, for example, by governments' budget plans and financial markets' projections of policy interest rates. These assumptions promote consistency among the country projections and also make it possible to identify tensions and problems that current policies portend. Meanwhile, the role of the country economists ensures that the projections benefit from the information gained and research conducted in their bilateral surveillance work. When the country projections are first aggregated by the Research Department at the start of a new forecasting round, the results are examined for inconsistencies. Subsequent iterations and interdepartmental discussions lead to revised projections until a final "baseline scenario" is derived that is broadly accepted by the staff as the most plausible projection under the assumptions adopted. This process allows the *WEO* to serve as an anchor to ensure the consistency across countries of the IMF's bilateral surveillance work.

The *WEO* report is written in a similarly collaborative process. It is drafted mainly in the Research Department, but interdepartmental review enables the main authors to benefit from the knowledge and views of economists across the IMF, while the engagement of academic consultants helps ensure that the analysis reflects the latest research outside the IMF. After discussions among the staff, and between the staff and IMF management, the *WEO* report is distributed to the Executive Board for discussion. Information provided, and views expressed, by Executive Directors may then lead to further revisions. In this way, the *WEO* becomes based on expertise that is much broader than that of its main authors, and representative of views more widely held, not only among the staff but also among Executive Directors and the authorities of member countries. In fact, the *WEO* process has often helped to advance discussion and forge consensus on policy issues among the staff and among the membership. But important differences of view often remain, and ultimately the *WEO* represents a consensus of views among the staff. This makes for consistency over time in the views expressed, regardless of the particular views and approaches of the staff working on the *WEO* at any one time—even those of the Economic Counselor and Director of the Research Department, who provides general direction for the *WEO* project, and the Deputy Director of the Research Department and Division Chief who direct the work. Views of Executive Directors expressed in the Board discussion are reflected in the "Concluding Remarks" of the Chairman, which are included as an annex to the *WEO* publication.

The basic rationale for the *WEO* and its use of projections is that the analysis of economic policies, at national and international levels, requires not only an understanding of the current economic situation and recent developments, nationally and globally, but also a soundly based view of future prospects under current policies. Like most other seasoned economic forecasters, however, IMF economists have tended to be modest about their ability to foretell the future, especially their ability to formulate accurate quantitative forecasts or to forecast breaks in trends and the timing of turning points in economic cycles. Economic forecasting is inevitably hampered by natural, political, and technological shocks, and by the complexity and instability of relationships among economic variables, which derive partly from the effects on economic behavior of immeasurable expectations and sentiment and from economists' imperfect understanding of the working of economic and financial systems. IMF staff have often emphasized that *WEO* projections do not even necessarily represent their view of the most likely future outcomes: to be useful for policy analysis they are not unconstrained forecasts, but projections conditional on such assumptions as unchanged policies and real exchange rates—assumptions often recognized as unlikely to hold.

Nevertheless every decade or so since 1988, the Research Department has engaged academic experts to examine whether *WEO* projections have met conventional statistical quality standards and how they compare with forecasts produced elsewhere in the official and private sectors. The results have been mixed. The 1988 and 1997 studies, which examined *WEO* projections for the each of the seven major industrial countries and regional aggregates of other countries, found that they mostly passed conventional statistical tests. For example, the 1988 study found that official forecasts from outside the IMF did not add information that could have improved the *WEO* projections—an indication of their statistical efficiency. But output growth had been persistently overpredicted for industrial countries in the 1970s, and more generally for developing countries, especially in Africa. The latter finding could be explained partly by the use in the *WEO* of projections used in IMF-supported policy programs, which assumed the full implementation of the programs—an assumption that was frequently disappointed. The 1988 and 1997 studies also found that projections of external current account balances had been relatively poor. The 1997 study highlighted the *WEO*'s failure to predict the global recession of the early 1990s—a cyclical downturn that should arguably have been more easily forecast than those of the mid-1970s and late 1980s because, rather than being due to an exogenous (oil price) shock, it appeared to have been endogenously driven. But it also found that errors in *WEO* projections and private sector forecasts were substantially the same. This last finding was confirmed by the 2006 study, which found a more general tendency to overprediction of growth and underprediction of inflation.

In response to the 2006 study, *WEO* reports beginning in April 2006 have included a "fan chart" for world GDP growth, showing confidence intervals around the central projection, estimated on the basis of the *WEO*'s past forecasting record and the staff's assessment of the current distribution of risks. The October 2007 *WEO*, for example, showed a central projection of 4.8 percent for global growth in 2008, with a 50 percent confidence interval of 4.1–5.3 percent. The greater part of the confidence interval is below the central projection, showing that the balance of risks is judged to be tilted to the downside.

A more important purpose of the *WEO* than precise quantitative forecasts is identifying actual and potential problems requiring policy action, including dangers arising from economic imbalances and from unsustainable prices in financial markets. Such warnings and advice are transmitted not only directly to member countries' authorities, including through the IMF's Executive Directors, but also by peer pressure, as countries encourage one another to implement needed policies. Warnings and advice based on the *WEO* can also be transmitted through other international forums than the IMF's Executive Board. The IMF's management and staff participate in a number of these, and are usually invited to lead the discussion on the global situation and outlook by presenting analysis based on the *WEO*. *WEO*-based presentations in other forums began in 1982, when the then Managing Director, Mr. de Larosière, participated in a meeting of finance ministers of the Group of 5 major industrial countries (G-5). Such participation by Managing Directors, in their "personal capacity"—meaning that they could speak independently of the Board—continued after 1986 with the Group of 7 major industrial countries (G-7). The IMF has also frequently contributed to multilateral surveillance discussions in other global groups as well as in various regional forums. Ministerial meetings of this kind are often preceded by preparatory meetings of senior officials or "deputies," in which the IMF's Economic Counselor participates.

The fact that the IMF is invited to provide *WEO*-based analysis as the basis for discussions of the global economy in these forums is testimony to the standing of the *WEO* in the official community, based partly on the unique global reach of the IMF's surveillance operations.

Publication of the *WEO* provides another vehicle for the IMF to influence policy—by contributing to public policy debate—apart from dialogue with country officials and peer pressure. The published *WEO* is also a source of data, information, and analysis for the private sector. It was in the vanguard of the IMF's increasing transparency, enabling the IMF to disseminate the findings of much of its staff's surveillance work for more than 15 years before the IMF's "transparency revolution" (Chapter 8). Dissemination has been enhanced from the beginning by press briefings by the Economic Counselor and other senior authors of the *WEO*, and, since May 1997, by the free provision on the IMF's Web site, www.imf.org, of the *WEO*'s full text and database.

How successful has the *WEO* been? Three external evaluations commissioned by the IMF or its Independent Evaluation Office (IEO) have delivered verdicts. The 1999 *External Evaluation of IMF Surveillance* (by John Crow, Ricardo Arriazu, and Niels Thygesen) found that "IMF multilateral surveillance is of generally high quality, and its work in this area, expressed through the *WEO* and the *ICMR*, received much favorable comment" from those consulted by the evaluators, including government officials, officials of other international institutions, academics, and private sector and NGO representatives. The 2000 *External Evaluation of IMF Research Activities*, by Frederic S. Mishkin, Francesco Giavazzi, and T. N. Srinivasan, reported that "Policymakers and academics told us that certain flagship research products such as the *World Economic Outlook* and the *International Capital Markets Report* were both of high quality and of great relevance to them" and added that "We were also impressed by the quality of these products." The 2006 IEO Report on *Multilateral Surveillance* found that "The *World Economic Outlook* (*WEO*) is especially well regarded" among the IMF's multilateral surveillance products by those consulted by the evaluators. The IEO also found that the *WEO* had "largely succeeded in identifying in a timely way relevant issues for analysis" and that "In terms of identifying relevant global macroeconomic and financial risks, both the *WEO* and *Global Financial Stability Report* (*GFSR*) also compare favorably with similar publications of other international and national bodies."

The remainder of this chapter discusses a few examples of how the *WEO* has provided warnings of dangers ahead; how it has put forward independent and sometimes unwelcome policy advice; and how its analytical work has been directed toward pertinent policy issues. Many issues to which the *WEO* has devoted attention—including the challenges involved in the transition from central planning, and in advancing economic growth and poverty reduction in low-income countries—are necessarily omitted.

Warning of dangers ahead

"If something is unsustainable, it will stop." Herbert Stein (1916–99), Chairman, US Council of Economic Advisers, 1972–74.

"Yes, but it will go on for longer than you expect." Rudiger Dornbusch (1942–2002), Professor of Economics, MIT, 1984–2002.

IMF staff members have not foreseen every economic crisis of recent decades, and they have expected some that never occurred. In any case, it would generally be irresponsible of the staff to be explicit publicly about crises they viewed as likely, because they might thereby themselves help to precipitate them. Nevertheless the *WEO* has, on a number of occasions over the past 28 years, provided warnings that have subsequently been vindicated.[74]

One of the main economic problems of the 1980s was the developing country debt crisis, which erupted in August 1982, lingered for several years, and seemed at times to threaten the global financial system. It was foreshadowed by the June 1981 *WEO*, which pointed to the weak balance of payments positions of oil-importing developing countries as one of the world economy's main adjustment issues. These countries had so far avoided excessive debt, but looking ahead, there was "cause for real concern," given recent increases in global interest rates, these countries' debt service burdens were "bound to grow more rapidly than in the past" and their medium-term prospects were "to say the least, disturbing." Thus policy action was needed by the countries concerned: "In the absence of adjustment measures [many of these countries] would soon find themselves unable to finance their deficits." In fact, they would "incur substantial increases in their debt-service ratios even if successful in implementing comprehensive programs of adjustment." The situation called for adjustment supported by international assistance. But insufficient action was taken to prevent the crisis.

Another major problem of international adjustment that erupted in the 1980s was payments imbalances among the major industrial countries—a US current account deficit of unprecedented size, with counterpart surpluses mainly in Japan and West Germany—and an associated misalignment of the US dollar in relation to other major currencies. The dollar appreciated through the early 1980s, reaching a peak in early 1985. The concurrent widening of the US current account deficit to about 3 percent of GDP, and associated deterioration in the US net foreign asset position (around this time the United States became a net foreign debtor, after many years as a net creditor) made the dollar's exchange rate look increasingly untenable. The April 1984 *WEO* sounded the alarm, referring to exchange rates among the major currencies as a "cause for concern." Noting "grounds for questioning the sustainability of the dollar's level," it expressed concern about a "potential shift out of the dollar" by investors. It argued: "If exchange rates and balance of payments positions are to be restored to more viable positions, policy adaptations are needed." It pointed to the US fiscal deficit as a major source of the problem (see Section 3 below) and called for international policy cooperation, including avoidance of protectionist trade measures.

This presaged two years of unparalleled policy coordination among the major industrial countries, involving official intervention in currency markets as well as macroeconomic and structural policy commitments, aimed partly at an orderly currency realignment. It began with a meeting of G-5 finance ministers and central bank governors in January 1985, which, the subsequent communiqué noted, involved the IMF Managing Director "for a discussion of the economic policies and prospects of the major industrial countries." The communiqué, the first by G-5 finance ministers and governors, noted "their commitment to work toward greater exchange market stability," including through monetary, fiscal, and structural policies, and also reaffirmed their commitment "to undertake coordinated intervention in the markets as necessary." Such intervention, on a large scale, in the next month helped initiate the dollar's return to more sustainable levels. After a pause in the decline, the G-5 forged the Plaza Agreement in September 1985. The communiqué noted that "some further orderly appreciation of the main non-dollar currencies" was desirable, and that this would be promoted by policies to "improve the fundamentals." Statements by each of the countries set out their policy commitments. The April 1986 *WEO* noted, with approval, that the dollar had moved substantially away from its peak; that the Agreement had committed the G-5 to actions that would change fundamentals in a way that would help a lasting currency realignment; and that the United States, in particular, had moved toward a major program of fiscal consolidation.

The seminal international financial traumas of the 1990s were the crises in emerging market economies that began in Mexico in late 1994, continued in Asia in 1997–98, and extended to Russia and Brazil in 1998–99. These crises all erupted when sharp deteriorations of investor sentiment caused large-scale capital outflows, putting massive pressures on the countries' exchange rates. The *WEO* Interim Assessment of December 1997, which reviewed the early stages of the Asian crisis, pointed to the virtual impossibility of forecasting the timing of such crises: "Just two or three months ago, neither economic forecasts nor the pricing of assets in financial markets foretold the depth and breadth of the economic and financial difficulties that have engulfed several southeast and east Asian economies and that affect emerging market economies more generally. It may well be that such developments are inherently unforecastable, as their occurrence and especially their timing are intimately linked to sudden changes in investor sentiment and financial market conditions." But this was not to say that it was impossible to identify the dangers. And, the *WEO* continued: "The risks of financial market turbulence not only could have been perceived: they were perceived, and with sufficient lead time to have permitted constructive actions to limit if not avoid current difficulties ... recent issues of the *World Economic Outlook* have repeatedly warned about the risks of disruptive changes in investor sentiment unless policies were adjusted to address overheating and to reduce unsustainable external imbalances, about the excessive narrowing of risk premiums for emerging markets, and about the dangers associated with financial sector weaknesses."

These warnings had begun as early as October 1992, when the *WEO* cautioned that while recent large capital inflows to a growing number of developing countries were welcome, there was also "need to recognize that capital inflows can be easily reversed and that appropriate policy adjustments are required to prevent overheating." A year later, a *WEO* chapter on "Domestic and Foreign Saving in Developing Countries" elaborated on these concerns: it emphasized the importance for successful economic growth of high domestic saving and policies to ensure adequate returns on domestic investment, and warned against reliance on external financing when these conditions were absent. Warnings continued in 1994, ahead of the crisis in Mexico—where low private saving was a weakness—although there was no specific warning about Mexico. The October 1994 *WEO* warned, in a chapter on "The Recent Surge in Capital Inflows to Developing Countries" that the risks were "likely to be most serious where capital inflows are relatively short-term and where fundamentals may not warrant large inflows on a sustained basis." It stated there were a number of countries where the latter, in particular, was true, either because of insufficient attention to macroeconomic adjustment or because capital inflows were contributing to inflationary pressures or "deteriorations in external current account positions that may not be viable over the medium term." Thailand's large current account deficit was to be a significant factor in the eruption of the Asian crisis. The chapter also warned that the dangers were augmented in many cases by weak financial systems: "Long-standing distortions in financial sectors and inadequate banking supervision and prudential standards could lead banks to engage in excessively risky lending behavior." Financial-sector weaknesses were to be prominent in the Asian crises.

Following the Mexican crisis, capital flows into Asia were generally sustained at high levels, and the October 1995 *WEO* noted a particular concern about risks of overheating in the region. It argued: "A key policy requirement of many of these countries is to strengthen the public sector's financial position in order to reduce pressure on interest rates and hence incentives for capital inflows." The same *WEO* contained a chapter on "Increasing Openness of Developing Countries—Opportunities and Risks," which devoted further attention to the risks of capital-flow reversals, and emphasized weaknesses in domestic banking systems and large short-term inflows as factors aggravating such risks. The May 1996 *WEO* viewed the dangers of overheating in Asia as having subsided in many cases, thanks partly to monetary-policy actions by the countries concerned, but nevertheless pointed to a need for additional measures of restraint in Indonesia, Malaysia, and Thailand. The October 1996 *WEO* again pointed to evidence of excess demand pressures in these countries, including widening current account deficits, and called for tighter fiscal policies. In the last *WEO* before the Asian crisis erupted, published in May 1997, the warnings were given particular prominence. In the first two pages of Chapter I, four main risks to the central projection for global growth were identified. Two of these were directly pertinent: the possibility of disruptions of capital flows to emerging markets, including the possibility of contagion, and the fragility of banking systems, particularly in some emerging market countries, linked to significant exposure to foreign exchange risk. Both these risks soon materialized in Asia.

During the emerging market crises, concerns about global payments imbalances reemerged in the *WEO* after a decade's absence. The October 1998 *WEO* noted a widening of current account imbalances among the major industrial countries—with the US deficit rising back to about 3 percent of GDP—and attributed this mainly to the absorption by the United States of much of the improvement in current account positions in the Asian emerging market economies and the US dollar's strength. It argued that the imbalances were unsustainable; that the inevitable adjustment might not be smooth, particularly if the return of confidence to emerging markets was delayed or if financial markets questioned the sustainability of the US deficit; and that policies in the United States, Japan, and the euro area (the G-3) should aim partly to rebalance their growth rates and reduce their payments imbalances. This was to be a refrain of the *WEO* over the next several years.

Another concern by late 1999 was the levels to which stock market prices had risen, especially in the United States. The "main concern" of the May 2000 *WEO* was a set of imbalances that included "very high stock market valuations around the world" as well as the imbalances of growth and external payments among the G-3 and the associated currency misalignments. The bursting of the high-tech stock market bubble followed in 2000, which led to the US recession of 2001 and the associated global slowdown.

Global imbalances remained a concern when the world economy emerged from the slowdown. The US dollar's trade-weighted average exchange value began to decline in early 2002, but in September 2002 the *WEO* estimated that the US current account deficit had reached 4½ percent of GDP, noted that the dollar was still overvalued, and warned that "an abrupt and disruptive adjustment remains a significant risk." By then, the current account surpluses of several Asian emerging market countries that were no longer suffering private capital outflows were becoming part of the concern. The April 2003 *WEO* projected a US deficit larger than 5 percent of GDP in 2003–4 and called for the global imbalances to be addressed with greater urgency. Meanwhile, the US dollar continued to decline—though not against the pegged currencies of some of the Asian emerging market economies in surplus. In April 2004 the *WEO* noted that the depreciation from early 2002 had helped to reduce the projected US deficit. But it continued to see global imbalances as a "serious concern" and called for a "credible and cooperative strategy" to facilitate their orderly correction.

This call was given added prominence as the imbalances subsequently widened and the dollar's depreciation stalled. In September 2005, the *WEO* showed in an analytical annex how a sharp decline in the demand for US assets, combined with protectionist measures resulting from the imbalances, could lead to a global recession. A year later, the US deficit appeared to be widening further, to 6½–7 percent of GDP, partly owing to the rise in oil prices since 2004; and China's surplus was becoming equally large. But the September 2006 *WEO* also noted some promising signs, especially more balanced growth among the G-3 associated with economic recoveries in Japan and Germany. In 2007, these signs strengthened, and in the October *WEO* the projected US deficit was reduced to below 6 percent of GDP. Moreover, the IMF's first Multilateral Consultation, conducted during 2006–7, had led to agreement by China, the euro area, Japan, Saudi Arabia, and the United States on a framework of policies to achieve an orderly reduction of global imbalances while maintaining global growth. But the October 2007 *WEO* still viewed the imbalances as a "worrisome downside risk for the global economy." In late 2007 and early 2008, the dollar's continuing weakness remained a major feature of financial market developments, and the dangers associated with global imbalances, of which the *WEO* had been warning consistently for almost a decade, continued to loom.

Another set of difficulties that unfolded in a number of economies in early 2008 related to the weakening of housing prices. The *WEO* first signaled this danger in May 2000, when it counted among the "imbalances" of concern a sharp rise in property prices in some economies. The April 2003 *WEO* focused on the danger in a chapter on "When Bubbles Burst," which argued that "price increases for housing in some countries have clearly reached a threshold that can be described as a housing boom." It indicated that international experience showed not only that 40 percent of all housing booms had been followed by busts but also that house price busts had typically led to larger recessions than equity price busts. A year later, the *WEO* noted that the risk of a rise in global interest rates was a particular concern for countries with buoyant property markets, and identified countries at greatest risk. The September 2004 *WEO* included an essay on the "Global House Price Boom," which observed that "House prices in many industrial countries have increased unusually rapidly in recent years and in some cases these increases do not seem to be fully explained by fundamentals." The April 2006 *WEO* reported that house price growth had slowed in many countries, but argued that, nevertheless, in some cases, including the United States, house prices had moved further away from fundamentals. It estimated that over 1997–2005, US home prices had risen by 10–15 percent more than would have been consistent with fundamentals, and viewed the housing market as a "key uncertainty for the US economy." By September 2006, the US housing market was, observed the *WEO*, "cooling quite rapidly," but concern remained that "a sharp adjustment in the housing sector would generate strong headwinds for the US economy." In April 2007, the *WEO* described a US housing market downturn that was deeper than projected earlier, but that still had "a way to run." This conclusion was strengthened in the next *WEO* by a new estimate that the proportion of the 1997–2006 house price rise in the United States that could not be explained by fundamentals was as high as one quarter.

Finally, a danger that a number of industrial countries have begun to face is the aging of their populations, and the associated fiscal pressures arising from public health and pension systems. The *WEO* began as early as 1989 to emphasize the need for fiscal policy in these countries to take these issues into account, and has subsequently, on a number of occasions, analyzed the challenge and considered the design of policies to address it.

"Ruthless Truth-Telling"

> *With countries naturally reluctant to cede any control over their own monetary and fiscal policies, it is likely that the IMF will have as instruments only the powers of analysis, persuasion, and, in Keynes's own favorite words, "ruthless truth-telling."'*
>
> —Mervyn King, Governor of the Bank of England

The authors of the *WEO* have considered their task to be not just conveying warnings about future dangers but also providing policy advice, even when unwelcome, based on their assessment of the current situation and outlook. The *WEO* has often included "ruthless truth-telling" of both kinds. It has provided advice on macroeconomic (fiscal, monetary, and exchange rate), structural, and international policies.

Unsurprisingly, the *WEO* has often argued for increased fiscal discipline. In the early 1980s, when the industrial countries were battling stagflation, it saw budget deficits as a widespread source of problems. They hindered monetary restraint and the control of inflation, or crowded out private investment and net exports by putting upward pressure on interest rates and exchange rates. At this time, with real interest rates in the United States rising to unprecedented levels, the US dollar increasingly overvalued, and the US current account in growing deficit, the *WEO* focused especially on the budget of its largest member. In May 1983 it called for immediate action, saying "in certain countries (notably the United States) policies to bring down budget deficits should be set in place now." In April 1984, the message was even more emphatic: "The single most beneficial change in the world economy in present circumstances would be a perception that the United States was taking action to contain and eventually reduce its underlying fiscal deficit." James Boughton has described how by 1984 "the IMF surveillance process was beginning to have an impact on the domestic debate in the United States, as critics of administration policy cited the IMF's views to buttress their arguments."[75]

In 1985, US fiscal policy moved in the direction urged by the IMF. The April 1985 *WEO* viewed the administration's recent budget proposals as "an important step ... if adopted ... but ... not sufficient," because it would stabilize the government's debt/GDP ratio at too high a level. A supplementary note to the internal version of that *WEO*, on the "Domestic and International Effects of the US Fiscal Position" provided estimates indicating that the benefits of a deficit reduction program would exceed the costs. This was circulated to the IMF's Executive Board but excluded from the published *WEO* because of objections by the US authorities. A year later, the *WEO* considered that "The increased determination of the US administration and Congress to deal effectively with the budget deficit is ... to be welcomed." Nevertheless both then and subsequently, the *WEO* spurred the US authorities on to more ambitious action.

There are many other examples of the *WEO*'s calling for greater fiscal discipline. In the early and mid-1990s, the *WEO* urged most industrial countries to adopt medium-term fiscal consolidation plans that would reverse the growth of public debt, and argued that in some cases debt positions were so adverse that fiscal stringency might actually boost demand and output, even in the short term, by increasing confidence and lowering interest rates. A decade later, despite progress in reducing budget shortfalls, concerns about many industrial countries' fiscal positions have persisted, partly because of emerging demographic pressures. Thus the October 2007 *WEO* called for "a more ambitious fiscal consolidation strategy" in the United States, for the benefit of the US economy and as part of a cooperative strategy to resolve global imbalances. It also observed that in the euro area the goal of medium-term budget balance was "unlikely to be met in a number of countries," including France and Italy, without policy action. With regard to developing countries, in 1992–94 the *WEO* identified fiscal discipline as key to economic success and pressed for reductions in fiscal deficits in much of the developing world. A decade later, in October 2003, a chapter on "Public Debt in Emerging Markets" showed how domestic public debt had grown to industrial country levels in many emerging market countries, and called for measures to reverse the trend.

But the *WEO* has not always favored budget tightening. It has always argued that automatic cyclical variations in the fiscal balance should be allowed to help stabilize the economy, unless the fiscal position is such that even cyclical increases in the deficit would jeopardize the government's credibility or otherwise undermine private sector confidence. And while it has usually been skeptical about the active use of fiscal policy for demand management—not least because of the implementation lags involved and the political problems that tend to confront fiscal tightening (or reversal of fiscal stimulus)—it has supported fiscal expansion in some circumstances. Thus for Japan, *WEO*s in the early to mid-1990s supported not only use of the automatic stabilizers but also fiscal stimulus packages, given the weakness of the economy and the country's strong budgetary position. And when Japan undertook tightening measures in 1997 as the economy began a fragile recovery, the *WEO* was sharply critical. The October 1998 *WEO* included a chapter on "Japan's Economic Crisis and Policy Options"—the only chapter that the *WEO* has ever devoted to one country—which viewed the tightening as "clearly, in hindsight, excessively ambitious," and also considered that it might "reasonably be asked whether the large degree of tightening actually undertaken was a prudent decision," *ex ante*. The *WEO* continued subsequently to support fiscal expansion in Japan as the recovery faltered and the scope for monetary stimulus became very limited. The *WEO* was also in favor of supportive fiscal policy in the Asian crisis countries once the seriousness of the economic contractions was clear. In October 1998, it noted, for instance, that "fiscal deficits have widened appropriately in Korea and Thailand, in face of worsening recessions and to accommodate the need to strengthen social safety nets and finance financial restructuring."

The *WEO*'s advice on monetary policy has been based on the view that it should aim, in normal circumstances, to secure reasonable price stability and to help moderate fluctuations in output and employment.

In the early 1980s, circumstances were not normal and these goals were seen as incompatible. High inflation was still a major problem globally, and the *WEO* emphasized the overriding need to reduce it, particularly through monetary restraint, as a precondition for sustainable economic growth. This meant there was little scope for active countercyclical demand management or "fine-tuning." This was part of the "medium-term strategy" adopted by the industrial countries at the beginning of the decade, along with fiscal consolidation and structural reforms to enhance growth and employment.

Like the monetary authorities of most of these countries, the *WEO* stressed the importance of reducing, and then maintaining at moderate rates, the growth of monetary aggregates, initially to help gain public acceptance of the higher interest rates involved in tighter policy, but also to help discipline fiscal policy and lower both the growth of nominal aggregate demand and inflation expectations. By the mid-1980s, monetary targeting had to be applied more flexibly because of difficulties related to innovation in the financial sector—difficulties that would soon lead most central banks to abandon monetary targets—but by then inflation in the industrial countries had been substantially reduced, to about 3 percent a year in 1987–88. The *WEO* lauded this achievement—while decrying the unsatisfactory progress with the other elements of the medium-term strategy—but as inflation rose again at the turn of the decade, to 4–5 percent, it emphasized the importance of further progress in reducing it, and flirted briefly in 1990–91 with zero inflation as the best objective for monetary policy.

When the world economy emerged from the 1990–91 slowdown with what seemed more settled low inflation, the *WEO* stressed that monetary policy should now be operated more symmetrically through the business cycle, and indicated it could favor monetary easing as well as tightening. The May 1992 *WEO* argued that "during a period of cyclical weakness, moderate and generally declining inflation, and sluggish growth of liquidity—as at present—... the instruments [of monetary policy] can be relaxed. This would not put credibility at risk as long as the resulting decline in interest rates does not lead to an excessive build-up of liquidity, and provided that the medium-term orientation of monetary policy remains firmly geared toward price stability (broadly defined as a low and stable rate of inflation that does not distort economic decisions)."

There followed several occasions when the *WEO* called for more forceful monetary easing by some central banks. In October 1993, for example, the *WEO* argued that in Japan there was "further room" for lowering short-term interest rates, and that in Europe, particularly Germany, "further actions to ease monetary conditions, supported by additional steps to rein in excessive budget deficits in the medium term and other confidence-building measures, are clearly necessary to stem recessionary forces." Again, in May 1996, the *WEO* argued that in Europe, "room for further declines in short-term interest rates ... is suggested by the large margins of slack, subdued price pressures, the strength of exchange rates, and modest growth of monetary aggregates in most cases" and that it was "especially important that the stance of monetary policies provide support for activity as fiscal consolidation efforts continue."[76] When the October 1996 *WEO* commented that the recent easing of monetary conditions in Germany had been appropriate and reiterated the view that "the proper conduct of monetary policy does not consist only of raising short-term interest rates," *The Times* of London carried a headline, "IMF delivers a spectacular recantation of monetarism" over an article on the *WEO* by its apparently surprised economics editor. More recently, in September 2003, the *WEO* argued that in Japan "much more aggressive monetary policy" remained essential to turn around deflation expectations.

The *WEO* has also differed from some central banks on whether and how monetary policy should take account of movements in asset prices. In the early 1990s, it argued that a lesson from the previous decade was that monetary policy needed to pay more systematic attention to asset markets. This was evident both from Japan's boom and bust in asset prices and from the resurgence of inflation that had followed the monetary easing by the US Federal Reserve in response to the October 1987 stock market crash. The October 1992 *WEO* argued that in many countries monetary policy had "inadvertently accommodated speculative increases in asset prices, while the monetary easing that occurred in response to the 1987 stock market crash was not reversed sufficiently quickly." The May 1993 *WEO* included an Annex on "Monetary Policy, Financial Liberalization, and Asset Price Inflation," which argued that "the indicators of inflation used by policymakers to judge the appropriateness of monetary and credit policies did not provide a complete and accurate assessment of the inflationary pressures that were building in the mid-to late 1980s."

These issues returned to the fore later in the 1990s as many asset markets surged while inflation remained subdued. The October 1999 *WEO* set out some policy guidelines, which again stressed the importance of symmetry: "Overheating in asset markets may call for monetary tightening, not only when it threatens an undesirable increase in product-price inflation through its effects on aggregate demand, but also when there is strong evidence that asset prices are rising to more and more unsustainable levels—generating correspondingly higher risks of a correction that would be significantly destabilizing for the economic and financial system. In the latter case, monetary authorities are confronted with one of their most difficult challenges: there is inevitable uncertainty about whether a rise in asset prices is in fact sustainable, since it may have arisen from a lasting change in wealth-holders' preferences or a lasting rise in the rate of return on capital; and furthermore, the effect of monetary tightening on asset prices is uncertain. Moreover, acting to slow or arrest a run-up in asset prices that may be generally popular is likely to be politically difficult, particularly for central banks whose independence is based on a mandate to control CPI inflation. But such action may be necessary to minimize risks of macroeconomic and financial instability that may carry greater costs. And it should be viewed as symmetrical to the response of monetary authorities to provide liquidity and ease monetary conditions in the face of sharp declines in asset prices that threaten disruption of the financial and payments system." This view is still a matter of controversy among central banks (and contrary to the views expressed on several occasions by former Chairman of the US Federal Reserve Board Alan Greenspan). No doubt views will evolve further in light of the recent episodes of house-price deflation in a number of countries.

Another monetary policy controversy arose during the emerging market crises of the 1990s. The *WEO* left no room for doubt that it viewed forceful monetary tightening generally as an essential part of the response to such currency crises. In a notable example of "ruthless truth-telling," the *WEO* Interim Assessment of December 1997 charged the monetary authorities of the crisis countries with much of the responsibility for the difficulties they were facing: "Large depreciations beyond what was needed have been due partly to the failure of policymakers to address problems in advance of the crisis and to move with sufficient force and determination once crisis had hit, undermining confidence throughout the region. Reluctance to tighten monetary policies with sufficient determination and persistence has been particularly important. For economies with substantial foreign currency debts, steep depreciation undermines the solvency of domestic firms and financial institutions as much as, or more than, temporary increases in interest rates. ... Unfortunately, the crisis having been prolonged, the extent of the economic slowdown is likely to be greater than would have been the case if monetary policy had been tightened more forcefully."

On exchange rate policies, the *WEO* has on several occasions pointed to the need for exchange rate adjustments. An important recent example is the *WEO*'s call for greater exchange rate flexibility in a number of Asian emerging market economies, including China, that have been experiencing current account surpluses and large increases in international reserves. This call has been a feature of every *WEO* since April 2003. For example, the September 2003 *WEO* argued that "greater upward exchange rate flexibility in emerging markets in Asia" would not only significantly facilitate the adjustment of global imbalances but would also be desirable for domestic reasons, including the ability to use monetary policy to control inflation, and the establishment of better balance between domestic and external demand. This argument was buttressed by an essay which found that it was difficult to rationalize economically the growth of Asian reserves in the previous 18 months "not least because of the high cost of continuing to pile up low-yielding claims on industrial country governments." By October 2007, China's reserves, in particular, had more than tripled from their end-2003 level, to more than $1.4 trillion. The *WEO* published that month called again for "further upward flexibility of the renminbi" along with a reform of China's exchange rate regime.

The *WEO* has also frequently emphasized the importance, for a country with a pegged exchange rate, of macroeconomic and structural policies that are consistent with the regime and the peg, and that effective resistance of currency pressures will usually require action on these policy fronts. It has viewed official intervention in foreign exchange markets to defend or otherwise influence a currency's exchange value as having only a limited role, but a potentially significant one in some circumstances. When the euro was close to its nadir, in September 2000, the then Economic Counselor, Michael Mussa, put it this way in response to a question at the press conference launching the October 2000 *WEO*: "There have been a large number of studies of the effectiveness of official intervention in influencing exchange rates, and I think the best conclusion from all that evidence is that official intervention, in particular so-called sterilized intervention—that is to say, intervention that does not involve any change in monetary policies in the countries involved in the ... intervention—has not zero but, on the whole, relatively limited effects. It does tend to be significantly more effective when that intervention is coordinated among the major countries and when those countries, in effect, send the signal that it is their joint judgment that markets have taken exchange rates substantially away from fundamentals and that some correction is warranted."

In Mr. Mussa's judgment, although "the circumstances in which the major countries would want to use intervention ... are relatively rare ... they do arise from time to time," and, with the euro that day falling below $0.85 for the first time, "one would sort of have to ask if not now, when?" Three days later, the central banks of the major industrial countries undertook coordinated intervention in defense of the euro. This marked the bottom for the euro, which by early 2008 had risen to about $1.45.

The *WEO* has also viewed the imposition of controls on international capital flows as having only limited value. During 1993–95, several *WEO*s argued that while the most effective responses to surging capital flows into developing countries depended on the circumstances, they were usually likely to include fiscal consolidation and, in some cases, currency appreciation and reform of prudential controls of the financial system. Market-based inflow controls might have a role, but they would carry costs. And broader controls on capital flows, in the words of the May 1995 *WEO*, "are rarely effective in stemming either inflows or outflows over the longer term, especially when they become a substitute for efforts to address macroeconomic imbalances and to correct unsustainable exchange rates." The October 2007 *WEO*'s chapter on "Managing Capital Inflows" reviewed these issues and drew similar conclusions.

While being skeptical about capital controls, the *WEO* has taken a consistently cautious view of capital account liberalization. In October 1995, for example—well before the Asian crisis—the *WEO* argued that, while opening up an economy to financial flows could bring considerable benefits in terms of investment, technology transfer, and growth, there were "valid concerns about the necessary pre-requisites to ensure that liberalization is viable" and that "countries that have made little progress toward macroeconomic stability and strengthening domestic financial markets need to be cautious about removing barriers to capital flows ... liberalization can be undertaken gradually."

Reform of financial systems is one of a range of structural reforms that the *WEO* has often advocated. Almost since its inception, the *WEO* has pressed for reforms of labor markets in Europe to cut unemployment and help reinvigorate growth. The May 1985 *WEO* referred to the upward trend of unemployment in Europe as "one of the most disturbing developments of the past decade" and viewed structural problems that resulted in real wage inflexibility as playing "a critical role." Twelve years later, the *WEO* reported that unemployment in the

European Union had recently risen to new postwar peaks, and pointed to the approach of EMU, within two years, as increasing the urgency of reform. The May 1998 *WEO* called the failure to reform labor markets "the Achilles' heel of the EMU project," and the first *WEO* with EMU in place, in May 1999, devoted a chapter to "Chronic Unemployment in the Euro Area: Causes and Cures." The October 1997 *WEO* had speculated that "EMU itself may promote labor market reform" and the Lisbon agenda of reforms adopted by the EU in 2000 added impetus. In April 2004, the *WEO* speculated further that conditions—including stronger international competition in goods and labor markets—had become conducive to an acceleration of reform, and more recent *WEO*s have reported significant progress in some countries. The October 2007 *WEO* found that "labor market performance in the euro area appears to have improved significantly over the past decade. ... Labor market reforms have made an important contribution."

Among international economic policies, the *WEO* has been a constant supporter of trade liberalization. Every issue of the *WEO* has contained warnings of the costs of protectionist policies, to the countries adopting them as well as to their trading partners. The *WEO* has also consistently supported multilateral trade liberalization rounds and urged countries to pursue free trade, pointing particularly to the benefits that the opening of economies has brought in the postwar period, especially to the opening countries themselves. This evidence was presented in a chapter on "Trade as an Engine of Growth" in May 1993, as the Uruguay Round was in deadlock, and again in a chapter on the global trading system in October 1999, ahead of the launch of the Doha Round. The *WEO* has, at the same time, stressed the importance of policies—such as the promotion of training and retraining, and strong social safety nets—to support those who suffer in the short run from structural changes resulting from trade and other causes.

Every *WEO* has also urged high-income countries to increase aid to the developing world, encouraging them to meet the UN target of 0.7 percent of their gross national income. Beginning in the late 1980s, *WEO*s have argued for debt relief and debt reduction for heavily indebted countries and have also emphasized the importance of using aid effectively. A box in the September 2003 *WEO* stated candidly that major challenges related not only to the administrative capacity needed to manage and use resources effectively, and to the volatility of aid receipts, but also to the potential for corruption, which pointed to the importance of good governance.

Extending the frontiers of knowledge for policy making

The *WEO*'s warnings of dangers ahead and its policy advice to countries have been written in language intended to be clear to policy makers, officials, and interested observers and commentators, but they have been based on theoretical and empirical analysis which has often been quite technical. Such analysis has made it possible, for example, since the mid-1980s, to construct alternative hypothetical policy scenarios illustrating the implications of adopting various alternative sets of policies relative to current policy plans, and to analyze the increasingly important international linkages among economies and macroeconomic effects of financial sector developments.

The *WEO* has also, from the beginning, reported innovative research intended to bring the latest techniques and available data to bear on important policy questions. Over the past 28 years, improvements in data availability and advances in information technology have made it increasingly feasible to test various hypotheses on large-scale international data sets, and to draw soundly based inferences from broad cross-country experience. This is apparent in the growing comprehensiveness and sophistication of the research reported in the *WEO*'s increasingly prominent "analytical chapters." Background research papers have also been published in companion volumes of "Staff Studies" or "Supporting Studies" and in academic journals. The wide variety of issues examined include, for example, the behavior of labor markets in industrial countries and the design of reform policies; various aspects of the international transmission of economic disturbances; the measurement of potential output, debt and growth in developing countries; the responses of external payments balances to exchange rate changes; aspects of the transition from central planning to market-based economies; the causes and consequences of booms and busts in asset markets; policy lessons from global economic development in the twentieth century; and the sources of currency crises.

One broad subject on which there has been considerable research over the past decade is globalization. Increasing international economic and financial integration was a frequent theme in the *WEO* from the beginning, but in the early 1990s the integration of the formerly centrally planned economies into the international market system gave the process a new global dimension. The word "globalization" seems to have first appeared in the *WEO* in October 1993, in a discussion of the growth of capital flows, and subsequent *WEO*s examined the policy implications of various aspects of the phenomenon. The May 1997 *WEO* included three chapters on the challenges and opportunities arising from globalization; the April 2005 *WEO* examined how globalization was affecting the scale and pattern of external payments imbalances and the ability to finance them; the April 2006 *WEO* considered how globalization was affecting inflation; the April 2007 *WEO* examined the extent to which labor markets had become globalized; and the October 2007 *WEO* examined the connections between globalization and inequality. The May 1997 *WEO* found that the fear in advanced economies that competition from low-wage economies would depress the demand for labor and adversely affect the distribution of income was largely misplaced, and that technical progress was a much more important influence on the pattern of labor incomes. This finding was strengthened by the October 2007 study, which determined that income inequality had increased in recent years in almost all economies, but that increased trade was not the culprit. Rather, technical progress, including its international diffusion through foreign direct investment, had disproportionately benefited the better educated. The lessons were not that technical progress should be prevented—this would damage growth—but that education and other social services should be provided to help people adapt. This study received significant positive attention in the media, and also, notably, in the "blog" of Professor Gary Becker, who won the Nobel Prize for Economics in 1992 partly for his work in the area of human capital and the working of labor markets.

Conclusion

The impact of the *WEO* on economic policies is virtually impossible to gauge. The *WEO* is one of many products in the public and private sectors that claim the attention of policy makers around the world. It also, to a large extent, represents the current consensus of the economics profession and the economic policy-making community. However, all the relevant independent external evaluations indicate that the *WEO* is unusually highly appreciated for its success in identifying and analyzing, in a timely way, issues and dangers requiring the attention and action of economic policy makers, and in formulating and advocating appropriate policy responses. This chapter has provided some examples of the *WEO*'s many contributions to policy debates and policy formulation. These contributions and the *WEO*'s acknowledged successes have been based partly on the operational role of the *WEO* in the surveillance work of the IMF and on the collaborative process by which the *WEO* is produced by the variety of economic specialists on the staff of the IMF. Most important, however, they have been based on the unique role of the IMF as the global institution dedicated to international cooperation in the field of macroeconomic and financial sector policies.

The IMF Staff's View of the World

Martin Wolf[2]

What is the International Monetary Fund for? The answer, at such a level of generality, is to provide public goods: liquidity in a crisis, smoother coordination of policies, information, and analysis. The *World Economic Outlook* (*WEO*) is an attempt—I would argue, the most important single attempt—to deliver the last three objectives. It is, accordingly, at the heart of the IMF's mission. It is what the Fund exists to do.

Graham Hacche has, as an informed insider, provided a brief, clear, and well-argued account of the history and achievements of the *WEO*. It is a mark of this achievement that it is impossible to imagine a world without it. As Hacche notes, the *WEO* matters not just because of its intellectual content but also because of the IMF's role as a monetary institution and, still more, because of its role in multilateral surveillance.

The *WEO*s provide the best available view of the evolution of the world economy as a whole. They show how the pieces fit together. They are, for this reason, invaluable to outside commentators, governments, market participants, and academics. They are precisely the sort of product that only an official institution could produce. They are, therefore, suppliers of indispensable public goods.

In his explanation of how the *WEO* works and what it does, Hacche brings out the following main points. First, the *WEO* benefits from being built from the bottom up, starting with projections for all Fund members. This ensures consistency. Second, the reports are written collaboratively and, as a result, represent the considered view of the staff as a whole. Third, the *WEO* offers not forecasts, but implications of the current set of policies and, in consequence, a clear indication of "actual

[2] Associate Editor and Chief Economics Commentator, *Financial Times*, London.

and potential problems requiring policy action." Finally, publication of the *WEO* influences the global policy debate.

Hacche also discusses three specific aspects of the *WEO*s.

One of these is its warnings of dangers ahead: the developing country debt crisis that erupted in August 1982, the global imbalances of the 1980s, the crises in emerging market economies of the 1990s, the reemergence of large global payments imbalances in the late 1990s and 2000s, the stock market bubble of the late 1990s, and the house price bubbles of the 2000s.

Another is "ruthless truth-telling": calls for increased fiscal discipline, tempered by the occasional argument for fiscal stimulus, as in Japan in the 1990s; demands that monetary policy should normally aim at "reasonable price stability," but with some attention to stabilization, particularly in Japan and Germany in the 1990s; arguments that central banks should pay greater attention to asset prices; attention to currency crises and, in particular, mistakes made in the lead up to such crises; the need for greater exchange-rate flexibility, notably in China in recent years; occasional calls for foreign currency intervention; arguments against controls on international capital flows, along with caution over capital account liberalization; and, not least, demands for structural reforms, trade liberalization and greater aid to the developing world.

A final aspect discussed by Hacche consists of attempts to extend the frontiers of knowledge for policy making: presentation of alternative policy scenarios and, in particular, many studies of aspects of globalization.

This, then, is a first-rate analytical account of the history of the *WEO*. The question the account raises is how well the *WEO* performs the functions set for it. My response is, inevitably, a partial one. I will start by focusing on what I find relatively less useful. I will then turn to what I consider most useful. Finally, I will consider what could be done better.

The least useful part of the *WEO* is, in my view, the forecasts themselves. This is because such numbers usually add little to the consensus of other forecasters, despite the systematic way in which they are built up. More fundamentally, it is impossible to forecast the timing of big changes in the world economy. So the forecasts tend to be rather good when nothing very exciting is happening and much less good when it is. Forecasts then are like umbrellas with holes in them: useful only when it is not raining.

What are most useful in the *WEO* are three big things. First, the *WEO* supplies invaluable data. It also allows users to download the underlying data sets. This is incredibly valuable for analysts around the world. Second, the *WEO* provides something far more useful than the forecasts themselves, namely, the building blocks of those forecasts. These analyses of what is happening around the globe and the discussion of how they interrelate are invaluable. Finally, the *WEO*'s background chapters on specific policy issues are almost always superb. My work would have been immeasurably poorer without the staff's effort to bring research, in the Fund and elsewhere, to the attention of readers. To me this is the single most useful contribution made by the *WEO*s over the years.

Finally, what could be done better? My answer to that question is, make the truth-telling more ruthless. The Fund's chief asset is its authority. This is even truer now that few countries need its money. Its chief job as an institution is to speak up with courage and clarity for the interests of the world as a whole. This will often mean criticizing the policies of powerful states. I well understand the risks that any decision to do so would run. But without ruthless truth-telling on the roots of global imbalances, on absurd trade policies, on the need for far better financial regulation, on moral hazard, on fiscal profligacy and so on and so forth, governments will continue to follow dangerously destabilizing policies. The IMF needs to be bolder if it is to make a difference. It is not enough to be clear to those able to read between the lines. It is also necessary to be clear to those who are able to read only the lines themselves.

My conclusion, then, is that the *WEO* is perhaps the best example of the Fund's ability to deliver public goods. The debate would be enormously impoverished without them. But it would be still more useful and influential if management and staff were prepared to be clearer and more courageous. Yes, maybe, that will lead to big rows from time to time. So be it. Rows are needed when mistakes are being made.

11
Conclusion

Eduard Brau and Ian McDonald

In late 2007 and early 2008, IMF credit outstanding was at its lowest level in decades, reflecting an absence of major balance of payments crises in member countries in recent years. But if history is any guide, some countries will experience financial crises in the future, and the lessons from the successful crisis recovery programs described here may well be useful to them. Even more valuable are the lessons on the domestic and international policies and initiatives needed to prevent crises in the first place. Indeed, it is partly because countries have heeded these lessons, to some extent at the urging of the IMF, that balance of payments crises have been avoided in recent years.

The staff of the IMF and many others continue to debate and study the programs and initiatives described in this book in order to distill enduring lessons from them. The IMF continues to seek from its experience ways to improve its policy guidance and strengthen its operations. The institutional memory within the IMF continues to gain from the knowledge derived from this valuable experience, which it works to share widely. This same institutional memory also enables the IMF to act quickly whenever a new need arises that it can help its member countries address.

Some lessons from the IMF-supported rescue programs are particularly important.

The IMF has been able to assist countries overcome crises that were remarkably different from each other. The economic problems faced by the six countries discussed in this book were very distinct. No two situations were the same and what was a weakness in one country was not a problem in another. Accordingly, the governments concerned and the IMF negotiated policy programs suited to each country's unique situation and specifically designed to overcome its difficulties. This is a far cry from what some have alleged to be a "one-size-fits-all" approach in the IMF's policy advice. The renewed growth achieved by all these countries is testimony to the IMF's ability to assist high- and low-income economies with equal success.

In each case, success was due primarily to the commitment of the country's policy-making authorities. Such commitment is more difficult to sustain when there is intense political and popular opposition to the needed policy actions. An important lesson, therefore, is that the authorities must develop support within their country's society for painful measures before there can be economic improvements such measures are designed to deliver. They must also be willing to make timely adjustments to economic policies when new information makes this necessary. A policy step agreed with the IMF can be carried out effectively by the authorities and explained well to the public, or it can be delayed, compromised, grudgingly adopted, and publicly "blamed" on the IMF. Confidence in the authorities by the population and by outside investors is critical to success. What domestic or foreign investor would risk investing in a country if there is doubt about the competence and willingness of the government and central bank to resolve the problems that caused the crisis? The population of a country senses immediately whether there is competence and willingness to adopt sound economic policies. Many recovery programs supported by the IMF have had desultory results until a government came to power that was truly committed to the policies agreed in the program.

Each IMF-supported crisis recovery program when it is approved has a probability of success that is never 100 percent, because relevant information is never complete when the program is designed, because economics is an inexact science, and because there are many future unknowables that can cause failure if not handled appropriately. Moreover, the design of each program is a compromise between what may be the first-best technical solution to the problem and what is acceptable to the member politically, at least adequate technically, and also acceptable to the IMF's Executive Board, which must approve the loan.

It is a major responsibility of the IMF's Managing Director, therefore, to recommend to the Executive Board for approval only such policy programs that, in his assessment, will be carried out and make a solid contribution to the economic performance and welfare of the country being assisted. This requires a judgment of the intent and capacity of a government that is confronting a difficult economic situation. There are two extreme approaches to reaching such a judgment.

One approach is to support only those programs where the government's capacity and willingness to implement the program appear to make the risk of failure small ("a sure bet"). With this approach, most programs would probably succeed, but the IMF would not have done its job properly because of the potential, but risky, successes it failed to support. It would be akin to a hospital not admitting very sick patients for fear that a possible sad outcome might tarnish the hospital's reputation. The IMF's Articles of Agreement are clear that the institution's responsibility is to try to help countries in economic crisis situations when the risks are inherently high.

Another possible approach would be to give wide benefit of the doubt to a government's expression of its policy intentions ("on a wing and a prayer") and to apply no effective conditionality. This would be akin to admitting all patients to the hospital and not asking them to take the treatment that they need to get well. In this case, many programs would fail and again, the IMF would not have done its job properly; in addition, it would have put its member countries' financial resources at risk.

The Managing Director and the Executive Board make a judgment between these extremes. They seek to give a government a reasonable benefit of the doubt that the agreed economic policies will indeed be carried out, but they will also make the disbursement of loans conditional on the implementation of the agreed policies. That reasonable benefit of the doubt will be maintained as long as actions taken by the government do not contradict it. No credit cooperative among countries such as the IMF could remain credible and be entrusted with large resources by its member countries without adhering to sound lending principles.

Was there an alternative to an IMF-supported crisis recovery program in the cases discussed in this book? Yes, there was an alternative, but the price would have been heavy. Each of the countries discussed in this book could have decided to resolve its economic problems alone. Or each of the countries could have turned to a rich ally or group of allies for help.

Let us examine these alternatives in turn.

It is possible to overcome a country's balance of payments and financial crisis without financial and policy help, but there is likely to be a price to be paid. This is because, without financial assistance, there will be a larger balance of payments gap to be filled. The price will usually be a larger and deeper economic contraction, which would be needed to achieve a larger compression of imports, than would have been the consequence if outside help were accepted. The price could also include a default on external-debt obligations when such a default should be unnecessary because the country was only experiencing temporary liquidity difficulties. Without help, a country would also be more readily tempted to export some of its problems to its trading partners by adopting an overly competitive exchange rate policy—which might be imposed on it by a currency collapse—import restrictions, or exchange controls.

A government that forgoes help to deal with a balance of payments crisis thus subjects its population to harsher-than-necessary economic costs, whether for policy mistakes that the government and not the population has made, or for negative economic shocks from abroad.

Because it is more difficult to overcome an economic crisis without outside help, any attempt to do so has less chance of succeeding. The result can be an absence of renewed economic growth and a lower standard of living for the population. It is for these reasons, of course, that very few governments confronted by a balance of payments crisis have not sought help.

Because it is much better to have help than not to have it, a government that can no longer borrow from private lenders may decide to seek assistance, but from a rich ally (or small group of friendly countries) rather than the IMF. One aim might be to avoid the policy conditions that the IMF would require in order to be confident that the country's economic problems would be overcome and the IMF be repaid. But the rich ally would then have a problem. If it granted a loan without policy conditions, the country's economic difficulties might not be solved and the loan might not be repaid. However, if it sought to negotiate economic policy conditions, it might be accused of seeking to exploit the country's weakness for its own political or commercial purposes. Even if the governments involved were able to ignore such accusations, the country in difficulty could not be assured it received policy advice that was based on wide experience and that was politically disinterested. The officials of the ally providing the advice and financial support would certainly not be subject to the expert checks and balances and international scrutiny that the IMF's Executive Board provides when it discusses and decides on IMF loans.

In conclusion, bilateral balance of payments loans from allies can be highly problematical. Experience has taught that they should not be given in isolation. Bilateral support loans have indeed been extended by rich-country governments, including in the cases discussed in this book. But they have been made only in support of IMF loans to enlarge the financing for the country concerned and not separately from multilateral support nor from the policy understandings reached between the country and the IMF.

The best answer to a financial crisis is to prevent the next one.

Some policy measures to reduce countries' vulnerability to financial crises must be implemented domestically, and other measures implemented internationally.

The necessary domestic measures depend on the circumstances of each economy. The IMF discusses such measures with each country, particularly during its surveillance consultations.

Only a well-functioning multilateral institution can create effective international financial crisis prevention initiatives.

International crisis-prevention initiatives seek to achieve among countries what prudential financial regulation seeks to achieve domestically: to establish systems that help to forestall financial crises. Domestically, compliance with regulations is ensured by the rule of law. Internationally, compliance comes only through voluntary participation, which in turn depends on a country's respect for the value of the initiative.

The IMF-monitored special data dissemination standard (SDDS) for countries' international reserves, which was set up in 1996 (discussed in Chapter 8), is now adhered to by many countries and is a very important measure. It achieves timely and comprehensive disclosure, in standardized form, of data that are vital to the avoidance of market disruptions. This eliminates the costly task of interpreting the idiosyncrasies of each country's particular, and often less than adequate, definitions.

It is very likely that Thailand's and Korea's economic crises in 1997–98 would have taken a milder form or been altogether avoided if this data standard had been adhered to by these countries at the time. There would then have been earlier market reactions to the loss of foreign reserves by these countries' central banks over many months, which, together with pressure on policy makers from citizens, would likely have led the countries' authorities to take policy actions before the countries' reserves ran out and an unavoidable sudden plunge in the exchange rate took the population by surprise. Without the SDDS, citizens and markets were in the dark.

The financial sector assessment program (FSAP) is also achieving highly beneficial results that could be attained only through a multilateral approach. As discussed in Chapter 9, this program involves delving deeply into a country's entire financial system, to identify its strengths and weaknesses and to recommend specific improvements that will enhance its ability to withstand negative shocks. This requires a technical, professional, and nonpolitical multilateral approach applied evenhandedly in all participating countries. No country would allow a team comprising experts from only one advanced country to undertake this task, for fear of revealing sensitive information on a bilateral basis. Moreover, what is needed is an approach that reflects a knowledge of best practices worldwide, not only a knowledge of practices in one advanced country whose financial system most likely has its own weaknesses.

Thus a well-functioning multilateral institution is needed to ensure wide consultation and legitimacy for such prevention initiatives, to encourage participation and oversee their wide implementation, to review their continued relevance, and to update them as needed.

It is up to each country to decide whether or not to participate in the two financial crisis-prevention initiatives just discussed. US Executive Directors at the IMF routinely encourage countries to participate in financial sector assessments, but the United States has not participated itself. As of the writing of this book, the United States and China have not yet completed a financial sector assessment, as contrasted with completed assessments for all other systemically important countries. Both countries have recently stated their intention to participate. As the international fallout from the sub-prime mortgage crisis in the United States demonstrates, other countries have a strong interest that systemically important countries do what they can to reduce the vulnerability of their financial systems.

The bright light of the *World Economic Outlook*

The uniquely valuable contributions of the *World Economic Outlook* to policy debates and policy formulation were discussed in Chapter 10. These contributions are made possible by the expertise of the IMF's staff on the economy of each of the IMF's 185 member countries and on cross-cutting issues affecting them, and by their ability to express their views without political interference.

It is particularly notable that the IMF's Independent Evaluation Office has found that the *WEO* had "largely succeeded in identifying in a timely way relevant issues for analysis" and that "in terms of identifying relevant global macroeconomic and financial risks, both the *WEO* and the Global Financial Stability Report (*GFSR*) also compare favorably with similar publications of other international and national bodies."

The *WEO*'s reputation for quality, objectivity, and timeliness helps to explain why the finance ministers of the G-7 and other country groups have long used *WEO* analyzes as the basis for their own periodic discussions of global economic issues. The IMF's success in maintaining this reputation tends to ensure that *WEO* analyses of key problems faced by the global economy are accepted by member countries as an objective baseline.

It is a big achievement to gain timely agreement among countries on the nature of the problems, given the natural political proclivity to point fingers at others, and it is essential to devising appropriate and timely policy responses.

Do past IMF successes matter for the future?

Yes, they matter for two reasons.

First, the stories told in this book underscore that many problems in the world economy have required multilateral cooperation to resolve them. The IMF has successfully brought member countries together to work on such problems many times in the more than six decades since its founding.

In the 1950s, for industrial countries (other than the United States, which already had a convertible currency), and later for most others, the IMF helped eliminate exchange controls on current account transactions and multiple exchange rates to establish convertibility for their currencies, a major achievement in progress toward an open world economy that is now often forgotten.

In the 1970s, the IMF helped many countries deal with the balance of payments impacts of the large increase in oil prices in 1973 and again toward the end of the decade, including extending policy-conditioned loans to Italy and the United Kingdom.

In the 1980s, for many countries in Latin America, and in the 2000s, for low-income countries everywhere, the IMF coordinated measures to resolve excessive indebtedness to public and private external creditors, and itself granted debt relief to many low-income member countries together with other official creditors.

In the 1990s, the IMF helped stabilize and integrate the formerly centrally planned economies of the Soviet bloc into the international monetary system through extensive policy advice, technical cooperation, and loans.

Second, the stories told in this book show that the IMF has extensive experience, a qualified and dedicated staff, and an ability to learn from mistakes and absorb lessons. They also demonstrate the ability of the IMF to respond to new issues effectively and to act promptly, if necessary, through decisions of its Executive Board, which represents the international community. There is every reason for confidence that the IMF can do the same in the future.

Globalization has, however, established a new economic environment in which the IMF carries out its mandate. Globalization has dramatically reshaped the economic world since the fall of the Berlin wall in 1989. A quantum leap in the economic and financial interdependence of countries around the globe has taken place in a short time span.

The average annual growth of world trade volume since 1990, at 6.7 percent, has been much higher than the average growth of world GDP, at 3.3 percent. As a result, the ratio of world exports to world GDP has increased from 19 percent in 1990 to 31 percent in 2006. In the United States, the ratio of exports to GDP has risen from 9 percent to 12 percent, meaning that some 18 million jobs depend directly on developments in foreign economies. Hundreds of millions of jobs in the advanced and developing economies likewise depend on foreign trade. The growth in world trade is set to continue, absent a geopolitical catastrophe. Cross-border financial capital flows have jumped from 4 percent of world GDP in 1990 to some 14 percent in 2006. Foreign direct investment flows nearly quadrupled.

Behind these numbers lie fundamental policy decisions by large countries. The countries of Eastern Europe and of the former Soviet Union have joined the world monetary and trade system. China and India, the homes of one-third of the world's population, have turned from inward-looking economic systems with heavy state intervention to market-oriented, outward-looking systems giving large scope to private economic initiative.

In this environment, any country's economic well-being depends ever more closely on the well-being of others, and vice versa.

Domestically, markets function well when there is a framework of respect for law and prudent regulation, and when there are strong economic governance institutions to ensure macroeconomic and financial stability, provide sound social safety nets, and foster the development of human capital. Internationally, markets function well when governments cooperate and respect mutually agreed rules. This is the spirit motivating the IMF, the World Bank, and the World Trade Organization. Through these three global economic institutions, governments have defined the rules they will observe on cross-border economic and financial transactions and through which they will cooperate for the common economic good.

This world economic system has played a key role in helping to bring economic prosperity on an unprecedented scale to most of the world since the end of the Second World War.

No economy has done well where the government has not made and implemented a fundamental decision: namely, to pursue an outward-looking economic policy that is open and encouraging to foreign trade and foreign investment. Expressed differently, every country—without exception—that has opted to interact economically as little as possible with others has failed to raise living standards over the long term. This is a truly remarkable fact. In India and China, for example, the absolute number of people living in dire poverty rose for decades after the Second World War. Only after these countries adopted market- and trade-friendly economic policies (in India since the early 1990s and in China since the 1980s) have hundreds of millions of their citizens escaped from dire poverty, and the economic growth of these countries has become sufficiently high to continue this progress.

The outward-looking market- and trade-friendly policies that are necessary for raising living standards everywhere create vast opportunities, but they also create risks.

Both the opportunities and the risks—"spillovers"—are transmitted among economies through the trade and financial flows that link them. Such spillovers are a normal and unavoidable by-product of economic progress. Spillovers will always occur when competition and innovation propel new investment and productivity growth, and outdated economic activity is replaced in the originating country and in its trading partners.

Good spillovers come from successful policies and economic growth in partner countries. Thus, for the first time in economic history, economic growth in developing economies accounts for half of the growth in world GDP in 2007–08. It is a major positive influence in maintaining high employment in industrialized economies through their flourishing exports to developing countries.

Bad spillovers can come from failed macroeconomic policies in a neighboring country. This was the trigger for Uruguay's crisis in 2002, as discussed in Chapter 7. Bad spillovers can also originate more narrowly in poor regulatory oversight of financial lending standards, as in the United States up to 2007, where problems from lax mortgage lending spilled over into wider credit-market seizures in the United States, Europe, and elsewhere, depressing confidence and economic activity.

This is an environment where more, and more effective, cooperation is needed among countries on common economic and financial challenges.

The IMF has the mandate to make the key economic and financial opportunities and risks transparent, and it has the tools needed to achieve effective cooperation. The IMF, however, needs reform of its own governance and a realignment of the voting shares of member countries to have the acceptance among all members to fulfill its mandate effectively.

Annex

How the IMF Operates

The IMF is the world's central institution for monetary and financial cooperation among governments and central banks. Its 185 sovereign member countries—virtually all the countries in the world—are committed to collaborating through the IMF to promote the common good by observing its charter—the Articles of Agreement. Some provisions of this charter concerning cross-border monetary matters have the force of law in the legal systems of all member countries. This charter defines the agreed code of conduct for all countries concerning the vital economic matters of exchange rate policies and exchange restrictions. In particular, members are required not to manipulate their exchange rates for competitive purposes, and to make their currencies freely convertible for current account transactions unless special arrangements have been made with the IMF. Currency convertibility is an essential prerequisite for the unhindered flow of lawful trade in goods and services, including travel, as well as of financial capital.

The policies that the IMF carries out are set by its member governments. Its supreme governing body is its Board of Governors, composed of a minister of finance or a central bank governor from each member country. The Board of Governors delegates much of its power to an Executive Board of 24 Directors, appointed or elected by the member countries, which is in continuous session in Washington, DC. Each member is assigned a quota which determines the member's financial obligations to the IMF as well as its potential access to credit from the IMF. Countries' quotas, together with the basic votes distributed equally to all members, also determine their voting power in the Executive Board. Quotas are intended to reflect the size of each member's economy. Thus, the United States currently has 17 percent of total votes and the only blocking vote among individual members for those fundamental decisions that require an 85 percent majority of votes; a small country such as Tanzania, for example, currently has 0.1 percent of votes. The Executive Board conducts the business of the IMF, and usually takes decisions by consensus, but by vote if necessary. The Board works with the Managing Director of the IMF—who is chairman of the Executive Board and chief executive—a First Deputy Managing Director, two Deputy Managing Directors, and a staff totaling some 2600 persons from more than 120 countries. The International Monetary and Financial Committee, a committee of the Board of Governors, meets twice a year and provides guidance to the Executive Board. The Board of Governors itself meets annually.

To promote stability and prevent crises in individual economies and in the international monetary system, the IMF reviews, assesses, and reports to its members and publicly on national, regional, and global economic and financial developments, issues, and policies. In this, its main activity, known as surveillance—which each member country accepts as an obligation of membership—it holds consultations with each member usually on an annual basis, and also monitors developments continuously and is in contact with members as necessary. In the course of its surveillance discussions, it provides policy advice to countries and helps transfer experience among them. It encourages them to adopt the policies most effective to tackle their economic problems and, in particular, to reduce their vulnerability to balance of payments crises. It serves as a forum for the discussion of the implications of individual countries' policies for others, and monitors any policies adopted by countries for undesirable economic and financial spillover effects on other economies. This is a peer-review mechanism that makes it possible for countries to critically comment, if necessary, on each other's policies without making a contentious diplomatic incident out of each such criticism.

Each country consultation ends with a statement "summing-up" on the Executive Board's analysis and advice, which represents, in effect, the view of the global community, and which is conveyed to the country's authorities. Apart from this country surveillance, the IMF is charged with overseeing the international monetary system as a whole to ensure its effective operation and therefore regularly examines developments and prospects for the global economy and financial system.

The IMF also functions as an international credit union that is able to help when a country faces a balance of payments crisis—when its exchange rate is collapsing or its foreign exchange reserves are falling to dangerously low levels, or it can no longer borrow on international capital markets, so that it has difficulty continuing to pay for its imports or meeting its other international payments obligations. Such a balance of payments crisis and its aftermath inevitably results in a broader economic crisis hurting living standards and employment.

The purpose of IMF help—comprising both financial assistance and policy advice—is to ease the adjustment required to resolve the crisis, and thus to minimize the cost to the country and its trading partners. Without IMF support, much more harm could be caused, for example, if the country failed to halt the collapse of its currency, or imposed restrictions on certain international payments, potentially wiping out jobs in its trading partner countries, thus repeating the mistakes of the 1930s.

If requested, the IMF therefore provides help by calling on countries in strong financial positions to provide it with financial resources, which members are obliged to make available up to the amount of their quota in the IMF (resulting in a total lending capacity of over $200 billion), and on which the IMF pays market-related interest. The IMF uses these funds to make a short- to medium-term loan to the country in crisis, subject to the country carrying out policies to overcome its problems, and charging it an interest rate that is higher than that paid by the IMF to the members providing the funds, but lower than typically obtainable in the international capital markets by a country in crisis.

The IMF also administers a separate loan window of concessional resources funded by donor countries and from partial sales of its gold holdings; these low-interest rate (0.5 percent a year) loans are made available to low-income member countries to help them overcome protracted balance of payments problems. This concessional lending was created in the 1970s in response to the needs of low-income members. In the 1990s and 2000s, the IMF participated with other multilateral institutions and individual official lenders in debt cancellation for the poorest countries.

The IMF provides vital elements of the infrastructure of the international monetary system. Together with other institutions, it gathers and publishes essential national and global economic and financial data used by public and private economic decision makers everywhere. This includes the supervision and provision of timely high-quality data on foreign exchange assets and liabilities of countries' central banks, information that was lacking publicly for most of the emerging market countries that experienced financial crises in the mid-1990s and late 1990s. It further includes the setting of standards of best practices concerning economic governance, such as the conduct of monetary policy by central banks, of fiscal transparency in government budgets, of public expenditure management, and other areas, and the monitoring and public reporting of countries' adherence to these standards. A final vital element of this infrastructure is the proactive, comprehensive, and detailed examination of countries' financial systems, in advanced and developing countries alike, by the IMF in collaboration with the World Bank, with a view to recommending improvements to make these systems more resilient and less vulnerable to crises.

Last but not least, the IMF is a repository of research and of expertise on macroeconomic policy management and institutions, including central bank and foreign exchange management policies, budgetary revenue and expenditure policies, financial sector and capital market policies, and others. This expertise is provided to countries under a large program of technical cooperation delivered by the IMF's staff and other experts appointed by the IMF to help countries, where needed, to acquire the policy and technical skills and the strong economic governance institutions that are essential for economic advancement.

This expertise is also transferred to officials of member governments via the extensive training programs conducted by the IMF in Washington, DC, and in several regional training centers.

Notes

1 Introduction

1. Except require a country to withdraw from membership if it does not fulfill its obligations to the IMF.

2 The Korean Crisis Ten Years Later: A Success Story

2. The team was led by Hubert Neiss and Wanda Tseng. Team members included James Gordon, Sharmini Coorey, Robert Dekle, Jeanne Gobat, Christian Thimann, Alexander Hoffmaister, Gary Moser, Pihuan Cormier, and Abdul Mahar. The financial sector team was headed by Tomás Baliño and included Peter Hayward, Daniel Hardy, Ceyla Pazarbasioglu, and Francine Koch.
3. This idea came from the experience of the financial crisis in India in the early 1990s, when the US Federal Reserve and the Bank of England provided a bridging loan.
4. The initial fiscal target for 1998 was a surplus of 1.5 percent of GDP. But this was predicated on a GDP growth projection of 2 percent. In the end, growth in 1998 declined by 7 percent and the eventual fiscal position was a deficit of 4.3 percent of GDP, but the latter was fully consistent with the program target.
5. There was pressure to increase interest rates further. After all, if as in mid-December, the exchange rate was falling by 10 percent per day; the ten-percentage-point increase in annual interest rates that had occurred provided poor compensation. The call rate peaked at 32 percent at end-December, 1997, and fell thereafter, dropping to the precrisis level by mid-1998 and to about 10 percent in 1999.
6. Unchan Chung, The Korean Financial Crisis: What is and What Ought to be Done, Mimeo, Seoul National University, December 1999; Paul Blustein, *The Chastening: Inside the Crisis That Rocked the Global Financial System and Humbled the IMF*, New York: Public Affairs, 2001; Marcus Noland, *Avoiding the Apocalypse: The Future of the Two Koreas*, Washington, DC: Institute for International Economics, 2000; and IMF Independent Evaluation Office, *IMF and Recent Capital Account Crises: Indonesia, Korea, and Brazil*, Washington, DC: International Monetary Fund, 2003.
7. In this context, at a conference on the Korean crisis in early 2000, the economist Jeffrey Frankel argued that the program's structural content demonstrated the IMF's ability to respond to changing global circumstances and characterized the expansion of scope to cover the financial system as "changing with the times" rather than "bureaucratic mission creep." *Ten Lessons Learned from the Korean Crisis*, NBER Conference, February 2000.

3 Poland: Stabilization, Transition, and Reform, 1990–91

8. The team was headed by Massimo Russo and included Peter Hole, head of the division covering Poland; Thomas Wolf, the expert on centrally planned economies; Hans Flickenschild; Timothy Lane; Rolando Ossowski; and Frank M. Lakwijk. Mark Allen and Rolando Ossowski were later posted as IMF Resident Representatives in Warsaw.
9. To this effect Mr. Camdessus met with the President of Poland, the Prime Minister, the Minister of Finance, the head of the Catholic Church, the Chairman of Solidarity, and leaders of Parliament.
10. These comprised the G-7 countries.
11. In an unprecedented program for its scope and coverage, the then Central Banking department provided assistance directly with its staff and coordinated a large number of experts seconded by several European central banks and the US Federal Reserve.

4 Turkey's Renaissance: From Banking Crisis to Economic Revival

12. Ashoka Mody and Martin Schindler, "Economic Growth in Turkey, 1960–2000," in *Turkey at the Crossroads: From Crisis Resolution to EU Accession*, Washington, DC: International Monetary Fund, 2005.
13. Caroline Van Rijckeghem and Murat Űçer, *Chronicle of the Turkish Financial Crises of 2000–2001*, Istanbul: Boğaziçi University Press, 2005. Intensifying market worries about problems in the private banks played a particularly important role in the run-up to the November 2000 crisis. The media highlighted lurid stories of corruption and malpractice in several private banks during the fall of 2000. At the same time, analysts and bank creditors became increasingly nervous about banks' foreign currency exposures. Rumors regarding potential funding difficulties for one bank with large debts in the overnight market were regarded by many as the trigger for the market panic on "Black Wednesday" (November 22).
14. IMF financing under the 1999–2000 program was initially set at a relatively modest $4 billion over three years. This had been boosted in December 2000 by an additional $7.5 billion in support of the government's efforts to contain the fallout from the November 2000 crisis.
15. Although the 1999–2000 program included measures to address the duty losses problem, it assumed that the broader vulnerabilities in the banking system (state and private) could be tackled over time by tightening the regulatory framework. This was one of several areas where policy implementation slipped during 2000, and in the event, time was not on Turkey's side. When the crisis hit, the Central Bank of Turkey (CBT) had very limited room to maneuver, as any monetary tightening to limit the fall of the lira was bound to cause the state banks additional losses.
16. Connected lending or lending to related parties occurs when a bank lends to its own shareholders or managers, including entities controlled by them or their family members.

17. Contrary to the IMF-backed program, this guarantee was lifted by the government in June 2000 but was reintroduced in December 2000 after the failure of Demir Bank, when some smaller banks faced liquidity withdrawals.
18. See, for instance: William E. Alexander, Jeffery M. Davis, Liam P. Ebrill, and Carl-Johan Lindgren, *Systemic Bank Restructuring and Macroeconomic Policy*, International Monetary Fund, 1997; David Folkerts-Landau and Carl-Johan Lindgren, *Toward a Framework for Financial Stability*, International Monetary Fund 1998; Carl-Johan Lindgren, Tomás J. T. Baliño, Charles Enoch, Anne-Marie Gulde, Marc Quintin, and Leslie Eng Sipp Teo, *Financial Sector Crisis and Restructuring: Lessons from Asia*, IMF Occasional Paper 188, International Monetary Fund, 1999.
19. In addition to Kemal Derviş as State Minister for Economic Affairs, the team appointed in the aftermath of the crisis comprised Sureyya Serdengeçti as Governor of the Central Bank of Turkey, Faik Öztrak as Secretary of the Treasury, and Engin Akçakoca as Chairman of the BRSA.
20. Before his appointment, Engin Akçakoca had been the General Manager of a medium-sized private bank owned by one of Turkey's most prominent business groups.
21. The mission had also closely coordinated its work with a financial sector mission from the World Bank.
22. There were four state banks: the large Ziraat and Halk and the smaller Vakif and Emlak. Emlak was merged into Ziraat. Vakif, whose legal owners were various foundations (but *de facto* state-controlled), was supposed to be quickly privatized, but as of mid-2008 only 25 percent of its shares have been sold to private investors.
23. Ziraat, for instance, which was created with a mandate to finance the agricultural sector, had previously been under the authority of the Minister of Agriculture.
24. Immediate technical assistance was crucial for the success of the scheme. BRSA faced rigid procurement procedures, and so MAE agreed to finance it. Later, a cost-sharing formula was worked out with BRSA.
25. Only the foundation-owned Vakif required a $137 million capital injection under the scheme.
26. A similar scheme had been used in Thailand with the same outcome, that is, shareholders preferred to invest their own money rather than to have the government participating in running their bank.
27. At the time, the law gave sworn bank auditors exclusive right to conduct on-site inspection of banks. This right was later removed, giving the BRSA more flexibility in the composition of on-site inspection teams.
28. A telling indicator of this restored confidence has been a marked shift by depositors since 2002 from foreign currency back into lira bank deposits.

5 Tanzania: Reform and Progress, 1995–2007

29. Known at the time of independence as Tanganyika, the country was renamed as the United Republic of Tanzania (including the mainland and Zanzibar) in 1964. The sole political party at independence was the Tanganyika African National Union (TANU) which was renamed the Chama Gha Mapinduzi

(CCM), "the revolutionary party," after merging with the Afro-Shiraz party of Zanzibar in 1977.

30. Mr. Kikwete eventually succeeded Mr. Mkapa as president ten years later and has continued the reform process.
31. July–June fiscal year. Earlier years are not comparable because of the impact of state-owned enterprises on revenue and expenditure.
32. Financing was a small surplus most years, but there were financing needs averaging 1.5 percent of GDP in 2004/5–2006/7, mainly because of the impact of drought on production of hydropower and agriculture.
33. Assuming population growth of 2 percent per annum.

6 Brazil: Anchoring Policy Credibility in the Midst of Financial Crisis

34. Fernando Henrique Cardoso, the former Minister of Finance, was elected president in October 1994, and Pedro Malan was appointed Minister of Finance. Mr. Malan was Minister of Finance during both presidential terms of Mr. Cardoso and they were successful in putting together very good economic teams.
35. The negotiations for the Stand-By Arrangement were led by Pedro Parente, Vice Minister of Finance, on the Brazilian side and on the IMF side by Teresa Ter-Minassian, Deputy Director of the Western Hemisphere department. Mr. Parente had worked earlier in the IMF's Fiscal Affairs Department and was well known to the IMF team. Michel Camdessus, the Managing Director of the IMF, and Stanley Fischer, the First Deputy Managing Director, closely followed the negotiations.
36. President Cardoso, in his 2006 book on his years in politics, gives a vivid description of this period, noting that Minister Malan offered to resign given the seriousness of the economic situation and the lack of clear agreement in the economic team. See Cardoso's "A Arte da Política, A História que viví," pp. 389–418.
37. Mr. Fraga was well known to investors and IMF staff from his work in an investment firm and from the time he was deputy governor of the central bank in 1991–92.
38. A cornerstone of the fiscal reform was the passage of a fiscal responsibility law to establish a general framework to guide budgetary planning and execution. Among other things, the law established prudential criteria for public indebtedness, provided strict rules for the control of public expenditures (including with sanctions against government officials who approved spending overruns), established rules to limit budget deficits, and prohibited any further refinancing by the federal government of states and municipal debt.
39. One of the authors was struck in a meeting with investors, sponsored by Citibank in Washington, DC, in the summer of 2001, by how skeptical these investors were about the capacity of Brazil to face the crisis on its own. Morris Goldstein of the Institute of International Finance (and a former senior IMF staff member) was representative of market watchers when he forcefully advocated a new IMF-supported program at this meeting.

40. In fact, such leaks did not occur.
41. Inflation averaged 7.5 percent in 1999–2001 and eventually reached 12 percent in 2002 before falling to single digit, in 2003.
42. See Arminio Fraga, "Monetary Policy in a Transition to a Floating Exchange Rate," in *New Challenges for Monetary Policy*, Federal Reserve Bank of Kansas City Symposium, 1999, pp. 149–54, for a description of this transition.

7 Uruguay 2002–3: Recovery from Economic Contagion

43. Subsequently, after receiving commitments from the government, the foreign shareholders provided some additional funding to the bank.
44. Sight deposits are transaction deposits, on which checks and other drafts may be written. Savings deposits also have no fixed maturity and can be withdrawn at will, although checks cannot be written against these accounts.
45. The fourth suspended bank was placed into liquidation after an attempt at a private sale failed. Depositors were similarly protected up to $100, 000 with government securities.

8 Opening the Economic Books of Governments and of the IMF

46. IMF Managing Director Camdessus commissioned Alan Whittome, a former senior staff member and Counselor to the Managing Director, to undertake a detailed study of the crisis.
47. Subscribers have a limited number of "flexibility options" to reflect specific circumstances.
48. For most data categories over 90 percent of the data are disseminated as described on the preadvertised dates. Interestingly, since around 2002 there has been some slight slippage, particularly with regard to fiscal data, and particularly in the case of some of the original subscribers.
49. As a central element of its work to improve information for financial markets, the IMF has identified a set of "core" and of "encouraged" Financial Soundness Indicators (FSIs). Around 60 countries have participated in an exercise to harmonize these indicators; up to now they have largely rested on national definitions that vary across country. At some point it is possible that FSIs may be included within the SDDS.
50. The FATF is based in Paris. It is the international body bringing together security experts as well as regulators and other relevant officials that sets standards for, and monitors countries' compliance with, measures to combat money laundering and the financing of terrorism. Its public "black list" of countries failing to meet its requirements prompted widespread efforts by the countries that had been identified to improve their practices to get off the list.
51. FSAPs are discussed separately in Chapter 9.
52. See John Cady and Anthony J. Pellechio, "Sovereign Borrowing Cost and the IMF's Data Standards Initiatives" (March 2006), IMF Working Paper WP/06/78.

53. Together with the 90 countries that participate in the GDDS, this means that almost 80 percent of the IMF membership participates in one or the other.
54. New Zealand does however disseminate the reserves template on the IMF Web site. It does not participate in the SDDS since it does not produce a few of the required data categories and considers that they are not needed in the New Zealand context.
55. The sixth edition of the *Balance of Payments Manual* is under preparation, and the international community is expected to move to its standards by 2012.
56. For a discussion of the introduction of IT in Indonesia and Turkey, see the relevant chapters in Charles Enoch, Karl Habermeier, and Marta Castello-Branco (eds) *Building Monetary and Financial Systems: Case Studies in Technical Assistance*, IMF, Washington, 2007.
57. See, for example, the IMF Managing Director's reports on strengthening the international financial architecture prepared for IMFC meetings in 1998 and 1999, the *Summary of Reports on the International Financial Architecture* prepared by the G-22 in October 1998, the *Declaration of the G-7 Finance Ministers and Central Bank Governors* (October 30, 1998), the *APEC Leaders' Declaration* (November 1998), views which were echoed by leading private sector analysts such as the Institute of International Finance.

9 Strengthening Financial Sectors and Preventing Crisis

58. In addition, some of these reserves were highly illiquid. For a summary discussion of the crisis in Asia in 1997 and what has been done since then, see Burton, David, *Asia: Ten Years on – Taking Stock and Looking Forward*, Singapore, June 5, 2007.
59. See, for instance, WEO, October 2007, pp. 29–31, and Rogoff, Kenneth S., Assism M. Husain, Ashoka Mody, Robin Brooks, and Nienke Oomes, *Evolution and Performance of Exchange Rate Regimes*, 2004, IMF Occasional Paper No. 229, Washington: International Monetary Fund.
60. IEO, *IMF Exchange Rate Policy Advice*, 2007, Washington: International Monetary Fund.
61. Thus, participation is not part of the obligations that the IMF has set for its members, in particular the obligation to hold periodical or ad hoc consultations with the IMF on economic policy (Article IV of the IMF Articles of Agreement).
62. The Basel Committee on Banking Supervision is a forum for cooperation on banking supervision. Its members are banking supervisors from Belgium, Canada, France, Germany, Italy, Japan, Luxembourg, the Netherlands, Spain, Sweden, Switzerland, the United Kingdom, and the United States. The Committee has issued international standards on capital adequacy, the Core Principles for Effective Banking Supervision, and the Concordat on cross-border banking supervision.
63. The team will include staff from the IMF and the World Bank—except for industrial countries where the World Bank usually does not participate—and experts in specific areas (for instance, banking supervision), mostly from cooperating institutions.

64. Communiqué of the Basel Committee, October 6, 2006.
65. These different approaches exist even among countries with financial systems at similar stages of development.
66. The aide-memoire is the only document that is not publishable, because it may include market-sensitive information.
67. Published reports are posted on the Web sites of the IMF and the World Bank and typically also on those of the relevant national authorities.
68. In particular, several African countries are presently undergoing FSAPs or have committed to participate; also, the United States has recently confirmed its participation.
69. Indeed, in some cases countries accelerate reforms shortly before being assessed in order to show stronger observance.
70. The World Bank and the International Monetary Fund, 2005, *Financial Sector Assessment – A Handbook*, Washington: World Bank and International Monetary Fund.
71. The G-7 (the United States, Canada, the United Kingdom, France, Germany, Italy, and Japan) set up this forum in 1999 to promote cooperation and coordination in the supervision and surveillance of the international financial system and to reduce systemic risk. In addition to G-7 countries, its membership now includes Australia, Hong Kong SAR, the Netherlands, Singapore, and Switzerland. The IMF participates in its deliberations and has seconded a staff member to the Forum's Secretariat.
72. For instance, an FSAP team cannot review credit files, detect any potential fraud or do any of the things that a supervisor—or someone interested in buying a financial institution would normally do.

10 The IMF Staff's View of the World: The *World Economic Outlook*

73. *ICMR* refers to the *International Capital Markets Report*, published annually by the IMF from 1980 to 2000. It was then succeeded by the *Global Financial Stability Report* (*GFSR*), which is published twice yearly. The contributions of the *ICMR* and *GFSR* are beyond the scope of this chapter.
74. In cases where the dangers have involved financial sector risks, the *WEO* has worked in tandem with the *ICMR* or *GFSR*, which has analyzed the nature of such risks more deeply and extensively.
75. Boughton, James M., *Silent Revolution: The International Monetary Fund, 1979–1989*, International Monetary Fund: Washington, DC, 2001, p. 143.
76. On April 18, 1996, the day after this *WEO* was released to the press, the lead front-page story in the *Financial Times* was about the *WEO*'s call for the Deutsche Bundesbank to cut interest rates. The story also reported that the staff's analysis had been contentious within the IMF, with the French and German Executive Directors protesting against it. The following day, however, the *Financial Times* carried news in the same space headed "Bundesbank makes half-point rate cut."

Index